The Sentinels of Culture

The Sentinels of Culture

Class, Education, and the Colonial Intellectual in Bengal (1848–85)

Tithi Bhattacharya

OXFORD
UNIVERSITY PRESS

OXFORD
UNIVERSITY PRESS

YMCA Library Building, Jai Singh Road, New Delhi 110 001

Oxford University Press is a department of the University of Oxford. It furthers the
University's objective of excellence in research, scholarship, and education
by publishing worldwide in

Oxford   New York

Auckland   Cape Town   Dar es Salaam   Hong Kong   Karachi   Kuala Lumpur
Madrid   Melbourne   Mexico City   Nairobi   New Delhi   Shanghai   Taipei   Toronto

With offices in

Argentina   Austria   Brazil   Chile   Czech Republic   France   Greece   Guatemala
Hungary   Italy   Japan   Poland   Portugal   Singapore   South Korea   Switzerland
Thailand   Turkey   Ukraine   Vietnam

Oxford is a registered trademark of Oxford University Press
in the UK and in certain other countries

Published in India by Oxford University Press, New Delhi

ISBN   0 19 566910 X

Typeset in AGaramond
By Le Studio Graphique, Gurgaon 122001
Printed in India at De Unique, New Delhi 110 018
Published by Manzar Khan, Oxford University Press
YMCA Library Building, Jai Singh Road, New Delhi 110 001

For Abhi

Contents

Acknowledgements

This book has taken shape over three continents and hence there is an international body of scholars and friends who has had a lot to do with it. I am grateful to David Arnold who supervised this in its dissertation form. His support and consistent critical comments helped transform most of my unformed thoughts into coherent arguments. John McGuire, David Washbrook, and Sudipta Kaviraj also guided this project in its infancy and I owe to them much of the theoretical scaffolding that holds up this book. My teachers in India, Kunal Chattopadhyay, Majid Siddiqi, and K.N. Panikkar, taught me the most crucial craft for a historian: the constant interrogation of established facts. They first instilled in me the idea that most of regular history was written from the point of view of the victors.

Mandakranta and Tirthankar Bose provided the unfinished project and me a home when we both needed it most. Much of this book, and my own life, have grown out of the compassion, warmth, and intellectual friendship that these two amazing individuals have given unconditionally.

I am grateful to the Felix Trust for funding the course of my Ph.D. work and to the Central Research Fund for providing a grant for my fieldwork research in India. The various staff members at the India Office Library, the School of Oriental and African Studies (SOAS) library, the West Bengal State Archives, the National Library at Calcutta, the Bangiya Sahitya Parishad, the Hiran Library, the Taltala Public Library, the Chaitanya Library, and the Bagbazar Public Library, made the tedious task of archival research easy and even pleasant. Parts of the chapters and the material that went into this book have been presented in seminars in London, Oxford, Edinburgh, Sussex, Portsmouth, Paris, British Columbia, Toronto, Quebec, Cairo, Dhaka, and Calcutta. I have greatly benefited from the comments and enquries that I was presented with on all these occasions. I would like to thank my friends and colleagues at Purdue University for providing the constant encouraging nudges that were so necessary in trying to finish a book while coping with a new job.

I would like to thank my parents for opening my mind to the world and my grandfather for showing me how to live in it.

It remains then to acknowledge the many friends who have, through the years, patiently tolerated mad theoretical debates, bad temper, and unreaonable requests. Without them this book would not have been possible. Sandy Nicoll, with his usual resilience, went through with me every agonizing moment, from the very first conceptual struggles to the last panicked proof-reading. He along with John Molyneux and Richard Peacock are responsible for introducing me to a world of Marxist thought that I never knew existed, both in the library and on the streets. Ian Wollington, Abhijit Bhattacharya, Bradley Hughes, Julie Devaney, Sunera Thobani, Indranil Roychowdhury, and Suvojit Bagchi have, over the years, defied various oceans between ourselves and kept up a steady stream of support and encouragement.

In many ways this project also belongs to the three women in my life who grew up with me: Shubhra Nagalia, Kavita Krishnan, and Parnal Chirmuley. They continue to colour my past and influence my future.

Pablo is perhaps the only person in the world who has had faith in me since I was two. Our discussions about spaceships and unicorns have been just as contributive to my thinking as our more recent ones about colonial capitalism.

Finally this book is for Abhi, without whom all of this would have been possible but none of it would have been worth it.

List of Tables

Glossary

Glossary

artha	Wealth
baiji	Dancing girl or courtesan.
bania	Indigenous merchant or man of business in the service of an European officer or trader.
bhrurjapatra	Handmade paper made from birch leaf.
chasa	Peasant
dadni/dadani	System of extending credit directly to the manufacturer by merchants.
dari	Bengali grammatical diacritic mark.
gurukul	Literally meaning the home of the Guru or teacher, but referring in general to the system of indigenous Brahmanical education whereby the students resided in the Guru's home and performed various household chores for the guru during the period of study.
half-Akhrai	The Akhrai was a genre of fold song which evolved in the Vaishnavite akhras or centres in the Nadia district in the 18th century. The Akhrai form was replaced by the half-Akhrai in the beginning of the nineteenth century developed in particular by Mohan Chand Basu, a disciple of the famous composer-poet Nidhu Gupta.
kerani	Clerk
lekha para	Literally meaning writing (*lekha*) and reading (*para*) but collectively denotes education as such
normal school	Teacher training school.
patta	Lease
panchali	A genre of narrative fold songs.

sradh	Funeral ceremony.
tulot kagaj	Stained paper, paper treated with the sulphate of arsenic.
vidya	Education, knowledge

Introduction

Some, perchance, here are,
Who, with a Newton's glance, shall nobly trace
The course mysterious of each wandering star;
And, like a God, unveil the hidden face
Of many a planet to man's wandering eye,
And give their names to immortality.[1]

In 1863, Vidya, or knowledge, in the form of a beautiful woman, appeared in a dream to an old pensioner, and asked him to reinstate her glory in the land of Bengal. The pensioner, Tarakrishna Haldar, had loyally served the colonial government, as a *munsif,* an acting deputy collector, and an additional *sudder amini,* for over twenty years. Eventually he had retired to Varanasi where he received the instructions of Vidya in his dream. Vidya directed him to cleanse the world by imparting to it some basic moral precepts. This task, however, was not as easy as it sounded. Vidya warned her new acolyte that the people of Bengal were presently under the influence of Maya, the very embodiment of Avidya (ignorance, or wrong knowledge). The wily Maya had so stupefied mankind that presently all moral instructions were received with ridicule and the moral instructor even risked losing his life. The only way that the blind multitudes could be reached was through a new social object which could be representative and disseminatory of Vidya herself: the printed book.[2]

---

[1] Madhusudan Dutt on his classmates at Hindu College in Kshetra Gupta, ed., *Madhusudan Rachanabali,* 11th edition (Calcutta: Sahitya Samsad, 1990), English poem no. 41.

[2] Tarakrishna Haldar, *Chamtkar Swapnadarshan* (Calcutta: N.L. Sheel's Press, 1867), pp. 6–8.

This story though unique in its particular form was by no means unusual in its content. Vidya made frequent trips to Bengal in the nineteenth century in the minds and acts of policy makers and intellectuals, though not often in dreams and rarely as a beautiful woman. The unifying concern of the colonizer and the colonized in the nineteenth century seems to have been the nature and extent of education. It formed the subject matter of textbooks, the central dispute of official policy, the topic of public debates, and, most importantly, the unquestionable root of social reform. Education and its handmaiden, reform, could make, or break, the known universe. It turned women into assertive subjects, lower castes into claimants of social justice, and the content colonial babu into a firebrand nationalist. Education and culture formed the two most significant elements that made up the world of the Hindu *bhadralok* gentry of the nineteenth century.

Indeed, education and culture were so characteristic of the bhadralok that both contemporary observers and present-day historians have conflated self-definitions of the historical subjects to be the objective truths about these subjects. An official report in 1928 described the school as 'the one gate to the society of the bhadralok'.[3] J.H. Broomfield in his study of twentieth-century nationalism, attributed to education the 'hallmark of bhadralok status'.[4] Even the postcolonial theorist accords specific importance to the world of culture and education. According to Partha Chatterjee, the domain of intellect and culture, or what he has famously called the 'spiritual domain', was equivalent to a civil society for the colonized, a 'sovereign territory from which the colonial power was excluded'.[5]

With such a wide range of opinions, from such diverse intellectual and political orientation, converging to nominate the world of culture as the representative register of the bhadralok world, it seems almost churlish to raise any further questions. But how did education become the defining

---

[3] Simon Commission, Volume VIII, p. 24, quoted in J.H. Broomfield, *Elite Conflict in a Plural Society: Twentieth-Century Bengal* (Berkeley and Los Angeles: University of California Press, 1968) p. 8.

[4] Ibid.

[5] Partha Chatterjee, 'The Disciplines of Colonial Bengal' in Partha Chatterjee, ed., *Texts of Power: Emerging Disciplines in Colonial Bengal* (Calcutta: Samya, 1996), p. 14. For a more detailed ennunciation of this argument see Partha Chatterjee, *The Nation and its Fragments: Colonial and Postcolonial Histories* (New Delhi: Oxford University Press, 1993).

template of the bhadralok? Was this always so? How was this defining stereotype maintained through time? These are some of the questions that the present work seeks to address. We seek to draw attention to the social implications of education. Education was, if anything, a charged concept. One editorial in the *Reformer*, owned and supervised by the Tagores, had its finger on the pulse when it tried to define the term:

Education when applied in the sense we are now using the term, does not mean the knowledge of English or any particular language; but the cultivation of the understanding, the improvement of the moral sense and of good and correct principle. It is not 'the art of speaking any language correctly' but the science of the mind, dependent on no particular pursuit.[6]

Culture and education, as this passage implies, were rarely unrelated to social and economic power. More often than not, the non-institutionalized appearance of the former, disguised access to the latter. Previous scholarly works on nineteenth-century Bengal and the bhadralok, with a few notable exceptions, *describes* the world of culture and education as an almost natural attribute of the bhadralok as a social group. It is the purpose of the present work to provide an *explanatory framework* for the obsessive importance accorded to such social categories as education and culture.

Fundamentally, we try to do two things in this book. One is to understand what constituted 'education', or vidya, in the nineteenth century and the other is to determine how and by whom the hallowed circle of the truly learned was formed. Admittedly, none of these questions can be adequately answered, either theoretically, or empirically, on the basis of Bengal's experience alone. Recent studies of other provinces point towards certain foundational similarities with Bengal but with interesting twists. Veena Naregal's work on the Maharashtrian public sphere, for example, has argued that the education policy in Maharashtra was 'a rubric for a whole set of inter-related assumptions and practices about knowledge, cultivation, textuality and identity'.[7] In this we share common ground, for it is precisely these peripheral 'assumptions' around education that we

[6] *The Reformer*, 19 September 1831, cited in Benoy Ghosh, ed., *Selections from English Periodicals of Nineteenth-Century Bengal*, Vol. 5 (Calcutta: Papyrus, 1978), pp. 47–8.

[7] Veena Naregal, *Language Polities, Elites and the Public Sphere* (New Delhi: Permanent Black, 2001), p. 146.

seek to unpack. Naregal's work provides us with an exciting contrast with our situation in her analysis of lower caste participation in the constitution of the intellectual terrain of Maharashtra. Maharashtra having experienced a much more robust assertion from the lower castes than Bengal, Naregal's material reveals how for all their reformist zeal 'the English educated intellectual elite remained dependent on the non-Brahmin leadership for gound-level support'.[8] In Bengal upper caste-ness, unfortunately, came to be naturalized as part of the bhadralok intellectual identity, as did its largely Hindu spirit. The question, however, still remains as to why this was so and when exactly this process of defining learnedness began.

We begin by asking why learnedness became the focus of social discourse from the middle of the nineteenth century. One obvious answer to this question, and one that scholars have pointed out in great detail, is that English education opened the door to gainful employment. Lal Behari Dey recalled in his autobiography the reason why his father urged him to leave his native village in 1834 and move to Calcutta:

A knowledge of English education, he (my father) said, was necessary to enable a man to earn a competence in life. People ignorant of English no doubt got berths, but berths to which only paltry salaries were attached. He felt his want of English everyday, and was therefore resolved to remedy that defect in the education of his son.[9]

Most of the renowned men of this period had similar administrations from their fathers. There were serious debates both in the learned journals and the popular press about the efficacies of education: that is, how and why education in the modern day was related to employment. But the discourse about learning and education was wider than being merely about English education. Indeed, learnedness was truly a 'discourse' in the Foucauldian sense. It was the ideological link between the cultural codes of society—language, values, schemes of perceptions—and the actual material institutions of that society—schools and colleges, employment possibilities, avenues of rule, and so on.[10] Hence the textbooks of the

---

[8] Ibid., p. 267.

[9] Lal Behari Dey quoted in B.T. McCully, *English Education and the Origins of Indian Nationalism* (New York: Columbia University Press, 1940), p. 44.

[10] See for details M. Foucault, *The Archaeology of Knowledge, and the Discourse on Language* (New York: Pantheon Books, 1972).

period, the key socialization signals to a new generation, regurgitated endlessly the importance of vidya and the dire consequences of its lack. The introduction of cheap print and the colonial grid of educational institutions made education available to all in *principle*. When Bhudev Mukhopadhyaya argued in 1864 that even the basest of men should have access to education, he was voicing the opinion of several of his peers.[11] The school system was layered into lower, middle, and higher class schools for the villages, district headquarters, and cities respectively. The geographical location of the schools formed an educational network with Calcutta as the centrifugal site of knowledge. The institutional hierarchy complemented a spatial hierarchy with the University of Calcutta as the end to a long chain of schools and high schools in the neighbouring towns and villages. As in the case Dey, 'going to study in Calcutta' formed the organizing metaphor for an educational project for several young boys of the nineteenth century. In this project he would have to cross the geographical distance between his native village and Calcutta, a journey which simultaneously served as a trope for his intellectual maturation. The meritorious village boy formed an important figure in the late nineteenth-century literature, who by his individual merit and wits overcame the hurdles placed in his path in this long epistemic pilgrimage from the village to the city.[12]

But was the acquirement of a formal degree the same as being educated? This is the more important question that the present work seeks to answer. A government report of 1919 stated four significant reasons why the educational migrant moved from the village to the city: ancient tradition, lack of local facilities, the fascination with and the glamour of Calcutta, and the opportunity to escape from the '*res angustae* of their home and

---

[11] Bhudev Mukhopadhyay, *Shikshabishayak Prastab* (Hooghly: Bodhodoy Press, 1864), pp. 2–3.

[12] Accounts of the childhood of famous men form the staple of this genre. See for example, Chandicharan Bandyopadhyay, *Vidyasagar Chatrajiban* (Calcutta: n.p., 1896). Several protagonists in contemporary literature also correspond to this powerful motif. Tagore's heores in *Tyag, Ek Ratri, Chuti, Samapti* are some of the more prominent examples along with Bibhutibhushan Bandopadhyay's Apu. For details, see Rabindranath Thakur, *Rabindra Rachanabali*, Vol. 9 (Calcutta: Government of West Bengal, 1988), pp. 68–72; 72–76; 110–14; 151–62; Bibhutibhushan Bandopadhyay, 'Aparajito Part 2' in *Bibhutirachanabali* Vol. 3, edited by Gajendrakumar Mitra, Chandidas Chattopadhyay, and Taradas Bandopadhyay (Calcutta: Mitra Ghosh, 1972).

village conditions into the fuller and less circumscribed life of the towns'.[13] The move to the city thus involved much more than the earning of a degree. It was a lesson in urban life, in new notions, experiences, and habits and, like the school system, there also existed a strict hierarchy of such experiences.

Several informal institutions of this period served as equally important arenas of schooling as the formal ones. The various associations and literary circles, which existed in almost all the major district towns, were key domains where social power was constituted and access to key social positions determined. There also existed libraries, reading rooms, and political organizations all carefully managed to be particular and selective. Rajat Sanyal's insightful study of voluntary associations goes as far as to state that although these bodies were theoretically open to all, in actuality they 'could be used by the privileged sections of the people as an instrument to keep lower classes further culturally distant'.[14] Not all scholarship on informal social practices, however, arrives at similar conclusions. Dipesh Chakrabarty's recent discussion of *adda* exalts this social practice as an indigenous improvement upon the notion of civil society. The concept of civil society according to Chakrabarty has built into it utilitarian motivations, *adda* on the other hand enjoys 'a sense of time and space that ... [is] not subject to ... instrumental purpose'.[15] While Chakrabarty lists for us the various humorous and sociable accounts of the numerous *addas* of the Bengali intelligentsia, there is no cautionary note in his account about how such informal social gatherings resecured traditional social roles and also acted as gatekeepers to others less privileged. To be considered truly educated in a manner that the editorial in the *Reformer* hinted at, a degree from the Hindu College was thus a necessary but not sufficient condition. It had to be bolstered by literary production, participation in social reform, and very importantly, and frequently, by opportune marriages.

---

[13] *Report of the Commission Appointed by the Government of India to Enquire into the Conditions and Prospects of the University of Calcutta*, Vol. 2, Part I (Calcutta, 1919), p. 314.

[14] Rajat Sanyal, *Voluntary Associations and the Urban Public Life in Bengal 1815–1876: An Aspect of Social History* (Calcutta: Riddhi, 1980), p. 8.

[15] Dipesh Chakrabarty, 'Adda: A History of Sociality' in his *Provincializing Europe: Postcolonial Thought and Historical Difference* (Princeton: Princeton University Press, 2000), pp. 204–5.

We suggest that the commentaries about education and being educated should be seen as key arguments in staking out the territory of a new emergent middle class. We examine the characteristics of this territory and the ways in which it was protected by conditions of entry that were either tacitly and practically required, or explicitly codified and legally guaranteed.

This brings us to the other chief concern for this work which is to determine the social location of the bhadralok. At the risk of simplifying our argument: our analysis of the bhadralok marks a departure from previous scholarly disputations on the subject in two important respects. First, we try to show the bhadralok as a *heterogeneous* category unified for a variety of political and ideological reasons. Sumit Sarkar's work on the *kerani* (clerk) forms an important marker for this argument.[16] While Sarkar points towards the existence of differing economic categories within the category of the bhadralok we extend the argument further to show why and how these divisions were socially maintained. We try to provide a material explanation as to why the category of the bhadralok appeared as a homogenous one and whose interests were best represented in such an ideological stratagem.

Second, we investigate the material aspects of bhadralok culture as opposed to providing a cultural explanation to material circumstances. In the course of the following chapters we suggest that the constituent elements of the nineteenth-century bhadralok world, education and culture, had not only material roots but also a material function. On the one hand what appeared as *subjective* social codes of comportment, style, and morals, were in reality the result of *objective* social and economic relations: birth, schooling, and other less formalized social networks. On the other hand, culture, or at least the rhetoric about culture, was something that gave a unified identity to the bhadralok as they came from extremely diverse economic and social backgrounds. Historical variables such as level of education, or social origin, usually appear as stable notions in society whose apparent explanatory power stems from the mental habits of common sense knowledge of the social world. In place of this, ours is an attempt to establish an exact relationship between well-defined concepts.

[16] Sumit Sarkar, *Writing Social History* (New Delhi: Oxford University Press, 1997).

Culture and Modernity: Raiding the Arsenal of the Postcolonial Theorist

The history of nineteenth-century Bengal, in recent years, has seen a veritable explosion in the study of cultural forms and practices. From the experiential components of a nation in formation, the literature has mapped the various practices of everyday life and its interruptions, like sexuality, protest movements, clock-time, and even garbage. While this list is by no means exhaustive of the cultural forms under consideration by scholars of colonial Bengal, a common theme that lends them unity is that they are all concerned with the production of a colonial *culture*. Appearing variously as problems of 'modernity', 'rationality', or dominant knowledge forms, these studies tell the story of the colonial encounter as an encounter between two alien *cultures*, either as assimilative, confrontational, or attributive. Every aspect of colonial culture thus becomes serious business and therefore it is worthwhile to outline our methodology in dealing with such an amorphous concept.

'Culture' in the scholarship of the postcolonialist assumes an immanent intellectual autonomy. Nicholas B. Dirks has called colonialism itself 'a cultural project of control', and claimed that 'in certain important ways culture was what colonialism was all about'.[17] This is an exceptionally wide latitude given to culture where it can claim to be about anything from the devastation of an economy to the translation of textbooks by the bhadralok. Also, the claim that colonialism is about cultural control is somewhat mistaking the tree for the forest. The simple 'control' of a people, or the forging of discourses about control, cannot be the reason for an almost three hundred year old empire, spread over three continents, although it may certainly be a justification for, or an outcome of, it.

Admittedly, all interventions made by the colonial state on the cultural life of India had to be within the paradigm of dominance. But does this also apply to the rising class of Indians who argued for certain changes in society? The discourse analyst would reply in the affirmative. Going by this logic one would have to end by arguing that a man such as Rammohan Roy was somehow corrupted by Enlightenment/colonial ideology and hence pushed for the abolition of sati. The impact this particular legislation had

---

[17] Nicholas B. Dirks, ed., *Colonialism and Culture* (Ann Arbor: University of Michigan Press, 1992), p. 3.

on the power of a certain caste and class of men to burn women alive then becomes inconsequential. Also in the case of another such legislation, the Widow Remarriage Act, the popular songs sung by ordinary people in the streets of Calcutta praising Vidyasagar for his efforts, are then, by a similar logic, of no consequence.[18]

Sumit Sarkar has recently made an extremely relevant point with regard to the postcolonial intellectual's ire towards Enlightenment rationality. Colonial middle-class thinking, he has argued, cannot be anachronistically judged from the point of view of rejection, or acceptance, of colonial discourse. Elegantly rescuing the nineteenth-century intellectual from the condescension of posterity, Sarkar has usefully pointed out that use of the rhetoric of liberal rights in the nineteenth century may have served as an important tool of criticism of specific aspects of colonial policy, particularly in the case of caste inequality, gender justice, and class conflict.[19]

We share with Sarkar the reluctance to reject the principles of European Enlightenment simply because it came to Bengal through the avenues of colonialism. This is so for two reasons. First, the political ideals of Enlightenment were the result of the struggle against the hierarchical order of the European ancient regime. In place of a segregated world of ranks and estates apparently sanctified by divine will, a new generation of philosophers and revolutionaries posited a society run by a participatory government premised upon the equality of its citizenry. The historical instantiation of the political ideals of Enlightenment, such as equality, or liberty, was however severely circumscribed. The ideals it seems came with tacit, or explicit, stipulations excluding women, the poor, the colonized people, slaves and many other groups from its scope.

The postcolonial theorist's solution to this problematic is a wholesale rejection of Enlightenment modernity, dubbing the entire modern project as a mere handmaiden of colonialism.[20] This brings us to our second

[18] For a history of such songs and doggerels see Sumanta Banerjee, 'Marginalization of Women's Popular Culture in Nineteenth-century Bengal', in K. Sangari and S.Vaid, eds., *Recasting Women: Essays in Colonial History* (Delhi: Kali for Women, 1989), pp. 127–80.

[19] Sumit Sarkar, 'Post-modernism and the Writing of History', *Studies in History*, 15, 2, (1999), p. 317.

[20] Dirks thus calls colonialism 'a theatre for the Enlightenment project'. Nicholas Dirks, ed., *Colonialism*, p. 6.

objection in rejecting the historical principles of modernity. The postcolonial approach seems to unconditionally ignore the single most important political and ideological contribution of the modern project: a thoroughgoing critique of premodernity. Indeed there has been a disturbing trend in historical writing on colonialism to actually celebrate premodernity as the natural alternative to colonialism.[21] Our disagreement with this position could not be clearer.

Hereditary institutions and rituals cannot find ready refuge in a rhetoric of divine right, or sanction, since the Enlightenment and the French Revolution. The individual and sovereign subjecthood of humanity has been established to such a universal extent that it can provide an effective paradigm against which any unfair practice may be measured. The abolition of a particular injustice, New World slavery, or Apartheid, merely highlights those that still demand rectification: women's oppression, or the exploitation of workers. The very generalization of the principles of modern equality, over both time and space, draws attention to any particular historical or local deviation from it.

This is an important rider for us when dealing with the nineteenth century in Bengal. Sekhar Bandyopadhyay's work on the Namasudras in Bengal incisively points out that for the majority of people, particularly from the lower castes, modernity was a distinctive improvement over premodernity.[22] Tanika Sarkar's contribution to the history of gender in the bhadralok world is perhaps the most creative treatment of this issue. Contextualizing premodern structures of dominance and oppression, she refuses to absolve the colonized upper caste–class bhadralok of 'complicity and culpability in the making of structures of exploitation'. Her detailed study of indigenous orthodox discourse on domesticity and gender shows that unlike the postcolonial claim that the colonized was overwhelmed and silenced by the colonial knowledge/power project, 'colonial structures

---

[21] The most prominent theoretical espousal of this position can be found in Partha Chatterjee, *The Nation and its Fragments: Colonial and Postcolonial Histories* (Delhi: Oxford University Press, 1995). A more empirical elaboration of the same theme can be found in Gautam Bhadra, *Iman O Nishan: Banglar Krishak Chaitanyer Ek Adhyaya* (Calcutta: Subarnarekha, 1994) where Bhadra valorizes the non-rational religious consciousness of the lower classes.

[22] Sekhar Bandyopadyay, *Caste, Protest and Identity in Colonial India: The Namasudras in Bengal, 1872–1947* (Richmond: Curzon Press, 1997), pp. 54–8.

of power' actually had a lot to learn from 'indigenous patriarchy and upper caste norms and practices which in certain areas of life, retained considerable hegemony'.[23] Indeed a *Western-liberal* rhetoric of individual rights could provide a much needed source of resistance to *indigenous* structures of oppression based on divine, or hereditary, sanction. Talking about a bhadralok modernity, as we do in this work, it is thus worthwhile to remember the anxieties and tribulations that outline the world of this numerically insignificant but socially momentous group. Their critique of colonialism is often framed by a nostalgia for precolonial times where the woman and the shudra knew their respective places. Consequently, their educational practices are marked by this combination of revivalist and anti-colonial concerns. Regarding colonialism as part of a larger global process effectively forms the framework of this book.

Colonialism, we argue, cannot be seen as merely a confrontation of two alien cultures. A recent study on the emergence of markets is a typical example of this approach. Accounting for the history of 'global expansion of European mercantile capital', Sudipta Sen argues that 'rather than being just a mechanistic structure of inevitable economic dominance' colonial expansion can be seen 'legitimately in the light of political and cultural confrontation, conflict, and compromise that *set the context* for such economic change' (emphasis mine).[24] To say that colonialism was a confrontation of two different universes of meaning is stating the obvious. The more important question is, why did one universe succeed over the other? The answer cannot be sought in numbers, brute force, hegemony, or dominance (though barring the first all the others are relevant), but needs to be viewed structurally as the success of a more productive mode of production over the other. Colonialism only makes sense as an outcome of capitalism. Seen only in its cultural implications the structural modalities of the political economy is subsumed under a 'clash of civilizations' approach.

The contradictions within both colonialism as a system, and the role of the classes within Indian society, cannot be understood without this view of the capitalist system as a whole. The concept of classes needs to

---

[23] Tanika Sarkar, *Hindu Wife, Hindu Nation: Community, Religion and Cultural Nationalism* (Bloomington: Indiana University Press, 2001), pp. 193–4.

[24] Sudipta Sen, *Empire of Free Trade: The East India Company and the Making of the Colonial Marketplace* (Philadelphia: University of Pennsylvania Press, 1998), p. 3.

replace that of an 'elite' in order to understand why a Bankim, Rammohan, or Vidyasagar inevitably had 'cultural' agendas, or why their projects had to be limited in terms of any real change. The non-Marxist view of history is ill-equipped to deal with such contradictions and this is nowhere clearer than in the history of colonial Bengal.

The Long Shadow of the Bengal Renaissance

Every student of nineteenth-century Bengal is aware of the resonance of the term 'renaissance' that is applied to this period. The derived meaning of the term, that is, the 'revival of art and literature', is closely tied to its historiography, in the sense that a large body of the literature on this period documents the various cultural and social achievements of the Bengalis in the field of art and literary production.[25] The ancillary implication of the word renaissance is a series of attitudinal changes in the social perspective which is often read as the formulating basis for the emergence of new art forms. Culture, as read by the discourse analysts, was a huge preoccupation of the age. The first text that sets the terms of this period is perhaps Shibnath Shastri's *Ramtanu Lahiri O Tatkalin Bangasamaj* (1909). Shastri, himself a product of the Brahmo movement and an active social reformer narrativizes the nineteenth century in terms of its key figures and significant events. However, he foregrounds his history under the assumptions of 'modernity' rather than that of a 'renaissance', a familiar position since the mid-nineteenth century, when a series of writers in self-proclamatory moments nominated the age as the beginning of the modern under various titles such as *adhunik*, or *ekal*.[26]

---

[25] The number of books on the subject in Bengali and English are too numerous to quote here, but most of them are on the celebratory aspects of the renaissance in terms of either its social reforms or art and literary production. See for example, A. Gupta, ed., *Studies in the Bengal Renaissance* (Calcutta: National Council of Education, 1958); J.K. Majumdar, *Raja Rammohan Roy and the Progressive Movements in India: A Selection from Records* (Calcutta: Art Press, 1941); B.B. Majumdar, *History of Political Thought from Rammohun to Dayananda (1821–84)* (Calcutta: University of Calcutta, 1934); N.S. Bose, *The Indian Awakening and Bengal* (Calcutta: Firma KLM, 1960); Susobhan Sarkar, *On the Bengal Renaissance* (Calcutta: Papyrus reprint 1985); R.C. Majumdar, *Renascent Bengal* (Calcutta: Asiatic Society, 1972); and Benoy Ghosh, *Banglar Nabajagriti* (Calcutta: Orient Longman, reprint 1979) among others.

[26] The most famous being Rajnarayan Basu, *Sekal ar Ekal* (Calcutta: Valmiki Press, 1874).

The writings of an age can reckon with change in two normative ways. One is by denominating change as the beginning of something new, or the loss of something old; and the other is by a ceaseless interrogation of the reasons for change. The writers of the nineteenth century did both. For them the reason for change was quite simple: foreign rule. Thus all discussions of the social phenomenon were conducted within a comparative rubric between Europe and India. The interrogation took many forms. Recent scholarship has emphasized the role of history as a discipline as one of the forms of this interrogation.[27] We are, however, concerned here with a different question. Comparisons between the West and the East took place in Bengali writing as a search for areas of excellence for the East. This was inevitably found in spiritual, or metaphysical, domains. Chandranath Basu's *Hindutva* (1892) is one of the most clearly formulated tracts on the subject.

In this text Basu raises the philosophical question of whether the creator and the universe are one and the same thing. In Hinduism, he says, they are, while Christianity distinguishes between the two. What then follows is that due to this basic metaphysical difference between the two belief systems: European culture is governed by a strong sense of the self, which is completely missing from all aspects of Indian thought. This merging of the Indian self into a sublime and all-encompassing universe creates an ontology for the Hindu self, which is one with the general ontology of creation itself. Herein lies the superiority of India over Europe:

In spirituality and mental strength none are her equal—all others are mere children in comparison. Europeans or Americans alike tremble at the thought of her adamantine road to meditative peace ... they are easily perturbed by the mundane and transient earthly concerns. The more their civilisation progresses the more agitated they get over material gains ... hence their scorn at the Indian *tapasvi*, [hence they shiver at *nirambu ekadasi* (the custom of widows fasting without either eating or drinking)], hence they condemn Indian widowhood as barbarity. It is not that they cannot bear any affliction, they certainly can. But that is more often than not to acquire earthly pleasures and wealth .... One cannot compare them to the Hindu. The Hindu's mind is depthless, the Hindu's spirituality limitless .... The Hindu progresses along this broad path, bearing his transcendental pains ... to merge with the Great Being.[28]

[27] For a recent exposition of this theme see Ranajit Guha, *History at the Limit of World History* (New York: Columbia University Press, 2002).

[28] Chandranath Basu, *Hindutva* (Calcutta: Medical Library, 1892), pp. 29–31.

Chandranath Basu was one of the more prominent opponents of the Age of Consent Bill for women in 1891 and can be squarely put in the anti-reformist camp. What is important for us here is that this divide between the material (Europe) and the spiritual (India), which forms the basic structure of Basu's argument is a rehabilitation of older Orientalist scholarship conducted by Europeans. The conflation of Indianness with an innate Hindu religion and spirituality forming an infrastructure of 'Eastern' civilization, was the theme of most Orientalist scholars of the Hastings era.[29] In Basu we can detect the more conservative derivations of this original divide, in this case employed in the service of preserving upper class/caste and patriarchal hierarchies.

Coming from a more liberal tradition, Anandachandra Mitra's explication of civilizational difference strikes a more generous note. A diligent activist and reformer for the Sadharan Brahmo Samaj, Mitra tried to come to grips with change in his *Prachin Bharat O Adhunik Europe Sabhyatar Bhinna Murti* (1876). Here, the cardinal difference between Europe and India is still located along the same lines of religion (India) and utility (Europe), but there are some interesting insights. Utility gains a unique meaning for Mitra. It is synonymous with principles and authorizes nationhood. Contrasting methods of warfare between ancient India and modern Europe, Mitra speculates that allegiance to a broader humanitarian virtue of dharma, abstracted from the mechanics of practicality, made the ancient Indians underestimate the evils of Muslim invaders and were consequently subjugated by them. Europeans, on the other hand, had a firm commitment to the general welfare of the many and thus conducted their wars not on principles of morality but under principles of greater national good. Wars were fought to facilitate trade, and for the enrichment of the motherland. The lack of a certain kind of morality in the Europeans is not a point of critique for Mitra, for the difference is celebrated by transferring one set of morality to the other. It is noteworthy that nationhood in the text is defined along almost Rousseauean lines of the General Will.

[29] See for example, Thomas R. Metcalf, *Ideologies of the Raj* (Cambridge: Cambridge University Press, 1995); Ronald Inden, *Imagining India* (Oxford: Blackwell, 1990); David Kopf, *British Orientalism and the Indian Renaissance 1773–1835* (California: University of California Press, 1965); and Carol A. Breckenridge and Peter van der Veer, eds., *Orientalism and the Postcolonial Predicament* (Philadelphia: University of Pennsylvania Press, 1993) among others.

Nations, according to Mitra, are composites of people's common aspirations and common welfare, and the lesser evil of fighting wars (in this case the Napoleonic ones) is sublimated under the greater good of prosperity that it brings to the nation as a whole.[30] This was not a unique position. As early as in 1828, twenty-two year old Kashiprasad Ghosh read an essay condemning James Mill's *History of British India* (1815) at the annual examination of the Hindu College. Ghosh perceived no barbaric society in the Hindu past held together by despotism. The power of the Hindu king was presented by Ghosh, almost along modern democratic principles, where he was supposed to have been 'restrained by the people and the law'.[31]

It is quite likely that Mitra was acquainted with certain Enlightenment literature.[32] What is more significant is his intermingling of a longing for a renaissance myth about an Indian past along with hopes for a future deliverance through an amorphous nationhood. Spirituality, unlike in Basu, is not zealously guarded, but contextualized. Europe's greatest art he feels lies in the general government offices, not in the ornate pureness of churches. The commemoration of human potential, the celebration of human prowess is the secret of Europe's difference with India. 'The place of the goddess in an Aryan town', he writes, 'is taken by the proud raised structure of the government house in Europe.'[33]

Mitra's association with the Sadharan Brahmo Samaj must have played a part in his ideological distancing from a fetishized Indian spirituality. Only a year later Keshabchandra Sen was to say in a public lecture that it was fruitless to revive the 'reign of quietism' that was the regime of ancient India. Meditative speculation had already done a lot of mischief in India and it was time to 'combine meditation and science' to prevent any 'relapsing into ancient mysticism'.[34] By the 1870s and the 1880s the

[30] Anandachandra Mitra, *Prachin Bharat O Adhunik Europe Sabhyatar Bhinna Murti* (Mymensingh: Bharatmihir Press, 1876), pp. 2–8.

[31] C. Ghose, 'Essay on Mill's British India', *Calcutta Gazette*, 14 February 1828.

[32] Henry Derozio, the rebel lecturer at the Hindu College set the trend of inculcating Rousseau's ideas in his students. For more details on this tradition see Benoy Ghose, *Bidrohi Derozio* (Calcutta: Bal Sahitya, 1961); and Sumit Sarkar, *A Critique of Colonial India* (Calcutta: Papyrus, 1985) among others.

[33] Anandachandra Mitra, *Prachin Bharat*, pp. 10–11.

[34] T.E. Slater, ed., *Keshub Chandra Sen and the Brahmo Samaj* (Madras: Society for Promoting Christian Knowledge, 1884), pp. 86–7.

reformist dreams of a renaissance improvement was already turning sour for a whole social group of educated Bengalis. The Brahmo Samaj had had a rather acrimonious split up, racial tensions were mounting with the passage of the Ilbert Bill, and Keshabchandra Sen was soon to renounce his lifelong principles in the scandal of his daughter's wedding with the Coochbehar royal family. On the other hand, liberal Western education had opened up vistas of opportunities in the professional and service sector. It is in this social world, within an admixture of hope and frustration, that these texts must be placed.

This brings us to our second problem for the cultural history of Bengal, its historiography. How does one interpret a body of available texts? Or to put it differently, what does a text represent? There are in the main three traditions of reading the nineteenth century. The first is the nationalist tradition. In the works of this generation of historians the sources were read as being concomitant to reality. The first symposium on the period was held in 1933 on the death centenary of Rammohan Roy. Leading figures of the early twentieth century who had actually lived a part of the era under discussion, such as Rabindranath Tagore and Bipinchandra Pal, participated in this symposium, their location in history normatively writing the text for history.[35]

The 1940s were a turbulent time for most people, and history-writing could not but be affected by the tremendous potential of the Royal Indian Navy (RIN) mutiny, the stark horrors of an exceptionally bloody partition, and finally the actual reality of a free India. For the members of a new and fairly weak Communist Party of India (CPI), this was the decade which moulded them ideologically as well as in activity, and it was the turmoils of this period that tempered most of their writing. The historical trend to read the sources as being ideological, that is assuming a certain level of mediation in their very formation, has been, in other parts of the world the classical Marxist tradition. For Bengal this had a more specific political agenda.

When the Seventh Congress of the Comintern met in 1935, the Nazis had taken power in Germany, thanks in part to the fatally sectarian tactics of a Stalinized International in the years after 1928, which made social democracy the chief enemy. From this ridiculous ultra-left position, the Comintern was now to be swung by the Stalinists to a position well to the

---

[35] Satish Chandra Chakravarti, ed., *The Father of Modern India* (Calcutta: Rammohan Roy Centenary Committee, 1935).

right of the social democratic parties, to a position of class collaboration—
precisely the position taken by the social democrats during and after the
First World War against which the founders of the Comintern had revolted.
The 'People's Front', a systematic class collaboration with the 'liberal
bourgeoisie' was to be the official line.[36] This perspective was presented
to the colonies as a project to create 'an anti-imperialist people's front'
and to 'draw the widest masses into the national liberation movement'.[37]
Thus nationalism, so far held at a critical distance by the Marxists, came
under renewed focus. For all intents and purposes, the Marxists in the
1940s, held, what can only be called a more nuanced nationalist position,
where a political affirmation of popular-front strategies ('People's War'),
led to a theoretical assertion of the progressive role of a national bourgeoisie.

The threat of partition, the horrors of the 1943 famine, British armed
repression, and the overwhelming bitterness against the mainstream
nationalists were enough to make the Bengali communist intellectuals stay
firmly with the CPI as the only possible alternative. In 1946, when the
students' movement in Calcutta was at its height, the eminent historian
Susobhan Sarkar wrote his *Notes on the Bengal Renaissance* under the
pseudonym, Amit Sen. All of the nationalist fervour generated both by the
genuine anti-colonial impulse and the CPI line, was brought to bear on
this tract. Bengal was elevated to a status of almost metaphysical superiority:

The impact of British rule, bourgeois economy and modern Western culture was
felt first in Bengal and produced an awakening known usually as the Bengal
Renaissance. For about a century, Bengal's conscious awareness of the changing
modern world was more developed and ahead of that of the rest of India. The role
played by Bengal in the modern awakening of India is thus comparable to the
position occupied by Italy ....[38]

[36] For details see Duncan Hallas, *The Comintern* (London: Bookmarks, 1985).

[37] Extract from the Resolutions of the Seventh Congress of the International,
quoted in Hélène Carrère d'Encausse and Stuart R. Schram, *Marxism and Asia: An
Introduction with Readings* (London: Allen Lane The Penguin Press, 1969), p. 248.

[38] Susobhan Sarkar, *On the Bengal Renaissance* (Calcutta: Papyrus reprint 1985),
p. 13. Sarkar's superiority as a historian, however, lies in the fact that by the 1960s he
had begun to point out how the 'renaissance' had moved 'on the axis of the upper
stratum alone of society', excluded the Muslims and the majority of the lower caste
Hindus and had failed to 'strike a consistent anti-imperialist note'. Sarkar, *Notes on the
Bengal Renaissance*, pp. 70–71.

This text was seminal in lots of ways. It won the CPI 'great prestige and ...
became a textbook or reference book for postgraduates in several Indian
Universities'.[39] A whole generation of young scholars, both Marxist and
non-Marxist, took their lead from this book and recreated for the troubled
era a glorious Bengali heritage of the 'renaissance'.[40]

The appellation 'renaissance' came under severe attack in the 1970s,
when radical hopes were awakened within intellectual circles once more
through the Naxalite struggles. Dismantling earlier notions about the glories
of the nineteenth century, and particularly the bhadralok's role in it, a new
generation of scholars undertook the project of an alternative reading of
the sources.[41] The radical peasant struggles of the period, the rebellious
attack of Naxalite youths on renaissance figures, and the concomitant
vibrant political culture of denouncing, rightly or wrongly, most things to
be either 'bourgeois' or 'comprador' had a profound effect on views of the
past. From being the 'awakening' to modernity, the renaissance was
projected as a narrow, subscribed effort of a handful of middle-class
intellectuals, severed from the masses. The oppositional and anti-colonial
content of the nineteenth century was entirely traded in for, in some
writings, to use a later formulation, a 'derivative discourse' of the bhadralok.
One scholar thus commented that the Bengali intelligentsia 'very much a
product of the osmosis of English education' had 'already invested
themselves in the colonial system and were totally dependent on the British

---

[39] P.C. Joshi, 'A Dedicated Teacher—Some Memories', in Barun De, ed., *Essays in Honour of Prof. S.C. Sarkar* (New Delhi: People's Publishing House, 1976), pp. 7–8.

[40] The most noted among the Marxists was Benoy Ghosh, *Banglar Nabajagriti*. From the non-Marxist tradition, Brajendranath Bandyopadhyay and Sajanikanta Das produced the multi-volume series of the biographies of the great and good of the nineteenth-century in their *Sahitya Sadhak Charitmala* between 1939 and 1952.

[41] See articles by Asok Sen, Sumit Sarkar, and Barun De in V.C. Joshi, ed., *Rammohan Roy and the Process of Modernization in India* (Delhi: Vikas, 1975); Asok Sen, *Iswarchandra Vidyasagar and his Elusive Milestones* (Calcutta: Riddhi-India, 1977); Dipesh Chakrabarty, 'The Colonial Context of the Bengal Renaissance: A Note on early Railway-Thinking in Bengal', Paper presented at the 33rd Session of the Indian History Congress at Muzaffarpur, Decmber 1972; Barun De, 'A Critique of the Historiography of the Trend Entitled "Renaissance" in Nineteenth Century India', Paper presented at the Indo-Soviet symposium on India and Russia in Moscow, May 1973. A more radical note is struck by Suprakash Ray on peasant movements in *Mukti-yuddhe Bharatiya Krishak*, first published 1966 (Calcutta: Bharati Book Stall, 1980); and others.

herrenvolk both ideologically and materially'.[42] On a similar note, Asok Sen added that the 'new Bengali middle class' was 'very much a creature of the dispensations of British rule and administration'.[43] The baby, in other words, was thrown out with the bath water.[44]

The youthful and largely justified historical fury of the 1970s matured into a systematic critique of 'elite' historiography in the early 1980s. Responding both to nationalist hagiographies and Stalinist apologies for nationalism, Ranajit Guha's Preface to the first volume of *Subaltern Studies* (1982) was a manifesto for the first concerted and regularized break with nationalist history.[45] It was a project to restore the 'subaltern' voice to history, which the collective justifiably argued had been censured by the clamour of nationalists and Marxists alike. In the varied documents of peasant uprisings, autobiographies of women, criminal and judicial records, this history attempted to read the sources against the grain of a dominant ideology.[46] In a way it was a reascription to the Marxist scholarship

[42] Rudrangshu Mukherjee, 'The Azimgarh Proclamation and some Questions on the Revolt of 1857 in the Northwestern Provinces', in Barun De, ed., *Essays in Honour of Prof. S.C. Sarkar*, pp. 480–1.

[43] Asok Sen, 'The Bengal Economy and Rammohan Roy', in V.C. Joshi, ed., *Rammohan Roy*, p. 111.

[44] A substantial amount of recanting was done by the earlier generation of scholars to catch up with the present empirical evidence as well as the political mood. See for example Benoy Ghosh, 'A Critique to [sic] Bengal Renaissance', *Frontier*, 4, 24–6 (September,1971), pp. 4–12.

[45] Even though the importance of the joint project cannot be overstated, it is worthwhile to remember that similar work had been undertaken by individual historians prior to this. The most notable examples being Majid H. Siddiqi, *Agrarian Unrest in North India: The United Provinces 1918–22* (New Delhi: Vikas, 1978); Ravinder Kumar, ed., *Essays on Gandhian Politics: The Rowlatt Satyagraha of 1919* (Oxford: Clarendon Press, 1971) among others.

[46] See, for example, Gyanendra Pandey, 'Rallying around the Cow: Sectarian Strife in the Bhojpur Region, c. 1887–1917', in Ranajit Guha, ed., *Subaltern Studies II* (New Delhi: Oxford University Press, 1983), pp. 60–129; David Arnold, 'Touching the Body: Perspectives on the Indian Plague', in *Subaltern Studies V* (New Delhi: Oxford University Press, 1987), pp. 55–90; Partha Chatterjee, 'Gandhi and the Critique of Civil Society', in *Subaltern Studies III*, pp. 153–95 (New Delhi: Oxford University Press, 1983); Gautam Bhadra, 'Four Rebels of Eighteen Fifty Seven', in *Subaltern Studies IV* (New Delhi: Oxford University Press, 1985); and Tanika Sarkar, 'Jitu Santal's Movement in Malda 1924–1932: A Study in Tribal Protest', in *Subaltern Studies IV* (New Delhi: Oxford University Press, 1985) among others.

undertaken so successfully in Europe by Christopher Hill, E.P. Thompson, George Rudé, and others. There was, however, an important, if unacknowledged, difference.

One of the principal points of departure for this body of scholarship from the social histories of the past was that its methodology was predicated on the idea of a heterogeneity of 'power' relations, best exemplified by a focus on 'practices'. Taking their lead from Foucault, this historiography tried to shift the focus from any concentric source of oppression—like the state, or the family—to what can be best described as a multiplicity of power relationships. The idea was to uncover sources of non-assimilable power born out of a plurality of relationships that form a matrix of institutions in society. The other major theoretical tool was the idea of an 'autonomous domain' of subaltern consciousness and culture. Now it is one thing to argue that contours of major historical events are necessarily shaped by 'pressures from below' and quite another thing to argue for 'autonomy' of consciousness. Ironically, Gramsci's writings were used in defence of this position.[47]

In his *Notes on Italian History* Gramsci sketches out what he calls the 'methodological criteria' for the history of subaltern classes. (Incidentally, on the question of Gramsci's writings, most academic writing does not take cognizance of the fact that the *Prison Notebooks* were written with the fascist state constantly looking over his shoulders. A lot of terms and concepts that he used, thus necessarily had to be vague to avoid prison censorship). Two of these were ultimately going to be the structural basis for the subaltern scholars. The first was the idea that the history of the subaltern classes was 'intertwined' with 'civil society' and not with the state 'until they are able to become a "State"'; and second, the 'formations' that the subalterns themselves produce assert their 'integral autonomy', but 'within the old framework'.[48] Two points need to be made in this regard. One, the distinction between the state and civil society in Gramsci is not as clear-cut as the idea of 'autonomy' as employed by the subaltern historians. In fact, there are several anomalies and ambiguities in his

[47] Ranajit Guha, 'On Some Aspects of the Historiography of Colonial India', in *Subaltern Studies I* (New Delhi: Oxford University Press, 1982), pp. 1–8.

[48] Antonio Gramsci, *Selections from the Prison Notebooks* (New York: International Publishers, 1971), p. 52.

usage of both terms, possibly for the reason stated earlier.[49] Second, subaltern 'formations' is clearly a reference to working class organizations, for in the line just previous to it he talks of the 'parties of the dominant group', that is, the ruling class, in opposition to which the 'formations' of the subaltern classes are asserted.[50]

The idea of the autonomous sphere of subaltern consciousness thus cannot be stretched endlessly. Guha's claim in his *Elementary Aspects of Peasant Insurgency* (1983), that there could be detected an underlying structure of peasant insurgent consciousness, is doing precisely this. The question of consciousness is admittedly a messy one and has preoccupied Marxist theoreticians for decades. For the sake of this argument, however, a reference to Gramsci's exposition of consciousness is sufficient.

He argues that there is a 'co-existence of two conceptions of the world' in the consciousness of subordinate classes in general, and the proletariat in particular. One conception is 'affirmed in words and the other displayed in effective action', presumably referring to class struggle. He further clarifies that:

The social group in question may indeed have its own conception of the world, even if only embryonic; a conception which manifests itself in action, but occasionally and in flashes—when, that is, the group is acting as an organic totality.

Hence

One might almost say that he ['the active man-in-the-mass', that is, the worker] has two theoretical consciousnesses (or one contradictory consciousness): one which is implicit in his activity and which in reality unites him with all his fellow-workers in the practical transformation of the real world; and one, superficially explicit or verbal, which he has inherited from the past and uncritically absorbed.[51]

The meandering over 'autonomous' consciousness is straightened out considerably in these passages. It is clear that what Gramsci has in mind is a coherent class-consciousness for the working class, which will eventually enable it to interpret the world and thereby change it. This is vastly, if not

[49] See for example the note by Quintin Hoare and Geoffrey N. Smith in Antonio Gramsci, *Selections*, pp. 206–9; also Perry Anderson, 'The Antinomies of Antonio Gramsci', *New Left Review*, 100 (November–December, 1976), pp. 5–75.

[50] Antonio Gramsci, *Selections*, p. 52.

[51] Antonio Gramsci, *Selections*, pp. 327, 333.

totally, different from Chatterjee's and Guha's notion of autonomy and is related fundamentally to the specificity of classes and class-consciousness.

Predictably, the first theoretical tool that was sacrificed at the alter of the new methodology, was that of class. Definitionally the term 'subaltern' is a step away from class, and simultaneously works as its implicit critique. Two issues are relevant in this context. One, that Gramsci's use of the term is very specifically located in an *analysis* of class forces, even though the term itself maybe open to ambiguities. In fact Gramsci uses the term in his account of the Turin factory council movement of 1919–20 where it of course unambiguously refers to the working class. Second, the Stalinist tradition of history-writing, in India as elsewhere, formed a major impediment to using the conceptual categories of Marxism. Against the backdrop of a sterile and economistic model, the move away from class, if not necessary, is understandable.[52]

The subaltern historians argued that in the absence of an uninhibited growth of productive forces under colonialism, the bourgeoisie, and consequently the lower orders, lacked an adequate degree of 'classness'.[53] In view of this model of 'insufficiency', which we shall come to later in this chapter, the bourgeoisie was problematized as unable to fulfil its historic tasks in economic and political leadership. Following from this absence of assertion by the bourgeoisie in the political, or 'public' domain, the subalternists gradually, but logically, shifted focus to a 'private' world of cultural practices, inarticulate visions, and unfulfilled dreams. It was in this theoretically reconstituted 'domain' that, in the words of its clearest proponent, Partha Chatterjee, the nation was 'brought into being'.[54]

The discourse of the private, or the spiritual, we would like to argue is not a 'given' as this historiography assumes it to be. Nor can it be read as an infrastructure of protest. To go back to our earlier query about sources: what do the various pronouncements of the 'elite' about the distinctness of Indian culture represent? One way of reading them, as the

---

[52] E.P. Thompson's overtly humanistic and erroneous definition of class is a good example of a generation's justified reaction to Stalinist crudeness. See Thompson, *The Poverty of Theory and Other Essays* (London: Merlin Press, 1978), p. 238; and *The Making of the English Working Class* (Harmondsworth: Penguin, 1991), pp. 8–10.

[53] Asok Sen, 'Subaltern Studies: Capital, Class and Community', in *Subaltern Studies V* (New Delhi: Oxford University Press, 1987), pp. 204–8.

[54] Partha Chatterjee, *The Nation*, p. 6.

historiography discussed earlier does, is to position them within their own realm of credibility. A postmodernist approach in which the text signifies the world. So Chandranath Basu's assertions about Indianness, or Keshab Sen's dilemmas about a Westernized modernity, can be either reclaimed as being the political, or cultural, language of resistance to colonialism; or can be read as being ideological, that is, as a displacement of, or as compensation for, something else. We think Chatterjee is quite right in his implication that this discourse had a political agenda. What is, however, wrong with this argument is an almost stagist theory of social development and change. According to Chatterjee, the 'elite' first arrived at a consciousness of the world within the 'private' and only then was it able to forge ahead with its 'political' confrontation in the public.[55]

Recently Sumit Sarkar has pointed to two of the major pitfalls of this argument. First, the 'material' and 'spiritual' divide that forms the core of Chatterjee's argument is essentially a rehearsal of the conceptual West/East divide that was 'almost classically Orientalist, much loved in particular by the most conservative elements in Indian society in both colonial and postcolonial times'.[56] (We have mentioned Chandranath Basu's work in this respect). And second, even in the 'spiritual' sphere Chatterjee draws attention only to forms of pre-colonial culture, necessarily 'elite', which may or may not appear as signs of conservative revivalist trends but forms, for Chatterjee, essential marks of opposition. The fundamental contradiction of colonialism then emerges as the contradiction between 'reified notions of "community" or "fragment" against [a] highly generalised category of the modern nation-state as the embodiment of western cultural domination'.[57]

Chatterjee's failure to discriminate between the text and the social context within which the texts are produced, leads him to homogenize the two poles of culture, the East and the West. Although Sarkar's discussion of this problem is valuable, it nevertheless has a major lacuna. The reason Chatterjee adopts the spiritual/material divide is because culture, education, and various forms of literary registers were an almost obsessive preoccupation with his 'elite' from the mid-nineteenth century. Sarkar himself accounts for Vidyasagar's success to be the skilful utilization of

---

[55] Ibid.
[56] Sarkar, *Writing Social History*, p. 97.
[57] Ibid., p. 93.

'the three basic determinants of nineteenth-century colonial middle-class life in Bengal: education, *chakri* [salaried job], print culture'.[58] The implications of this statement remains rather underdeveloped in Sarkar's overall analysis, and it is this argument that forms the basic premise of the present work.

We are in agreement with Sarkar that print, jobs, and education were fundamental to the constitution of the middle class in the nineteenth century. This was not lost to the contemporary social agents. It is no small coincidence that most of the prominent nineteenth-century figures were either connected with printing, publishing, education, or as in the case of Vidyasagar, all three. A cursory glance at the first batch of graduates from the Hindu College proves this above supposition in material terms. Rajnarayan Basu, the Brahmo reformer, lists in his autobiography some of his classmates from this group, not with the fond nostalgia for a lost youth, but with the quiet confidence of social distinction. Amongst his associates were: Michael Madhusudan Dutt the poet, Pearycharan Sarkar, a professor at Presidency College and the writer of one of the most popular textbooks of the times, Gyanendramohan Tagore, a barrister, Bhudev Mukhopadhyay, Yogeshchandra Ghosh, deputy magistrates, Anandakrishna Basu, a famous scholar and personal tutor to Raja Narendrakrishna and Rajnarayan Deb, Yagadishnath Roy, the first Bengali to become a district police superin-tendent, Nilmadhab Mukhopadhyay, a renowned doctor, Girishchandra Deb, the Principal of the Hare School, and Gobindachandra Dutta, a high-ranking officer in the Treasury Department.[59] Every arm of the state, every inch of the upper layers of the service sector was fitted out by this new band of eager professionals. It was an age of famous men— remembered for their scholarship, their reforms, and their literary merits. Nineteenth-century Bengal, both in its history and historiography appears as a dramatic world orchestrated by these great men.

Self-definitions are curious artefacts. Besides serving as sociological shorthands for the past they also retain a broad charismatic authority. The term 'bhadralok' is one such definition. Sarkar gives us a near precise analysis of the constituent elements of this definition. In their own perception this was a 'middle class (*madhyasreni*, *madhybitta*), bhadralok world which situated itself below the aristocracy' but 'above the lesser folk'

[58] Ibid., p. 232.
[59] Rajnarayan Basu, *Atmacharit* (Calcutta: Kuntalin Press, 1909), pp. 27–9.

engaged in manual labour and generally from the lower castes, or the Muslims.[60] But what distinguished them from either was education of a particular kind, so much so that in common sense terms, the pronouncements about education became the sole criterion for defining the bhadralok, and was, we shall argue in the following chapters, the basis of a class-based nationalist ideology. The understanding of this as an ideology is not apparent in Sarkar but as this proposition is fairly central to our understanding of the bhadralok, it is worthwhile to pause and analyse it further.

Ideology and Class

Göran Therborn has drawn our attention to a broad definition of ideology, where ideology is 'that aspect of the human condition under which human beings live their lives as conscious actors in a world that makes sense to them in varying degrees'.[61] This conception of ideology as related to consciousness in a social sense makes it irreducible to either discourses, or specific institutions. Persons have ideological beliefs, not classes. However, they do so because of social mechanisms, thus, an ideology is that consciousness that is socially caused. As Jon Elster puts it, 'the study of ideology purports to explain why many similarly situated individuals come to accept the same views, or to produce them simultaneously'.[62]

The literature on the bhadralok tries to get around this problem by either ignoring it, or through a misrecognition of the principle of education. Ranu Basu thus writes the 'education and social awareness, rather than class' was the 'most important criteria' in determining 'elite status' in mid-nineteenth-century Bengal.[63] Richard Cronin makes a more substantial analysis:

[60] Sarkar, *Writing Social History*, p. 169.

[61] Göran Therborn, *The Ideology of Power and the Power of Ideology* (London: Verso, 1980), p. 2.

[62] Jon Elster, *Making Sense of Marx* (Cambridge: Cambridge University Press, 1985), p. 464.

[63] Ranu Basu, 'Some Aspects of the Composition of the Urban Elite in Bengal, 1850–1872', in *Studies in Bengal*, Papers presented at the Seventh Annual Bengal Studies Conference (East Lansing: Asian Studies Centre, Michigan State University, 1975), p. 108.

While *bhadralok* status was generally limited to members of the three highest Bengal castes, membership in this social elite depended primarily upon the acquisition of education, both Western and Sanscritic ... high caste alone did not guarantee *bhadralok* status. Nor did *bhadralok* status insure a comfortable existence. In fact the growing surplus of educated and partially educated white-collar job seekers, and the increasing subinfudation of landholdings, had brought about a situation in which many former prosperous *bhadralok* families had been reduced to poverty.[64]

Then the obvious question that springs to mind is: why did the 'acquisition of education' become the primary determinant of bhadralok membership? Sumit Sarkar's answer to this is colonialism's limiting of all other channels of social mobility except education. While this is true, it raises the further question about ideological dominance. To put it differently: Sarkar's analysis is a pointer to *why* educational sensibilities are dominant but not *how* they become so and are maintained thus. Let us recall Elster's definition of ideology as that which is socially caused. The primary sense in which ideologies are socially caused is that they are expressions of interests. Ideologies exist, or arise, to fulfil the needs of agents occupying particular positions within the relations of production. To make sense of the world from that particular class position. Thus, ideologies play an *objective* role in the social formation and have, what Althusser has called, a 'material existence'.[65] The materiality of ideological beliefs, thus, derives from the fact that they are embodied in particular social practices. The present work is an examination of these social practices which gave rise to the ideology of education.

A group of persons subscribing to the same ideology does not, however, constitute a class. In his seminal work on the English working class, E.P. Thompson makes a distinction between class experience and class consciousness:

Class happens when some men, as a result of common experiences ... feel and articulate the identity of their interests as between themselves, and as against other men whose interests are different from (and usually opposed to) theirs.[66]

[64] Richard P. Cronin, 'The Government of Eastern Bengal and Assam and "Class Rule" in Eastern Bengal, 1905–1912', in J.R. Mclane, ed., *Bengal in the Nineteenth and Twentieth Century* (East Lansing: Asian Studies Centre, Michigan State University, 1975), pp. 99–100.

[65] L. Althusser, *Lenin and Philosophy and Other Essays* (London: New Left Books, 1970), p. 158.

[66] E.P. Thompson, *The Making of the English Working Class*, pp. 8–9.

This is, though widely quoted, is not the most satisfactory definition of class. Class does not 'happen', nor are classes supra-individual persons but groups of agents with a shared position in the relations of production, which *may* form themselves into collectivities, although not inevitably. Class cannot be conflated with experience, the latter being purely subjective. Marx's own discussion of the concept of class is eminently unsystematic.[67] It is, however, possible to arrive at a consistent definition of class from Marx's writings. G.E.M. de Ste Croix does precisely that in his magestrial study of ancient Greece:

Class (essentially a relationship) is the collective social expression of the fact of exploitation, the way in which exploitation is embodied in a social structure. By *exploitation* I mean the appropriation of part of the product of the labour of others .... A *class* (a particular class) is a group of persons in a community identified by their position in the whole system of production, defined above all according to their relationship (primarily in terms of the degree of ownership or control) to the conditions of production (that is to say, the means and labour of production) and to other classes ... The individuals constituting a given class may or may not be wholly or partly conscious of their own identity and common interests as a class, and they may or may not feel antagonism towards members of other classes as such.[68]

Given this definition of class, the bhadralok posits a great theoretical dilemma. The term so far has had a somewhat ambivalent legacy of definition. It has been denoted variously as a class in the Marxist sense,[69] a status group in the Weberian sense,[70] and even as a 'mere category'.[71] Chatterjee and Sarkar both avoiding the term bourgeoisie, have called it the 'new middle class', the former focusing his attention more on the

---

[67] As Althusser rather eloquently put it: 'The reader will know how Volume Three [of *Capital*] ends. A title: Classes. Forty lines, then silence'. See, L. Althusser and E. Balibar, *Reading Capital* (London: New Left Books, 1970), p. 193.

[68] G.E.M. de Ste Croix, *The Class Struggle in the Ancient Greek World* (London: Duckworth, 1981), pp. 43–4.

[69] S.N. Mukherjee, 'Class, Caste and Politics in Calcutta, 1815–38', in E. Leach and S.N. Mukherjee, eds., *Elites in South Asia* (Cambridge: Cambridge University Press, 1970), pp. 33–78; Pradip Sinha, *Calcutta in Urban History* (Calcutta: Firma KLM, 1978).

[70] J.H. Broomfield, *Elite Conflict*, pp. 13–14.

[71] Ranajit Guha as cited in S.N. Mukherjee, 'Class, Caste', p. 51.

'middleness' of it as a descriptive term about its emergent consciousness.[72] This problem of definition is tied to two factors, one subjective and the other objective. Subjectively, the historiography of the bhadralok, with a few exceptions, takes the bhadralok's own history about itself too seriously. A self-descriptive cognomen is imputed onto a social group in a unproblematic and apparently homogenous way. Hence, in most writings, the term is used freely to give the impression that the bhadralok is, or was, a cogent group of individuals who shared a similar if not equal social position, culturally and economically.

Proceeding with Ste Croix's definition of class, it is important that this analytical and structural category is not used in this subjective sense. If class is determined by the subject's position (control, or lack thereof) within the conditions of production, then it is impossible to call the bhadralok a class. Describing a man as a bhadralok tells one nothing about his job, let alone his relation to production. He would not be a peasant, or a worker, Muslim, or lower caste, but he might be a state official, a man of letters, a professional, a merchant, a banker, a low position clerk in a government, or private office, or an academic. He might simply live from the income he derived from urban or rural property, or from money invested, perhaps in government securities.

We mentioned before that there are some notable exceptions in this historiography. John McGuire's quantitative study of the bhadralok for the last half of the nineteenth century is a graceful analysis of the actual class position of a section of the bhadralok.[73] McGuire has shown the dominant production relation of the bhadralok to be that of rentiers. As large as 30 per cent of the men were a part of this class. The size and location of property, whether urban or rural, would vary greatly, for even clerks in petty jobs could have a plot of land back in the village.[74] The channelling of indigenous capital into rural and urban ground rent had a

---

[72] Partha Chatterjee, *The Nation*, p. 35; For some of the different definitions of the term bhadralok see J.H. Broomfield, *Elite Conflict*; Anil Seal, *Emergence of Indian Nationalism* (Cambridge: Cambridge University Press, 1971); Pradip Sinha, *Calcutta*; Rajat K. Ray, *Social Conflict and Political Unrest in Bengal* (New Delhi: Oxford University Press, 1984) and others.

[73] John McGuire, *The Making of a Colonial Mind: A Quantitative Study of the Bhadralok in Calcutta, 1857–1885* (Canberra: Australian National University, 1983).

[74] McGuire, *The Making of a Colonial Mind*, pp. 16–47.

profound impact on social relationships of the indigenous entrepreneurial families, which from the mid-nineteenth-century 'in contrast to the earlier period' became 'much more uniform'. McGuire concludes that while, until the late 1840s, 'there was an emerging merchant bourgeoisie and a potential industrial bourgeoisie as well as the rentier class', by 1857 they were all uniformly a part of the latter group.[75]

This brings us to the chronological bracket of this work. The two dates (1848 and 1885) are not in themselves absolute historical benchmarks. They are merely more dramatic sequential points of a broader process of historical development. Thus, the fall of the Union Bank in 1848 did not in itself signify an entirely new beginning but rather represented in a single event the more general trend of the political economy at that time. All the prominent families of Calcutta were affected by the collapse of the bank. The event also prompted a major shift in their already changing investment pattern. The bhadralok, as they appeared in their social arena of print, education, and jobs for the better part of the next century, was very much a product of this shift. The change from trade to rentiership as a social relationship was combined with a disproportionate development of Calcutta as an urban centre due to colonial needs. As a result, urban life became the focus of activity, which has led scholars to correctly point out that even the rural landholders squandered 'most of their peasant fleeced money in urban luxuries and vices'.[76] In the later chapters we shall see how these urban activities became the core of a social identity and gave rise to the ideology of education.

The reason for stopping at 1885 with the formation of the Indian National Congress is, again, not of any isolatable significance. One of the theoretical agendas that the book grapples with is that of nationalist ideology and national mobilization. The formation of the Congress was a formal articulation of an ideological process that occurred throughout the course of the nineteenth century. Once it gained official recognition in an institution the ideological imperatives as well as the mobilizing strategies began to change. In this study we are more concerned with tracing the beginnings of that process. The dates 1848 and 1885 are thus only convenient highlights in the service of a narrative. The events that they point at are historical indicators of larger processes of social change.

[75] Ibid., p. 16.
[76] Benoy Ghosh, 'Social Change', in *Renascant Bengal*, p. 16.

Ideology and Material Practice

Ideology, as we have argued, is necessarily embedded in real material practice. Print, education, and a salaried job, we shall argue following Sarkar, were the three main areas of 'primitive accumulation' of class *awareness*. A word of clarification is in order here. Following Anthony Giddens, we shall distinguish between class awareness and class consciousness. Of the former he writes: 'in so far as class is a structural phenomenon, there will tend to exist a common awareness and acceptance of similar attitudes and beliefs, linked to a common style of life, among members of the class'. But this class awareness, according to Giddens, does not involve the recognition by those having it that they belong to the same class. Class awareness stems from a shared class position but does not acknowledge its existence.[77] The attitudes ascribed to the bhadralok become clear in this light. What contributed to the making of the bhadralok was the ideology of education, which while emanating from a class, was not confined to it. Hence, while there existed an awareness of difference with other *social groups*, (Muslims, lower castes, etc.) not classes, we must constantly remind ourselves, it could not be called a class-consciousness in the strict sense, as that would involve the organization of the bhadralok into one single class.

It is with this understanding that the term 'intelligentsia' is deployed in this work. The term refers to the social role played by the bhadralok as a social group. The intelligentsia by its very nature is a social group which maybe composed of members of different classes. This indeterminacy in its composition ensures that as a social group it sees its interest at varying moments with different classes. Thus, the intelligentsia in colonial Bengal could play a revolutionary role against the British state while its counterpart in Russia, in 1905, threw in its lot with the bourgeoisie. It is our objective to understand, in the following chapters, the material circumstances which gave rise to the intelligentsia in Bengal. It is also our project to understand whether the heterogeneity of class composition within the bhadralok had any effect upon its overall social position.

The methodological focus of the present work is first on the privileged of colonial Bengal. This is not a history of the 'subaltern' but rather one

---

[77] Anthony Giddens, *The Class Structure of the Advanced Societies* (London: Unwin Hyman, 1981), pp. 111–13.

about the 'elite'. It is unfortunate that this obvious fact needs emphasis, for in the current historiographical climate, the centrality of the oppression of the Hindu upper-caste bhadralok is often too well documented.[78] Recent histories about the bhadralok have thus seen an aggrandisement of his role as the nationalist hero, tragic or otherwise.[79] His overt declarations of nationalist resentment is too often disassociated from his covert policies and attitudes towards the non-bhadra. The present work does not cover the results of such policies and attitudes. It does not, for example, look into the series of lower-caste mobilizations that occupied the nineteenth century, sometimes in direct opposition to upper-caste bhadralok mobilization.[80] Second, this book deals only with the Hindu bhadralok. It is important, however, to remind ourselves that the Muslim intellectual was not absent from the public life of Calcutta: a rather difficult feat given that nearly half the population of the city was Muslim in 1866. Men such as Abdul Latif Khan, or Mir Mosarraf Hossein, were as much a part of the intellectual/pedagogic life of the age as Bhudev Mukhopadhyay or Bankimchandra Chattopadhyay, but with an important distinction. The contours of intellectual topography were decidedly becoming Hindu from as early as the 1850s. For reasons that we shall explore in the coming chapters, the Muslim response to Western education and modernity was, as a *community*, fairly unenthusiastic. This, of course, did not apply to Muslims as *individuals*, who made significant contributions to the mental world of nineteenth-century Calcutta. Of relevance here is Rajat Sanyal's comment about the Mohomedan Literary Society. Started by Abdul Latif, the society organized regular lectures on educational and literary topics in Urdu, Persian, Arabic, and English. According to Sanyal, the society, for all its efforts, was not the result of an organic expansion of Western education amongst Muslims. It was rather the 'society of a hesitant

[78] Partha Chatterjee has dubbed this phenomenon as the 'subalternity of an elite'. Chatterjee, *The Nation*, p. 37.

[79] Sudipta Kaviraj's study of Bankimchandra Chattopadhay outlines the tragic aspect in cultural terms while Brian Hatcher's study of Vidyasagar tries to show the subalternity of the brahmin pundits. Kaviraj, *The Unhappy Consciousness: Bankimchandra Chattopadhyay and the Formation of Nationalist Discourse in India* (New Delhi: Oxford University Press, 1995) B. Hatcher, *Idioms of Improvement Vidyasagar and the Cultural Encounter in Bengal* (Calcutta: Oxford University Press, 1996) see particularly p. 18.

[80] For this see Sekhar Bandyopadhyay, *Caste, Politics and the Raj: Bengal 1872–1937* (Calcutta: University of Calcutta, 1990).

community with an enthusiastic leader'.[81] In a certain sense, here we also indulge ourselves in the luxury of hindsight. As the intellectual and pedagogic discourse about Hinduness becomes transposed onto a larger and more specifically political agenda from the early twentieth century, we try to trace its material origins in the pronouncements and practices of some of its architects in the nineteenth century. Again, as mentioned before, this is a study of the select few, but it is one in which their selectiveness is seen as that which is achieved at the expense of other social groupings and something that is maintained at the cost of other lives and livelihoods.

Print and printing form important areas of focus in this work. If one talks about a 'print culture' then we have before us the edifying moral texts produced by the Sanskrit Press of Vidyasagar, diligently working towards providing a 'scientific' and 'rational' world view for the young minds embarking upon their journey in the world of learning. We also have at the same time and working with a similar printing press, the likes of Kalidas Chakravarty, who make an appearance in the pages of history as an entry in the police files for being arrested for selling 'improper' books, which the commissioner of police believed to be 'unfit for circulation'.[82] Both the genres had wide readerships. While a vast number of books were being printed and circulated from presses such as the Sanskrit Press on the importance of the 'right' kind of education for women, lesser known figures such as Kali Das Chakravarty plied the newly-educated female reader with semi-erotic wares.[83] Print formed an arena of practices whose sole register was their availability. As long as a book was available in the market, it was going to be read by someone. Hence print and education in the nineteenth century, we stress again, were practices that embodied a particular ideology.

One of the important disjunctures that a printed book can bring about is between its production and reception. The work on print by the

---

[81] Sanyal, *Voluntary Associations*, p. 140.

[82] Government of Bengal, Judicial Proceedings, 27 February 1874, Nos. 402–3.

[83] Bamasundari one of the neo-literates conducted a scathing attack upon this practice of women reading 'improper' books. While she was an ardent advocate of female education, she chided the misuse of the ability to read. She concluded that such women were best left illiterate and foolish as education clearly had been counter-productive for them. Bamasundari, *Ki Ki Kusanskar* (Calcutta, 1876), p. 20.

French historians such as Roger Chartier and Jacques Revel demonstrate that 'with printed texts often a particular form is invested with values that are foreign to it or interests expressed elsewhere'. Thus, a particular text may be read within an entirely different context from its intended production. In a way, this is not a grand discovery. Ideas do not usually bear trademarked labels of non-appropriability, and the traffic happens both ways. What European historians of print attempt to show are the actual mechanics of this appropriation.[84]

The idea of diffusion of the printed word and the variegated levels of its impact among various social sections, is a method that we borrow from this historiographical inquiry. Where we depart from this scholarship into an older mode of social history is in our understanding of this cultural history in terms of the topics of inquiry. Can a history of culture work, if it is shorn of all theoretical assumptions about culture's relationship to the social world—if indeed, as Chartier has claimed, its agenda is conceived as the undermining of all assumptions about the relationship between culture and the social world?[85] To take a concrete example, a text like Samuel Smiles's *Self Help* was produced in Britain long after the consolidation of the nation state. The priority of Smiles was to establish the individual as being an extractive ideal of the social, where the former represented the latter even as an isolatable entity. Its Bengali translation, however, was invested with an entirely different set of priorities. The individual, for the Bengali translator Somnath Mukhopadhyay, was an embodiment of the *jati* and the latter needed to be emphasized through the edification of the former. If we concentrate, as Chartier does, on the autonomous reception of this text then we overlook the expansive universe of interests and animosities that already existed which a text like *Self Help*

---

[84] See for example, Robert Darnton, *The Business of Enlightenment: A Publishing History of the Encyclopédie, 1775–1800* (Cambridge, Mass., London: Bellnöp Press, 1979).

[85] In their investigation of cultural practices historians such as Chartier and Revel have perhaps been influenced by Foucault's criticisms of the fundamental assumptions of social history. Foucault's demonstration that there are no 'natural' intellectual objects finds a unique echo in Chartier: 'madness, medicine, and the state are not categories that can be conceptualized in terms of universals whose contents each epoch particularizes', they are historically grounded and by implication always changing: Roger Chartier, ed., *The Culture of Print: Power and Uses of Print in Early Modern Europe* (Cambridge: Polity, 1984), p. 4.

coincided with and helped to articulate. The mechanics of reception in isolation from the history of reception does not answer for us questions, such as, what informed the choice of certain ideas at any given point. The gulf between a book and the way it was read cannot be filled by tracing the discontinuity to any particular book but to the social world where men and women of the nineteenth century were dealing with their own social reality.

While we will be looking at the debates around print and education, they both undoubtedly possessed unquestionable significance. The secretary of the Calcutta Literary Society, a typical social organization of the nineteenth century, concretized the significance of this in the following terms:

Men of *literary culture* start Journals and magazines, and become leaders of *society*, in course of time.

The *true greatness of a Nation* consists in the number of its literary men, and the Journals and Newspapers, which the reading public supports and encourages. If you wish to criticise the action of *men-in-authority*, you should do so either by a speech, or by contributions in the columns of a *Newspaper* [emphasis given].[86]

There is much social self-assurance behind such a remark and rightly so. It is the project of this book to delineate the coordinates of this social poise. It is also its project to show that there is no reason to assume, as the postmodernists do, that phenomena like language, culture, or representation, cannot be studied with tools provided by Marxism. There is a connection here between political objective and scientific method. Though the nineteenth century seems a long way away from present-day political undertakings, it is important to rescue the past from the outcome of its interpretations.

[86] *Annual Reports of the Calcutta Literary Society* (Calcutta, 1875), p. 1.

1

The Curious Case of the Bhadralok
Class or Sentiment?

*The English-speaking natives, though to be found in almost every village,
are generally employed in the larger towns, and are only occasional visitors
to their homes ... They are chiefly remarkable for the loss of the good manners
for which their forefathers were so distinguished, and they confuse a desire
for independence with an awkward appearance of incivility.*[1]

The question 'who were the bhadralok' is a rhetorical one as the bhadralok
themselves have left voluble testimonies as answers. The debate is rather
over their idenity as a sociological entity. In Broomfield's study, the bhadralok
is defined as a homogenous 'elite' group for whom status instead of class
was a more appropriate register of definition.[2] Marxists, such as, Sumit
Sarkar and Sumanta Banerjee have called it a 'new middle class' and described
in some detail the historical context of their 'happening' in the Thompsonian
sense.[3] Classes, as we have previously pointed out, cannot be studied only
in their effects. The way a social group behaves in a particular historical
context is *related* to class positions but it cannot be equated with class
behaviour. (The rise of the Black Panthers in America, for example, definitely
has much to do with the group's class position, but their radical Black
nationalist struggle, or anti-racist moves cannot be reduced to class.) Class,
as a theoretical category, loses its use if stretched endlessly. We thus need to
ascertain in the course of this chapter which classes make up the social

---

[1] *Annual Report on the Presidency Division for 1872–73*, No. 77JG (dated 16
September 1873), West Bengal State Archives (hereafter WBSA).

[2] J.H. Broomfield, *Elite Conflict*, pp. 13–14.

[3] E.P. Thompson, *The Making of the English Working Class*, pp. 8–9.

group called the bhadralok and what the implications of such a composition are. Accordingly, the chapter addresses the following issues: first, the identity and social composition of the bhadralok and whether they were in any sense homogenous; second, if there was any change in the composition and concerns of the bhadralok between the first and second half of the nineteenth century; last, but not the least, the distinctions between national mobilization and class mobilization.

Rethinking the Bhadralok

As early as in 1823, an excellent sociological account of the bhadralok was provided by Bhabanicharan Bandyopadhyay (1787–1848). Born in 1787, Bhabanicharan, belonged to a generation of men who saw the unfolding of the effects of Cornwallis's land settlement and witnessed the changes it brought in the rhythms of urban life in the city of Calcutta. The self-sufficiency of the outlying areas being systematically undermined due to colonial pressures, Bhabanicharan's father was one amongst the many who came to the big city in search of employment. He moved from his native village of Narayanpur in Burdwan to Calcutta. Bhabanicharan himself moved to Calcutta at an early age when his father bought a house in Kolutala in north Calcutta.

Moving to Calcutta, however, did not mean an immediate integration. The young Bhabanicharan like many of the youngsters of his times went back to his native village a couple of times in the year to visit the rest of the family and to attend social occasions. As an adult, when he wrote *Kalikata Kamalalaya* (1823), his own tribute to the city, perhaps in memory of his own experience, but more likely as an astute social observation, he claimed it to be a guide for the newcomer from the village. The city in all its glory and its mysteries was still a relatively new cultural entity for Bhabanicharan's social group, even though the best part of their lives had been spent there.

Kalikata Kamalalaya (henceforth *Kalikata*) is a dialogue between a newcomer to Calcutta and a local. Through the eyes of the newcomer, the reader is given a tour of the city and its strange ways. The most amazing object of the city is of course its people and their way of life which strikes the stranger as being completely alien to his own. Having said this, the newcomer himself is not without his own alienness to the local, for he is referred to as a *videshi*, which literally translates as foreigner. Clearly, urban life had not reached its later cosmopolitan and impersonal status. A stranger in town still evoked older boundaries of social interaction, whereby what was known was spatially bound within everyday personal contact and interaction; a long way indeed from any concept of an abstract 'imagined community'.[4] In the dialogue of these two men unfolds the history of the bhadralok:

Foreigner: I hear that many in Calcutta have forsaken all customs and rituals. They have a meal and leave their *bashas* early in the morning and go to work where the entire day is subsequently spent. Some even return as late as *dui danda, chari danda* at night, some even at *ek prahar*, whence they have another meal and just go to bed.

Local: what you have heard is true but such ways are not of the Hindu, those who lead such lives are merely Hindus in disguise. I cannot say much about them. But let me tell you about the ways of the bhadralok.[5]

The use of the word *basha*, a house rather than a home, is again tinted with the impermanence and transience of the residents. Indeed the local, in his persuasive defence of the city, complains of the way in which distinguished members of the bhadralok community are yet to treat Calcutta as their *basha*, and how they keep going back to their village of origin for social ceremonies.[6] Two other things are of particular significance in this conversation. The first is the notion of work and the second the concept of time. Sumit Sarkar has drawn our attention to both these factors as constitutive of the bhadralok's identity. The use of *danda* and *prahar*, in *Kalikata*, indicates the still surviving categories of a previous time scale unconnected to the routine of work and schedule. It is also of interest that Hindus are said not to partake in this onerous business of going to work.

Bandyopadhyay himself worked for various British firms in his lifetime. Till the mid-nineteenth century, however, the more tedious clerical jobs

[4] Even around 1885 the Bengali bhadralok was not well travelled beyond Bengal. In Haraprasad Shastri's account of a meeting with the Russian scholar Ivan Minayeff, Shastri admits that within his circle of friends and acquaintances, including Bankimchandra Chattopadhyay, Hemchandra Bandyopadhyay, Rameshchandra Dutta, Rajanikanta Gupta and several others, only Rameshchandra Dutta had travelled beyond Bengal. Satyajit Chaudhuri et al., eds., *Haraprasad Shastri Rachana-Sangraha*, Vol. 2 (Calcutta: Paschim Banga Rajya Pustak Parishad, 1981), pp. 40–1.

[5] Bhabanicharan Bandyopadhyay, *Kalikata Kamalalaya* (Calcutta: Pratibhash, reprint 1986), p. 7.

[6] Ibid., pp. 5–6.

were mainly done by Armenians, Eurasians, and the Portuguese.[7] The spread of education had not generalized to the point where these jobs were accessible to Bengalis in large numbers. Only a privileged section with a knowledge of English, like Bandyopadhyay himself, worked as *bania*s for British business. We have already noted that the bhadralok is equated with the Hindu in *Kalikata*, what were his other attributes?

Three kinds of bhadralok were listed in *Kalikata*. The first were those who were in 'high office', that is, were *bania*s, or dewans, to the British. The second were the *madyabitta*, the middle class, who were 'not rich but comfortable'. The third were the 'poor but bhadra' group who worked as accountants, or *sarkars*, and had to put up with the humiliating treatment meted out to them daily by the dewans.[8] This categorization brings us to the crux of the problem about the bhadralok. The basis for division *within* the group for Bhabanicharan was wealth, but clearly wealth was not a constitutive factor for the group as compared to the rest of society. The staying power of this ambiguity around wealth was immense, for even thirty years later, the Inspector of Schools, Henry Woodrow commented that 'The *Bhadralok* (the respectable), not the *Dhanilok* (the rich) send their children to the Bethune School'.[9]

The predominantly Hindu, upper caste, and Bengali composition of the bhadralok has not escaped the notice of scholars.[10] It is significant, however, that the exclusionary mechanism worked not only to skim off the lower, but also the upper layers of society. The Setts and Basaks, the traditional trading partners of the British till 1753 and the earliest inhabitants of the city, never enter the chronicles of bhadralok studies.[11] Nor do the

[7] See James Long, 'Calcutta in the Olden Times—Its People', *Calcutta Review*, 35, 69 (September, 1860), pp. 170–2.

[8] Bandyopadhyay, *Kalikata*, p. 7.

[9] Cited in Narahari Kaviraj, 'Banglar Jagoron O Bhadralok', in Narahari Kaviraj, ed., *Unish Shataker Banglar Jagoran: Tarka O Bitarka* (Calcutta: K.P. Bagchi and Co., 1984), p. 226.

[10] See for example, Sumit Sarkar, *Writing Social History*, Broomfield, *Elite Conflict*; Anil Seal, *The Emergence of Indian Nationalism*.

[11] The Setts and Basaks were the merchants of cotton-piece goods whose influence waned with the discontinuation of the *dadni* system in 1753. In the nineteenth-century they were predominantly moneylenders in the city. See B. Ghosh, 'Some Old Family Founders in Eighteenth Century Calcutta', *Bengal Past and Present*, Vol. 79 (January–June, 1960), pp. 42–55.

Marwaris of the Barabazar area. The inhabitant of Calcutta in *Kalikata* clarifies for us the yardstick against which the rich were measured:

Someone is a shopkeeper, a kayastha, he has made some money from his shop, the house he lives in is pukka, but if you offer him a book on zamindari accounts, what sense will he make of it? Another is disguised as a doctor, he carries a medical bag in his hand, but he treats people of the hari, shuri, dom castes with roots and leaves, now you go and offer him Bharat Mallik's annotated works on medicine, what use is that to him? One is a weaver, all his life he has spun his wheel and amassed a huge fortune. You think he is a bhadralok and you offer him a printed copy of the *Hitopodesh*, what can he say to that? Someone is a *bania*, possessor of great riches, he is going towards Chinabazar, jingling his keys, you might think because of his appearance that he is a decent soul, offer him a book, do you think he will show any enthusiasm?[12]

Books, and the knowledge therein, become coextensive with the social identity of the bhadralok in this passage: an idea of the social power that was built on the edifice of books, journals, newspapers, and magazines. We shall deal with the centrality of this idea later, but here we should simply remind that men such as Bhabanicharan and Nilratna Haldar (associated with the *Bangadoot* (1829)) were amongst the very first men in colonial history whose livelihood and social position was largely dependent on the printed word. Similarly, of Gangakishor Bhattacharya, the compositor at Serampore Press, the *Friend of India* said that he appeared 'to have been the first who conceived the idea of printing works in the current language as a means of acquiring wealth'.[13] Our local in *Kalikata* gives form to an idea which was eventually to become the pre-eminent site for the constitution of the bhadralok identity.

Bhabanicharan's contempt for wealth shorn of knowledge was matched only by his contempt for the caste of men he described, inadvertently pointing to another distinction of being bhadra. This unreserved derision for lower castes who had managed to make money, was a relatively new development. Only eight years previous to the publication of *Kalikata*, Walter Hamilton had observed: 'The men of opulence now in Bengal are Hindu merchants, bankers, and *banyans* of Calcutta, with a few at the principal provincial stations'.[14] The majority of these men came from

[12] Bandyopadhyay, *Kalikata*, pp. 24–5.

[13] *Friend of India Quarterly Series*, Vol. 1 (Serampore, 1822), pp. 35–6.

[14] W. Hamilton, *The East India Gazetteer* (London: Printed for J. Murray by Dove, 1815), p. 136.

intermediate caste origins and were certainly not marked for their education, or knowledge. In 1822 Radhakanta Deb, himself a bhadralok, compiled for H.T. Prinsep 'The accounts of all respectable and opulent natives of the Presidency'.[15] This remarkable list was further revised in 1839.[16] Of the twenty-three men mentioned in the list (the list was by no means definitive) only three were of Brahmin origin. It is quite significant that neither Bhabanicharan himself, nor his more distinguished contemporary Rammohan were included in Deb's list. The latter's exclusion, S.N. Mukherjee has speculated, was perhaps due to the strong animus that Deb bore towards him.[17] While this may be true, it is perhaps more useful to see it in a different way. The reason for the exclusion of a certain kind of men, was perhaps because the categories for being a bhadralok had not yet taken shape, and people with Rammohan's importance were not yet recognized by the political economy. Scholars have often commented on the satires of the nineteenth century, which heap criticism on opulent decadence. One should note, however, that between *Kalikata* and *Nababubilash* (1825), the first few of its kind from Bhabanicharan, there was a time lag of good two decades before this genre became firmly established and the attacks upon wealth and conspicuous consumption consolidated, in the likes of *Alaler Gharer Dulal* (1858) and *Hutom Penchar Naksha* (1862). Bhabanicharan's works are thus merely an indication of things to come. During his time, wealth was still a stable referential to the men who made their precarious fortunes under the East India Company in the first half of the nineteenth century. The two decades between *Kalikata* and *Hutom* are of vital importance in our analysis of the bhadralok, and this disjuncture is often overlooked in its historiography. Ranu Basu, for example, homogenizes the bhadralok as displaying 'an unique combination of intellect and business acumen'.[18] Intellectual activity and education were certainly not the hallmarks of prominence in the first half of the century and the starkness of this distinction needs to be fully appreciated.

[15] Reprinted in B.N. Banerjee, 'Raja Radhakanta Deb's Services to the Country' in *Indian Historical Records Commission*, Vol. 9 (1926), pp. 105–9.

[16] Cited in Brajendranath Bandyopadhyay, *Sambad Patre Sekaler Katha*, Vol. 2 (Calcutta: Bangiya Sahitya Parishad, 5th edn, 1994), pp. 753–8.

[17] S.N. Mukherjee, 'Class, Caste' pp. 46–8.

[18] Ranu Basu, 'Some Aspects' p. 109.

The Merchants of Empire

The men who found their place in Radhakanta's list were all newcomers to the city and had risen to their present opulence in the latter half of the eighteenth century. All of them had made their fortunes either as dewans, or *bania*s, to the Company. James Long quotes a contemporary definition of the *bania* in his account of Calcutta in the earlier half of the nineteenth century:

> *Banyan* is a person either acting for himself or as the substitute of some great black merchant by whom the English gentlemen in general transact all their business. He is interpreter, head book-keeper, head secretary, head broker, the supplier of cash, and cash-keeper, and in general also secret-keeper.... In short he possesses singly many more powers over his master than can in the country be assumed by any young spendthrifts, steward, money-lender, and mistress all together.... There is a powerful string of connections among these Banyans who serve all the English in the settlement of Bengal, as well in all public offices as in their private offices. Since the great influence acquired there by the English, many persons of the best Gentoo families take upon them this trust of servitude and even pay a sum of money for serving gentlemen in certain posts; but principally for the influence they acquire thereby, and the advantage of carrying on trade ... duty-free, under cover of their master's dustucks.[19]

Raja Binaya Krishna Deb, writing the history of the town in 1905, noted that several 'eminent native gentlemen' settled in Calcutta 'previous to the English settlement and after the battle of Plassey'. Dewan Ramcharan, *bania* of Vansittart and founder of the Andul Raj, settled in Pathuriaghata. Dewan Ganga Govinda Sing, dewan of the board of revenue under Warren Hastings, had his house in Jorasanko. Darpanaryan Tagore, the founder of the Tagore wealth, who had worked as the dewan of a French company, founded his establishment in Pathuriaghata.[20] It was mercantile wealth, riding on the back of a new town and the infinite possibilities that the agency houses offered.

The first half of the century witnessed a tremendous commercial potential for the indigenous merchants. Between 1780, when the first agency house was set up in Calcutta, and the fall of the Union Bank in 1848, the city, as the commercial and financial centre of India, was dominated by the dynamic entrepreneurs of this era. A man such as Dwarkanath Tagore

---

[19] James Long, 'Calcutta in the Olden Times' p. 184.

[20] Raja Binaya Krishna Deb, *The Early History and Growth of Calcutta* (Calcutta: Riddhi, 1977, Ist edn, 1905).

combined in his person the multiple roles of a zamindar, a major financier, the dewan of the Salt Department, and an investor in indigo, steam-boats, coal, and several other commercial ventures.[21] At a time of violent de-industrialization, when in Bengal alone more than a million people employed in the cotton trade are estimated to have lost their jobs,[22] Calcutta presented to the manufacturing interests of Britain 'the spectre of a second Lancashire on the bank of the Ganges, which could beat the original with cheap Indian labour and raw material'.[23] In 1833, the value of bonds held by Indians in the joint-stock market was calculated to be worth nearly £7,000,000.[24]

The first of the agency houses was formed in the 1780s by Britishers who had left the Company to try their luck in private trade. As agents for the investment and remittance of private savings of the servants of the Company, the agency houses used the money of their associates to finance the import and export trade. Gradually, competition forced them to expand their sphere of activity. They built and operated ships, served as bill brokers, formed banks and insurance companies, and undertook ventures in mining, manufacturing, and plantation projects. The number of agency houses steadily increased over the first half of the nineteenth century. In 1790 there were fifteen such agency houses, in 1828, twenty-seven, in 1835, sixty-one, and by 1846, ninety-three.[25]

The *bania* dominated the social and economic stage of the age. Valued for his knowledge of the internal markets and sources of supply, he served the Company before the advent of the agency houses. Warren Hastings' famous *bania*, Kantababu, helped him to conclude the contract of supplying bullocks for transport to the Company, among other things, which allowed Hastings to send home to Britain a profit of £950. Between 1742 and 1769, Kantababu rose from being a *dadni* merchant working for Hastings' personal *bania* to a *bania* working for Sykes. It has been estimated that in

[21] For more details see Blair B. Kling, *Partners in Empire: Dwarkanath Tagore and the Age of Enterprise in East India* (Berkeley: University of California Press, 1976).

[22] Amiya Bagchi, 'De-industrialization in India in the Nineteenth Century: Some Theoretical Implications', *The Journal of Development Studies*, 12, 2 (1976), p. 143.

[23] Quoted in Amales Tripathi, *Trade and Finance in the Bengal Presidency 1793–1833* (Bombay: Orient Longman, 1956), p. 228, cited in Kling, *Partners*, p. 50.

[24] K.N. Chaudhuri, ed., *The Economic Development of India Under the East India Company* (Cambridge: Cambridge University Press, 1971), p. 299.

[25] S.B. Singh, *European Agency Houses in Bengal (1783–1833)* (Calcutta: Firma KLM, 1966), pp. 1–35.

this period he had invested over Rs 40,000 in properties, this is excluding the land settlements that he obtained by several *pattas* or leases.[26] As the British learned more about the Indian market, the *bania* became less necessary to market imports, or collect products for export. But after 1813, with the abolition of the Company's monopoly, there was an arrival of new adventurers from Britain who came with little capital of their own and the *bania* once more acquired prominence, this time as a source of finance. With the financial crisis of 1830–3, his importance continued to grow, when the British became reluctant to invest capital in India. By the 1840s, some *banias* had become leading figures in the agency houses. The shipping magnate, Ramdulal Dey is an ideal example of the *bania* of this period.

Dey was an orphan who began his career as a bill collector at a low salary of Rs 5 a month at Madan Datta's office in Calcutta. With the growth of consignment trade and the agency houses he became a *bania* attached to Fairlie, Fergusson, & Company. But he also worked as an independent agent. American traders, in particular, found it more profitable to do business with Dey than with the established English houses, since he charged them a commission of not more than 1 per cent. He established contacts with merchants in New York, Boston, Newberry Port, and Philadelphia. His American business friends named a ship after him, and sent him a portrait of George Washington as a token of their friendship.[27]

Motilal Seal is another instance of new money of this period. Born in Calcutta to a small cloth merchant family, he started off by selling empty bottles and corks. By 1820 he had established himself as a leading merchant, working as a *bania* to various agency houses, investing in various business ventures and landed properties. After the crisis of 1830–3, he started in a firm of 'general merchants and agents' in partnership with Europeans and opened the Oswald and Seal Company.[28] Seventy-three of the 202 proprietors of the Union Bank in 1838 were Indians, and of them seventy were Bengali Hindus, two Muslims, and one Parsi.[29] There were four Indian

[26] Somendra Chandra Nandy, *Life and Times of Cantoo Baboo* (Calcutta: Allied Publishers, 1978), pp. 28–45.

[27] Girish Chunder Ghosh, *A Lecture on the Life of Ramdoolal Dey, The Bengali Millionaire* (Calcutta: Riddhi, India, 1978, 1st edn 1868), pp. 18–20.

[28] S.N. Mukherjee, 'Class, Caste', p. 48.

[29] *The Bengal Directory and Fourth Quarterly Register for the Year 1838* (Calcutta, 1838), pp. 322–3.

directors of the Bank; three being Bengali Hindus—Ashutosh Dey, the son of Ramdual Dey, Radhamadhab Banerjee, and Dwarkanath Tagore.[30]

The city carried in its mapping the intonations of both sets of newcomers: the *bania* and the English. Buildings and actions interpenetrated in the courtyards, arcades, and stairways and gave life the appearance of a spectacle. Divided radically into its native and white areas of residence, our story of the *bania* developed in the native part of town, in the din of the markets in Shovabazar, the squalor of Beadon Street, the prostitute quarters of Sonagachi, the printing presses of Chitpore Road, and the palaces of the rich in Jorasanko.

The rate of growth of the city can be ascertained by the growth in population. In just five years, between 1703 and 1708, the population of the town doubled, and grew a further three-fold in the next forty years.[31] In 1821, 179,917 people were reported to be living in Calcutta, of whom 118,203 were Hindus, 48,162 Muslims, 13,138 Christians, and 414 Chinese.[32] The next fifteen years saw a further increase of nearly 30 per cent, according to W. Birch, the Superintendent of Police of Calcutta, who made the following assessment based on house tax.

TABLE 1.1 Population of Calcutta[33]

English	3,138	Western Hindus	17,333
Euro-Asians	4,746	Bengali Hindus	120,318
Portuguese	3,181	Moguls	527
French	160	Parsees	40
Chinamen	362	Arabs	351
Armenians	636	Mugs	683
Jews	307	Madrasees	55
Western Muslims	13,667	Native Christians	49
Bengali Muslims	45,067	Low Castes	19,054
		Total	229,714

[30] *The Bengal and Agra Directory and Annual Register for 1848* (Calcutta, 1848), p. 318.

[31] Harisadhan Mukhopadhyay, *Kalikata Sekaler O Ekaler* (Calcutta: K.P. Bagchi, 1915), pp. 443–4.

[32] D. Bhattacharya and B.B. Bhattacharya, ed., *Census of India 1961: Report of the Population Estimates of India (1820–1830)* (New Delhi, 1963), pp. 234–5.

[33] Cited in S.N. Mukherjee, 'Class, Caste', p. 37. The total in the above estimate excludes the number of people who came to the city on a daily basis, as either migrant worker, or office-goer.

The Bengali Hindus thus formed the bulk of the population, being nearly 53 per cent of the total. One would assume that given the social prominence of the *bania*, the category 'lower caste' here does not include men like Nabakrishna Deb or Radhakrishna Basak, but was a reference instead to the lower castes among the very bottom of society. The Bengali Hindus lived in the 'native' part of town, close to the Barabazar, where most of the commercial transactions of the city were conducted.

The contours of this mercantile economy constituted the space for the inscription of wealth in nineteenth-century Calcutta. The display of abundance was not conducted in the individual anonymity of the private, but was grandly performed everyday upon the public life of the city. Whether as actual participants in the grand ceremonies, or reading about them in the newspapers and satires, or recounting doggerels about the good life of the rich, the commoner was firmly situated in the spectacle of excess and patronage.[34]

A contemporary journal described the funeral ceremony of Raja Nabakrishna Deb's mother as follows:

There were full thirty days between the death and the *sradh* day and Nubkissen's countrymen made good this advantage. At first the beggars, Bhats, and Pariahs undertook the journey. Next there were those whose conditions oscillated between decency and beggary. Lastly, men even in competent circumstances, tempted by large expectations and urged by greedy wives, complied with the small chance of being distinguished in the crowd, followed ... As presents were given per head the very babies were brought and when many of them died of suffocation, the parents preserved them for the occasion and exhibit [sic] them as if they were alive, added to their incomes.[35]

Nabakrishna, the famous *bania* of Robert Clive was amongst the first generation of the so-called 'opulent natives' of Radhakanta's list whose dwelling houses in Shovabazar, were noted for their grandeur and style,

[34] Good humoured and indulgent criticisms of the high life of the rich formed the topic of tales and verses of this period. The babu's predilection for prostitutes was an acknowledged theme of Kalighat paintings, verses, and songs. The cultural forms of *jatra, kheur, akhrai,* and *hap-akhrai,* mediated the social lives of the high and the low within a common sharing of ribald humour, and narratives. For a detailed study of these expressions of cultural homogeneity see Sumanta Banerjee, *The Parlour and the Street: Elite and Popular Culture in Nineteenth Century Calcutta* (Calcutta: Seagull Books, 1989).

[35] Quoted in Pradip Sinha, *Calcutta in Urban History*, pp. 220–21.

and according to a late nineteenth-century journal were 'the only two specimens of palatial buildings in a city styled the City of Palaces'.[36] According to the Persian records, between 1766 and 1769 Nabakrishna appears as an intermediary between the Indian princes and nobles on the one hand, and the Company's government on the other.[37] In 1767, he secured the job of the political *bania* to the Company.[38] In 1774, he obtained the unusual right of holding the farm of Shovabazar in perpetuity, and the bazaar became the property of the Deb family. This deed was further bolstered in 1778 when he was given the taluk of Sutanati, with an exclusive right to collect the ground rent and grant leases.[39] Similarly, in the late eighteenth and early nineteenth century, the Malliks of Barabazar are mentioned as *bania*s in connection with various business transactions.[40] The pages of *Samachar Darpan* document vividly the accounts of this family, particularly when the Malliks held a *sradh* ceremony and villagers within a thirty miles radius of Calcutta poured into the city to partake in the grand festivities of the Mallik babus.[41]

Wealth depended not so much upon rational calculation and sustained industry as upon speculation and varying degrees of idleness. The wealth of the *bania* was not contingent on his official income from the Company. It was not a salaried wealth bound to a rhetoric of thrift, or saving. At the time of the now famous funeral of his mother on which he is reputed to have spent Rs 9 lakh, Nabakrishna's official salary was only Rs 60. In 1766, when Clive awarded Nabakrishna the title of maharaja, he was offered a salary of Rs 2000. The uncrowned raja, now made official, refused this and demanded only Rs 200! However, he rode home from the ceremony on an elephant literally throwing currency notes around him.[42] Prosperity was awarded, or withheld, by a certain degree of chance in the commercial enterprises of the *bania*. Walter Benjamin in his writings on Paris notes that

[36] *Mukherjee's Magazine* (1861) quoted in Raja Binaya Krishna Deb, *The Early History and Growth of Calcutta*, p. 54.

[37] *Calendar of Persian Correspondence 1767–69*, Vol. 2 (1767–69), p. 93.

[38] Sinha, *Calcutta in Urban History*, p. 68.

[39] See N.N. Ghose, *Memoirs of Maharaja Nubkissen Bahadur* (Calcutta: K.B. Basu, 1901).

[40] *Calendar of Persian Correspondence*, Letter No. 1517.

[41] Brajendranath Bandyopadhyay, *Sambad Patre*, Vol. 2, pp. 538–9.

[42] Ibid., p. 46.

in trade, or speculation, the link between (labour) time and money is severed and its corollary was thus indolence.[43] The cultural life of the *bania* corresponded strongly with this idea. Far from being a private assertion of culture, the cock-fights, entertainment by the leading *baijis*, the elaborate weddings and funerals were a theatre of leisure, a part of the fluid, unbounded time of the merchant.

The spectacular display of wealth was not, we should note, authoring Babu Calcutta, as education and literature was to later, but rather the display of wealth was a naturalized social semiotic of eminence. Ganga Govinda Singh, a head servant to Warren Hastings, spent, it was said, Rs 1,200,000 at his mother's funeral. His expenses, noted the missionary William Ward, were principally incurred as presents to Brahmins.[44] In Ramdulal Dey's garden-house at Belgachia, about a thousand people were fed on a daily basis. Dey himself erected thirteen temples at Varanashi, and to mark the occasion, his wife weighed herself in gold and distributed the proceeds. The merchant did not merely stand out from the homogeneity of the crowd in his wealth, the crowd was an active ingredient in his ritualistic display. So much so that Ramdulal's son actually owned a pet rhinoceros. The humongous solidity of the creature, on display in the babu's house, at Beadon Street, was in many ways an iconic presence. It condensed the social form of the times in its specific image of excess.

There was a definite structure to this display of material wealth. The bourgeoisie in Victorian England had their own display of surplus wealth in over-cramped living rooms and halls filled with curios, artefacts, and a cornucopia of things, ranging from heavily inlaid snuff boxes to pen-knifes of different shapes. It was the richness of things, private and interiorized, which moved wealth into an inner domain of private individual consumption. The only act that linked the bourgeois notion of opulence to a wider sphere of the many was the act of buying, the sole practice that related the individual consumer to a public sphere. In contrast, our examples of the rich and colourful festivities of the early nineteenth-century babu, in his myriad funerals, weddings, and feasts bespoke a social connection that was very much a public language of splendour.

[43] See Graeme Gilloch, *Myth and Metropolis: Walter Benjamin and the City* (Cambridge: Polity Press, 1997), pp. 157–60.

[44] William Ward, *View of the History, Literature, Religion of the Hindus including a Minute description of their Manners and Customs and Translations from their Principal Works*, 2 (Serampore: Mission Press, 1815), p. 145.

The *bishayi* bhadralok of *Kalikata* started his day by 'meeting and conversing with various sorts of people', as he returned back from work there was a *baithak* in waiting and then he either met up with people who came to him for some purpose or he went to visit his peers.[45] The hierarchization of the *bania* was not in the abstraction of either commodities, or a discourse of knowledge, but a very concrete relationship between him and the faces that surrounded him in his daily rituals. Pradip Sinha notes a reflection of this phenomenon in the way the town of Calcutta was planned in this period. While the basic tendency in the economic organization of the European town of Calcutta was to cut down the number of people in transaction, a reverse tendency operated in the Indian town, 'a tendency reinforced and carried forward by the comprador–landlord who caused the development of a spatial organization based on the idea of "peopling it"'.[46] This face of the city was uniquely lacking in spatial boundaries and divisions. Spaces and buildings interpenetrated and merged in an unplanned and chaotic urban landscape where the spatial anarchy rehabilitated the old and the new, the public and the private, the sacred and the profane all at the same time. The home far from being the sanctuary and haven from public life, the site of private fantasies, was a space where the street migrated to. Certainly the sphere of domesticity was demarcated along gender distinctions in the upper echelons, but never in the interiorized sense of the bourgeois 'private'.

The common motif that restored the 'people' to their 'spaces' and dominated the signifying range of the age was that of land. It is worthwhile to remind ourselves that this was a generation that arose from the after-effects of 1793 and the legacy of land and its ideological imperatives was as yet a part of both the material reality and the universe of imagination. Most of the older urban families of Calcutta claimed descent from the 'jungle clearing inhabitants' of the city. This, Sinha has noted was an expression of the *talukdari patta* repeated 'in an altogether different setting'; and the land was cleared not in conformity with notions of urban residential space but within the trope of the rural, where it would yield immediate income. The houses of the opulent classes in this period were, as Sinha has pointed out, 'surrounded with huts or embedded in slums' in order to maximize the rent income.[47] The older social semiotic of land relations folded in itself the new stories of an urban life. This was not surprising for one way to create a

---

[45] Bandyopadhyay, *Kalikata*, p. 117.

[46] Sinha, *Calcutta in Urban History*, p. 18.

[47] Ibid., pp. 18–19.

recognizable experiential grid would be to reorganize urban spatiality to represent the manageable rural reality that one had left behind. S.N. Mukherjee has forcefully demonstrated how the initial forays into urban living were conducted by the rich of Calcutta in the form of rural existence.[48]

This splendour and excess of the early half of the century was, however, short-lived. The spectacular city-scape of Calcutta and the dream life of the *bania* were soon to be become a longing memory in the social angst of a new generation.

From *Byabsa* to *Chakri*

English Policir ei ek bidhi, dhan tor amar budhdhi
Ami manib, tui mutsuddi, labhya amar, tor kshati
Aha mari ki ashcharya, roge shoke, majlo rajya
Athacha bojhena arya, santane samaj gati
Banijye basate Lakshmi, aneke ihar pabe sakshi.[49]

(This is the way of English policy, the capital is yours but the brains belong to me; I am the master, you are the *mutsuddi*, the profits remain mine, while you pick up the loss; O how strange! the land dies of ailment; Yet you fail to comprehend: only trade begets prosperity).

Thus ran a popular song composed in the mid-nineteenth century. The Bengalis, by then, were no longer harbouring ambitious commercial dreams of building railway lines, but were instead manning, in large numbers, administrative, intellectual, and professional occupations. Positing byabsa (trade) against chakri (salaried job) and pointing out the slavishness of the latter against the independence and obvious superiority of the former, was one of the most potent tropes of regret and nostalgia in the literature of this time.[50] Unfortunately, this shift to the service sector has been interpreted

---

[48] S.N. Mukherjee, *Calcutta: Myths and History* (Calcutta: Subarnarekha, 1977).

[49] A poem by the popular bard Rupchand Pakshi reproduced in Benoy Ghosh, ed., *Samayikpatre Banglar Samajchitra*, Vol. 4 (Calcutta: Papyrus, 1966), p. 957.

[50] The examples are numerous on this account. For leading articles in contemporary newspapers urging Bengalis to trade see *Gyananeshawn*, 21 April 1838; *Sambad Prabhakar*, 23 November 1853; *Tattobodhini Patrika*, 14 May 1870; *Somprakash*, 29 July 1878; also see less famous tracts like Chandrashekhar Sen, *Ki Holo* (Calcutta: Peoples' Friends Press, 1875), pp. 46–7; Tarakrishna Haldar, *Chamatkar Swapnadarshan*, pp. 16–24; For an interesting discussion on how the notion of chakri was caught up in the formulation of enslavement in a larger context also see Tanika Sarkar, 'Rhetoric Against Age of Consent', *Economic and Political Weekly*, 28, 36 (1993), p. 1870.

by some scholars again within a framework of status and social values, where it has been argued that 'these careers were more in accord with the bhadralok value system'.[51] Amiya Kumar Bagchi's work on the nature and extent of foreign investment in Bengal is seminal to our understanding of the processes of decline and economic subordination of indigenous entrepreneurship.[52] John McGuire has also given us a material interpretation of the situation. He has identified three main reasons why the local entrepreneur had to move out of the capital accumulation network of the agency houses and the East India Company. The most evident cause was the financial crisis of 1830–3 when the leading agency houses collapsed and then again in 1848–52 when the economy was depressed following the fall of the Union Bank. Great panic had seized a section of the city and one newspaper reported: 'All rich men have lost their riches .... All men of property have been frightened. There are brisk and false transfers of property'.[53]

Second, the development of a monopoly through the managing agency houses served as a link with major finance groups in the city of London, which provided the channel for the import of British finance capital thus freeing the agency houses from their dependence on indigenous capital. Another reason for lessened interest in merchant capital was the growing attractiveness of investment in rural ground rent. After 1806, the prices of holdings began to rise so that despite depressed periods, they averaged over 500 per cent of that of the original settlement by 1857.[54] By the time we

---

[51] Kling, *Partner*, p. 7. Morris D. Morris also makes a similar argument about entrepreneurial responses being determined by particular community value of the group involved; See Rajnarayan Chandravarkar's reply to this position, 'Industrialization in India before 1947: Conventional Approaches and Alternative Perspectives', *Modern Asian Studies*, 19, 3 (1985), p. 645.

[52] A.K. Bagchi, *Private Investment in India 1900–1939* (Cambridge: Cambridge University Press, 1972); also see his more recent *The Evolution of the State Bank of India: Roots: 1806–1876, Parts I and II* (Bombay: Oxford University Press, 1987).

[53] Cited in N.K. Sinha, *The Economic History of Bengal from Plassey to the Permanent Settlement*, Vol. 3 (Calcutta: Firma KLM, 1956–62), pp. 70–71.

[54] John McGuire, *The Making of a Colonial Mind*, pp. 2–16. Also see Benoy Chaudhuri, 'Land Market in Eastern India 1793–1940 Part 1: The Movement of Land Prices' *IESHR*, 12, 1 (1975), pp. 1–42; Amit Bhaduri, 'The Evolution of Land Relations in Eastern India Under British Rule', *IESHR*, 13, 1 (1976), pp. 45–58; and Ratna Ray, 'Land Transfer and Social Change Under the Permanent Settlement', *IESHR*, 11, 1 (1974), pp. 1–45.

come to our period of study, the leading Bengalis of Calcutta had large zamindaris and taluqdaris in Bengal, Bihar, and Orissa. Though these families continued to invest in the joint-stock market, in each case the families, or individuals, concerned were also big rentiers.[55] Indigenous capital, in the face of competition from British finance capital was mainly channelled into ground rent. Also, there was a great expansion of overseas trade in 'primary produce' like cotton, jute, tea, and oilseeds. As a result, exports nearly doubled, making the possession of land even more lucrative from the mid-nineteenth century and land prices continued to rise.

Most of the *bania*s who made their money before 1800 had easy opportunities of investing in land.[56] The families which remained closely connected with the leading European agency houses, or tried to compete with them in the usual export trades, were less lucky. The fortunes of the Burrals, *bania*s to Alexander and Company for at least two generations sank when that firm closed its doors in 1832. Only those Indians whose fortunes could not be forfeited by virtue of belonging to nominal partners of European agency houses and who managed to create some substantial property in land, or real estate, escaped. Amiya Bagchi has noted that the 'fall of the Union Bank merely marked the end of a process'. The 'defaulting European merchants decamped with the money' and were virtually untouched by the crisis as they sailed 'through the portals of the courts as insolvent debtors', while their Indian *bania* and partners were 'sold up for the debts of the firms'.[57]

Let us now recall the classification for the bhadralok in *Kalikata*: the rich *bania*, the comfortable middle class and the 'poor but bhadra' bottom rung. The rich *bania* had disappeared from the socio-economic stage, and Calcutta was left with the remaining two categories. It was this 'comfortable middle class', as Bhabanicharan called them, that we shall see gave rise to the educational ideology and it was the 'poor but bhadra', the lower rungs of a petty bourgeois class, who had been forced into higher education, that became a part of it. The implications of this skewed nature of the political

[55] The number of directorship in the joint-stock companies held by aristocrats increased from three to fifteen between 1857 and 1866. See McGuire, *The Making of a Colonial Mind*, p. 127.

[56] Gokul Ghosal the *bania* of Verelst and the Bhukailas Raj family are prominent examples.

[57] Amiya Kumar Bagchi, *Merchants and Colonialism*, Occasional Paper, 38 (Calcutta: Centre for Studies in Social Sciences, 1981), pp. 21–22.

economy has not received enough theoretical attention and merits some discussion.

These two social groups were the basic constituents of the bhadralok community. The *social* composition of the bhadralok, however occupied two *class* positions united by the common ideology of education. A man such as Pearychand Mitra (1814–83), who was on the board of directors for several business ventures including the Great Eastern Hotel Company, the Port Canning Land Investment Company, the Howrah Docking Company, the Bengal Tea Company, and so on, cannnot be equated with either Vidyasagar, a man of modest means, or to a *kerani*.[58] This fact has been overlooked by most scholars who work under the assumption that the bhadralok is somehow a homogenous category. This is due to a fundamental misrecognition of the term. What is essentially an ethic, or a sentiment, held for various reasons by individuals from different class positions, has been read as a social whole, even as a single class. Social commentators of nineteenth-century Britain often made the same error about the category of the 'gentleman'.[59]

There is not much confusion about the class position of the first group of the bhadralok and McGuire's analysis is very much relevant to this class. Their families had made their fortunes as dewans and *banias* to the Company and with the change in the structure of the economy invested in rural and urban property. One of the scions of this class, Kaliprasanna Singha (1840–70), wrote a scathing critique of its origins in 1862:

Soon after the Company conquered Bengal [1765] and just before Nandakumar was sentenced to be hung [1775], our Babu's great-grandfather was made the dewan to the salt department, in those days there was a lot of money in this; and thus the babu's great-grandfather worked only for five years and left a legacy of nearly five lakh rupees—since then the babu has become a respected man in society.[60]

---

[58] Brajendranath Bandyopadhyay and Sajanikanta Das, eds., *Sahitya Sadhak Charitmala: Pearychand Mitra* (Calcutta: Bangiya Sahitya Parishad, 1948), pp. 179–80.

[59] Clerical workers have been described in 1871 Britain to 'reside in a fairly genteel neighbourhood, wear good clothes, mix in respectable society, go sometimes to the opera, shrink from letting their wives do household work'. B.G. Orchard quoted in Alex Callinicos, 'The "New Middle Class"', in A. Callinicos and C. Harman, eds., *The Changing Working Class* (London: Bookmarks, 1989), p. 21. Also see David Lockwood, *The Blackcoated Worker: A Study in Class Consciousness* (London: Allen and Unwin, 1958).

[60] Arun Nag, ed., *Satik Hutom Penchar Naksha* (Calcutta: Subarnarekha, 1991), pp. 30–31.

Kaliprasanna's own family had made its money as dewans to the British. The founder of the family, Santiram Singha, was a dewan to Sir Thomas Ramsbold and to Middleton in Patna. Radhakanta Deb, was a descendent of Nabakrishna Deb. The Duttas of Hatkhola, Ramchandra Dutta, Jagatram Dutta, were dewans and *banias* to the Company. Madanmohan Dutta was a shipping magnet and his descendent, Prannath Dutta (1840–88) was the editor of the well-regarded satirical journal *Basantak* (1874–6). Keshabchandra Sen's ancestor, Ramkamal Sen, was a dewan in the Bengal Bank. The history of the Tagores, the leading intellectual family of Calcutta, has been mentioned already. When the brief heydays of the great *banias* were over, they invested their accumulated wealth in various urban and rural properties. The rent from these investments allowed the Tagores a life of comparative ease, if not excessive affluence like before, leaving them free to pursue culture and the arts.

This group responded in class terms to most social issues, as their relationship to production was much more clear-cut. Allegiance to cultural and social values were disregarded in class mobilization. Thus, Dwarkanath Tagore, who supported Rammohan's ideas on social change could sit easily with a pro-Sati activist like Radhakanta Deb, when it came to the protection of zamindari rights on land, on the Landholder's Association in 1838. This association also included Muslims zamindars like Munshi Muhammad Amir; class allegiance overrode all other issues.[61] Again in 1843, the likes of Prasannakumar Tagore, Ramdulal Dey, radical Young Bengals like Dakshinaranjan Mukhopadhyay formed a committee to decide on the government's policy on house tax. The committee limited its membership not along the lines of any elusive 'status', or cultural convictions, but only to those who paid tax over Rs 25.[62]

Except in minor ways, this was not a class noted for its cultural achievements, barring a few literary figures like Peary Chand Mitra and Kaliprasanna. (It is, however, noteworthy that it was precisely these individuals who launched a critique of opulence and privileged education and knowledge over wealth in their most famous works). Their inclusion in the bhadralok rhetoric often sublates this. The bulk of them were not a part of the Hare School/Hindu College nexus which developed later. Indeed,

---

[61] For a detailed contemporary report of the event see *Gyananeshawn*, 24 March and 16 June 1838.

[62] *Bengal Spectator*, 16 March 1843.

some of their forays into the world of culture were received with scepticism, even ridicule. The review of Raja Kalikrishna's translation of Sanskrit *shlokas* in the *India Gazette* is an indication of this:

The Raja ... is an evidence and representative of the beneficial effects that has been produced upon the wealthy Hindoos by the progress of education.... Fifteen years ago a Hindoo of this description would have plunged into sensuality and expended his superfluous riches in the most evanescent gratifications. Instead of following in this respect ... he is laudably desirous of benefiting his countrymen.... Yet because the mode he has adopted does not fully meet the wishes or expectations of the reformers, he is met with a storm of obloquy.[63]

The editor of the *Mukherji's Magazine* confirmed in 1873 that 'mercantile men' were 'usually impatient of literature'.[64] But what exactly were the 'expectations' of the 'reformers' and who were they? To answer that question one needs to delve into the second class of the bhadralok: the salaried men.

The *Friend of India* commented in 1859 that the 'leaders of society' in Calcutta were the 'salaried men'.[65] S.N. Mukherjee has provided for us an important statistical account of the number of Indians employed in government service, particularly in the Revenue and Judicial departments for the whole of Bengal.

TABLE 1.2   Number of Indians employed in government service

Year	Europeans	Natives
1800	7,719	49,322
1810	10,715	77,125
1820	11,676	121,238
1830	15,701	96,897
1840	16,303	102,055
1850	26,803	126,910
1851	27,159	138,142

Source: S.N. Mukherjee, 'Class Caste', p. 40.

[63] *India Gazette*, 21 October 1831.
[64] Sambhuchandra Mukherji to Bholanath Chandra, 13 January 1873 in Manmathanath Ghosh, *Manishi Bholanath Chandra* (Calcutta: Gurudas Chottopadhyay and Sons, 1924), p. 172.
[65] *Friend of India*, 21 July 1859.

There are several factors involved in this growth of employment in the service sector, the most important being the importance of Calcutta as the capital of British India and the seat of commercial capital for the Empire. A substantial portion of the colonial trade passed through the city which was simultaneously the heart of the colonial administration. According to one estimate, in Calcutta alone, 18,950 people were employed in the government services in 1901, while the number of professionals was 22,530.[66] These figures, compared to the number of people engaged in trade and commerce, were very great indeed. In 1891, there were only 57,615 people in trade, including banking, money lending, etc., which was nearly half of the sum total of the former.[67] Obviously, the marginalization of the natives from the areas of capital accumulation in any real sense, accounts for this disproportionality.

Despite the flattering comment in the *Friend of India* about salaried men, the salaries of these men were remarkably unflattering. Out of 2,813 Indians employed as uncovenanted servants in 1849, only 493 received salaries above £240 per year (roughly Rs 200 per month) and 1,147 received salaries between £24 to £120 per year (Rs 20–120).[68] The *Hindoo Patriot* had a better grasp of the situation:

There are now in Bengal only two, perhaps three, families which can boast of a clear annual income of above fifty thousand pounds, or five lacs of rupees a year. The source of their income is, of course, property in land ... [for] families of incomes ranging between ten and fifty thousand a year ... the number ... would be a hundred. The major part of this class ... are ... land owners ... about half a dozen of that class which combines banking with trade may be found in the list, but not one salaried or professional man. The next class ... in receipt of incomes ranging from five to ten thousand a year.... Their number may be a little above a hundred ... the landowners form a still larger majority in this class; there are a few bankers and merchants in the list, and we know of but a single income derived from professional sources that exceeds five thousand pounds or fifty thousand rupees a year. The fact that there is not a single salaried income which amounts ... to that figure has not only economical but a political significance.[69]

[66] *Imperial Gazetteer of India, Provincial Series: Bengal,* Vol. 1(Calcutta, 1909), p. 402.

[67] See Amiya Bagchi, 'Wealth and Work in Calcutta, 1860–1921', in Sukanta Chaudhuri, ed., *Calcutta: The Living City,* Vol. 1(Calcutta: Oxford University Press, 1990), p. 215.

[68] S.N. Mukherjee, 'Class, Caste', p. 41.

[69] *Hindoo Patriot,* 11 October 1855, reprinted in Benoy Ghosh, ed., *Selections from English Periodicals of Nineteenth-Century Bengal,* Vol. 3 (Calcutta: Papyrus, 1980), pp. 196–7.

The ownership of land by the salaried masses is an unusual but relevant factor. Landed property and rent thereof, was, as mentioned earlier, the only sphere of the economy left open to Indians. The amount of land owned, however, varied according to class. The first class that we talked about, controlled substantial amount of land from the mid-nineteenth century. For the majority of the salaried class, however, this was not the case. According to the 1891 Census, one-third of the shopkeepers, a tenth of schoolteachers, one-fourth of the doctors, pleaders, and lawyers and one-sixth of the clerks had 'some interest in land, generally as intermediate tenants'.[70] The crucial fact to keep in mind in this regard is that most of the people who manned the various public offices and low paid clerical jobs in the cities, or sudder towns, were originally from some outlying village, where they had some landed property already. The landless peasant, or the poor cultivator, did not come in search of office jobs to the cities, it was generally people who had already had some access to education, and a knowledge of English, even if, only a smattering.[71]

Sumit Sarkar has listed some of the factors responsible for this migration in the early part of the nineteenth century. For the Brahmins, the loss of patronage due to the changes in the land arrangement settlement, was a strong motivation. On a more general scale the famine of 1770, the decline of traditional crafts and the shift of the flow of the river made Calcutta a much more attractive option.[72] Those that came to the city, the men to be precise, from this class of small landowners, left their families behind in the village. Writing in the earlier part of this century on the Faridpur District, J.C. Jack observed that 'clerks, lawyers and Government officers' who work in the headquarter towns 'very rarely bring their wives and still more rarely their children to the town to live with them'. This, he concluded, was 'partly due to the difficulties and expense of conveyance'.[73] It was thus a class of

---

[70] C.J. O'Donnell, ed., *Census 1891*, p. 291.

[71] Vidyasagar's father Thakurdas picked up English from a friend of his patron Jaganmohan Nayalankar in whose house he stayed at when he first came to Calcutta. This private tutoring was necessary even in his minor job as a bill collector. See Chandicharan Bandyopadhyay, *Vidyasagar* (Calcutta: Standard Publishers, reprint 1990), pp. 9–11.

[72] Sarkar, *Writing Social History*, pp. 222–4.

[73] J.C. Jack, *The Economic Life of a Bengal District: A Study* (Oxford: Clarendon Press 1916), p. 77.

petty landowners, who came to the city under duress to become the white collar worker or the much maligned kerani. While ownership of even a small holding in the village provided a degree of status, the city in all its impersonal homogeneity and pecuniary hardship robbed him of even that. A large literature of this period was thus devoted to positing a nostalgic green village where all was well, against a hard concrete city where life was a treadmill of chakri and humiliating drudgery.

This genteel poverty was essentially the social and class origins of the bulk of the intelligentsia of the late nineteenth century. Ramtanu Lahiri (1813–98) came from such a family of petty landowners and salaried men. It is said that his grandfather, being of a pious turn of mind, chose the ancestral *shalgram shila* and some *debuttar* land when the family fortunes were being divided up amongst the brothers. On his mother's side, he was related to the Rais, who were dewans to the Raja of Krishnanangar. Much of the landed property of the Raj, auctioned after the strictures of 1793, had been bought up by them.[74] We learn from Sibnath Shastri's account that they also had investments in indigo. Ramtanu's father, Ramkrishna, however, only had a small plot of land from which he derived some income and had to supplement it with his salary as the manager of the estates of the wealthy Lala babus, to maintain his large family of ten children.[75] He did manage to send Ramtanu to Hare School as a free student in 1826. Shastri gives us an expressive description of his admission to this prestigious school which is indicative of the social circumstances of this class.

Ramtanu's elder brother Kesab was a clerk at the Judge's Court in Alipore. In 1826, he brought Ramtanu to Calcutta to provide him with the panacea of an English education. This was not an easy task on his salary of only Rs 30 a month, so a mutual acquaintance introduced the young Ramtanu to Gourmohan Vidyalankar, a friend of David Hare. On an appointed day Ramtanu was taken by Vidyalankar to Hare with the object of getting him admitted as a free student. Hare, however, was in no mood to confer a favour as in those days he could hardly step out of his house without having a band of young hopefuls running alongside his palanquin with poignant pleas of 'me poor boy, have pity on me, take me into your

[74] Kartikeyachandra Ray, *Swargiya Dewan Kartikeyachandra Rayer Jibancharit* (Calcutta: Indian Association Publishing Company reprint 1956), pp. 2–3.

[75] Roper Lethbridge, ed., *A History of the Renaissance in Bengal, Ramtanu Lahiri: Brahman and Reformer* (Calcutta: Edition Indian, 1972), pp. 19–20.

school', etc. He thus turned Vidyalankar down saying that the quota for free students had been filled for the year. The canny pundit was not easily defeated and decided that a little importunity could win the day for Ramtanu. He thus instructed the boy to run with Hare's palanquin for a few days, which he did accordingly for about two whole months. Eventually Hare, convinced of this great urgency for an English education, relented and Ramtanu was admitted as a free student.[76]

The need and value attached to an English education has been the subject of much scholarship.[77] The important point to keep in mind, however, is that this was the only avenue of survival for the entire petty bourgeoisie from the 1850s onwards. The emphasis of previous scholarship has been upon the hegemonic function of the English language, but we are more concerned here about the fact that education and salaried jobs had become by this period a social imperative. So much so that a contemporary text on the history of education cited the following incident as proof of this compulsion:

Some gentlemen coming to Calcutta was astonished at the eagerness with which they were pressed for books by a troop of boys who boarded the Steamer from an obscure place called Komercolly. A Plato was lying on the table and one of the Party asked a boy whether that would serve his purpose. 'O yes', he exclaimed, 'give me any book'. The gentleman at last hit upon the expedient of cutting up an old Quarterly Review and distributing this [sic] articles among them. In the evening when some of the party went ashore, the boys of the town flocked around them, expressing their regret that why [sic] there was no English School in the place and saying that they hoped that the Governor General to whom they made an application on the subject when on his way up the country, will establish one.[78]

There was, around this time, a renewed effort on the part of the Bengalis to start their own private educational institutions to meet this need.[79] By 1876

---

[76] Shibnath Shastri, *Ramtanu Lahiri*, pp. 45–6.

[77] See for example, Gouri Viswanathan, *Masks of Conquest: Literary Study and British Rule in India* (London: Faber and Faber, 1990); Svati Joshi, ed., *Rethinking English: Essays in Literature, Language, History* (New Delhi: Oxford University Press, 1991); Ania Loomba, *Colonialism/Postcolonialism* (New York: Routledge, 1998).

[78] Cited in Upendranath Mukhopadhyay, *Hindujati O Shiksha*, Vol. 1(Calcutta: Srikali Ghosh, 1915), pp. 316–17.

[79] Motilal Seal started his 'Seal's College' in 1843, while the local bhadralok community of Krishnanagar raised Rs 13,000 to assist the government's project of opening a college in 1845. Jogeshchandra Bagal, *Banglar Uchchashiksha* (Calcutta: Vishwabharati Press, n.d.), pp. 33–7.

there were only five colleges and normal schools which were purely government institutions.[80] Hunter provided a rough summary for the number of people engaged in the service sector and petty trade in the twenty-four parganas in 1870–3. According to him, there were 18,303 men employed under government, municipal, or other local authorities; 33,996 men engaged as 'Professional persons, including professors of religion, education, literature, law medicine, fine arts, surveying and engineering'; and about 31,395 men in small trade and shopkeeping.[81] The Lieutenant Governor of Bengal, Richard Temple, commented that the position of this class engaged in public and private professions was 'in some respects ... improving fast; [but] in other respects it ... [was] becoming harder and harder'. Clerical labour, he observed, was becoming so cheap due to its super abundant availability that it failed 'to afford reasonable remuneration to those engaged in it'.[82] This was not big news, for already in 1860 James Long had remarked that the Bengali kerani could be employed at one-third the cost of Eurasians.[83]

There was a general recognition of the diverse composition of the salaried masses. Sumit Sarkar's elegant analysis of the recurrent myth about the present as *Kaliyuga* draws attention to this declining world of the kerani.[84] In a later chapter we shall see how this class was the main consumer of the Battala texts from the mid-nineteenth century. In one such text, a fabulous reason was provided for the penury of the professions and particularly of the kerani, by one Taran Sharma. In his grand venture titled *Keranipuran*, Sharma recounted a conversation between the Creator Brahma and his trusted sage Narad. Brahma was feeling sorry for the kerani, having cursed them previously to a life of hardship, as they had plucked all of Brahma's swan's feathers in order to write with them. Narad was accordingly dispatched to Earth to alleviate their woes. Narad found the keranis to be of three

---

[80] *Report on the Administration of Bengal 1874–75* (Calcutta, 1876), p. 79.

[81] W.W. Hunter, *A Statistical Account of Bengal*, Vol. 1 (London: Trübner and Co., 1875), pp. 45–9.

[82] *Report on the Administration of Bengal*, p. 44.

[83] James Long, 'Calcutta in the Olden Times' p. 170.

[84] Sumit Sarkar, 'Renaissance and *Kaliyuga*: Time, Myth and History in Colonial Bengal' in *Writing Social History*, pp. 186–215. *Kaliyuga* is defined by Sarkar as follows: 'Kali is the last and the most degenerate of the four *yugas* (eras—the preceding ones being Satya, Treta, and Dwapar) in the traditional high-Hindu concept of cyclical time.' Sarkar, *Social History*, *ff*.186.

castes: the first were the *kulin* amongst keranis who earned between Rs 200–400; the second were the *bangsaj* with a salary of Rs 100–200; below them were the *moulik* earning only Rs 30–100 a month. Below the Rs 30 range were those who were the menial mouliks and above the Rs 400 mark were the chief kulins.[85]

The term petty bourgeois is extremely confusing, particularly because we insisted that class should be used in Marxist sense and not merely as a sociological category based on occupation, etc. Marx refers to the 'lower middle class' as one comprising the small manufacturer, the shopkeeper, the artisan, and the peasant, who may assist the working class in its struggle against the bourgeoisie, but only to prevent itself from sinking into the ranks of the proletariat. They are the owners of small capital, economically trailing behind the big bourgeoisie and politically between the worker and capital. Their class position demands they be reactionary, even though at particular historical junctures they may play a revolutionary role against the bourgeoisie.[86] The main enemies for the kerani in the *Keranipuran* are thus 'mass education' and female education.[87] Although the sole avenue of survival for them was English education, access to higher education was strictly differentiated according to class. The bottom rung of the petty bourgeoisie thus became the kerani, while the top layer was recruited to the slightly higher rungs of the colonial state. In 1833, the office of deputy collector was created for Indians, in 1837 that of principal sudder, and in 1843, the deputy magistrate. A large section of the intelligentsia, Bankimchandra Chattopadhyay, Shibchandra Deb, Vidyasagar, Bhudev Mukhopadhyay, Rangalal Bandyopadhyay formed a part of this layer. It is this section of the original petty bourgeoisie that we shall term, following Sarkar, the new middle class.

While part of the same *class*, deputy magistrates, like Bankim, with their annual incomes ranging between £480–600 were of course quite different from the junior clerks in government or private offices who barely earned Rs 30, a month. Eric Olin Wright's theoretical category of 'contradictory class location' is of use here. Theoreticians like G.A. Cohen have forcefully demonstrated that the ownership of the means of production

---

[85] Taran Sharma, *Keranipuran* (Calcutta: Tarinicharan Das, 1886), pp. 1–8.

[86] K. Marx and F. Engels, *Selected Works* (London: Lawrence and Wishart, 1968), p. 44.

[87] Sharma, *Keranipuran*, pp. 40–1.

is maintained by what he has called 'power' which is screened by legal rights. Cohen cites a significant passage from the *Grundisse* to support his claim:

The bourgeois economists have a vague notion that it is better to carry on production under the modern police than it was, e.g., under club-law. They forget that club-law is also law, and that the right of the stronger continues to exist in other forms even under their 'government of law'.[88]

The 'other forms' in which the rights of the stronger exist, Cohen rightly argues is the 'real content filling the bourgeois legal form'.[89] Thus, *real* control over the means of production can preclude simple legal control. In this context Wright then argues that within these effective or real controls of the means of production there are some positions which occupy 'objectively contradictory locations within class relations'.[90] Wright places managers, supervisors, and semi-autonomous employees in this category. The former have a varying degree of control over allocation of resources and labour power while the latter have control over '*how* they do the work, and have at least some control over *what* they produce'. The former thus fall between the bourgeoisie and the proletariat while the latter between the petty bourgeois and the worker.

We cannot use Wright's definition in its entirety due to the specificities of a colonial economy. What we can retain, however, is the concept of a contradictory class location, whereby the higher income group of what we have called a petty bourgeois class was in its class allegiance pulled upwards, while the middle and bottom layers were constantly pushed downwards to make ends meet. Another eloquent description of the clerk was presented in a little known tract from the end of the nineteenth century. The clerk, in this tract, somehow manages to barely survive with his family on his paltry salary of thirty rupees a month. The only capital he owned was his ancestral house in the village, the rest of his *bramhottar* land having been appropriated by others due to his absence from the village on account of his *chakri* in the city.[91] What united the clerk with the likes of Bankim was this

---

[88] Marx quoted in G.A. Cohen, *Karl Marx's Theory of History: A Defence* (Oxford, Clarendon Press, 1979), p. 225.

[89] Ibid.

[90] Eric Olin Wright, *Class, Crisis and the State* (London: New Left Books, 1978), p. 61.

[91] Prasad Das Goswami, *Amader Samaj* (Serampore: Tamohar Press, 1895), p. 17.

landed property, but this again, in the former's case, was much more likely to be lost.

The top layer of this class, on the other hand, was constantly being offered limited control in the colonial bureaucracy. Most of them began their careers from within the hallowed portals of the Hindu College. In a vast country run by a handful of foreigners the connections between the top layers of the state and academic professions were very fluid and most students entered government services with the recommendations of their professors. In 1831, for example, the Surveyor General, Col. Everest authorized Tytler, the Professor of Mathematics at Hindu College to select from among his students a 'number of talented young men ... for the purpose of carrying on the computation of the Great Trigonometrical Survey of India'. As a result Shibchandra Deb and Radhanath Sikdar were nominated as computers at a monthly salary of Rs 30 each. Unlike the fate of clerks, this job for Deb was only a first rung in his career. In 1838, he was made the deputy collector for Cuttack at a salary of Rs 300 per month 'including Rs. 50 for office establishment' and 'when employed in the Mofussil ... authorized to draw an additional sum of Rs. 50 per month'.[92] In 1854 he was further promoted to a salary range of Rs 600 per month.[93]

These promotions up the ladder of the colonial bureaucracy came with the ruler's approbation. Deb had to his credit numerous letters of praise from higher British officials extolling the discharge of his duties. One collector, Bayley, said that he did not know anyone 'who could have done the same duty with so much clearness and success to his superiors and so little annoyance to those with whom he has to deal'.[94] The sociologist John Goldthorpe has argued that members of what we have called the new middle class, have a relationship with their employers which necessarily involves an important measure of *trust*, and accordingly they are 'accorded conditions of employment which are also distinctive in the level and kind of rewards that are involved'.[95] The ruling colonial power was forced to delegate part

[92] Abinashchandra Ghosh, ed., *Naradeb Sibchandra Deb O Tatsahadharminir Adarsha Jibanalekshya* (Calcutta: Birendranath Mitra, 1918), pp. 58–63.

[93] Ibid., p. 77.

[94] Ibid., p. 76; also see pp. 64–6, 73–5, and 78 for similar letters of approval.

[95] J. Goldthorpe, 'On the Service Class, its Formation and Future', in A. Giddens and G. Mackenzie, eds., *Social Class and the Division of Labour* (Cambridge: Cambridge University Press, 1982), p. 170.

of its role to these employees, and needed to be able to rely on these delegates to exercise the discretion involved in a manner conducive to their own interests, and therefore offered those in these contradictory class locations financial awards. A rather obvious corroboration of Macaulay's infamous thesis.[96]

The Associations of Power

We have tried to describe in this chapter the class location of the social category of the bhadralok. Summarizing then, the bhadralok was a composition of a landed rentier class, and the petty-bourgeoisie which colonialism forced to occupy contradictory class locations. The importance of education for this layer had diverse implications and different objective results. For, the rentier class indulgence in literary occupations was not so much a matter of necessity. After all men like Digambar Mitra had huge investments in rice, silk, and indigo and, of course, land.[97] *Hutom*, the best self-critique of his own class, calls the likes of Mitra, 'more dangerous than a snake, more vicious than a tiger'.[98]

For the salaried class of the bhadralok education was not merely a source of material sustenance, but because it was such, the only register of self-identity. For the upper layers of this class, the rent from whatever small land-holding they might have was not enough to maintain a life of luxury and yet just enough to provide entry into élite educational institutions of the city. McGuire reckons that the Hindu College acted 'as a key socialisation agency for this earlier generation of *bhadralok*', as entry into these institutions assured one a place in the colonial bureaucracy.[99] We have noted earlier the brilliant trajectories of the first batch of its graduates.

Having said this it is, however, important to re-emphasize that the new middle class was not the ruling class in the nineteenth century, nor were

---

[96] The reference is to the infamous comment of Macaulay on the object of English education in India in his Minute on Education (1835): 'to create a class of persons, Indian in blood and colour, but English in taste, in opinions, in morals, and in intellect', quoted in Stanley Wolpert, *A New History of India* (Oxford: Oxford University Press, 1997) p. 215

[97] Sibnarayan Shastri, *Kolkatar Paribarik Itihas*, Vol. 1 (Calcutta: Ramakrishna Sahitya Kutir, 1933), pp. 12–19.

[98] Nag, *Satik Hutom*, pp. 46–7.

[99] McGuire, *The Making of a Colonial Mind*, p. 47.

they an incipient bourgeoisie. This is why positions of historians like Anil Seal, analysing nationalism in terms of jealous self-interests, somewhat miss the point.[100] The new middle class was clearly distinct from the colonial ruling class in two important respects. First, in the nature of controls involved. Some writers have distinguished between two forms of effective possession of the means of production. On the one hand, there is 'allocative', or 'strategic', control, 'the power to employ resources or to withdraw them, in line with one's own interests and preferences' and on the other hand, there is 'operational' control, 'control over the day-to-day use of resources already allocated'.[101] Strategic control corresponds to Wright's category of control over investment and resource allocation. This is essentially the prerogative of the ruling class. The new middle class was involved in operational control, making decisions within a framework laid down by those with strategic control. The practice of *suparish* (recommendation), and essentially managerial functions, in the colonial context reveals the disparity between the classes.

The *Keranipuran* lamented that neither education nor intelligence were prerequisites to obtaining a job, whose imperatives rather were: very slight efficiency, *salams*, auspicious offerings at the right places and the benign glance of the Saheb.[102] Our new middle class also had a limited but significant role to play in this economy of favours. Sumit Sarkar makes passing comment on Vidyasagar's ability to acquire 'fairly important posts for some friends and clients' in the 1840s and 1850s.[103] An indication of his importance in this regard is demonstrated by the fact that once when he was ill and off-duty for two weeks, a daily stream of notes and requests for jobs, around twenty-five everyday, used to pour in for his commendation.[104] Amongst

---

[100] Seal attests the irrelevance of Marxist class analysis for the nineteenth and twentieth century, and claims that social change and nationalism should be studied as reflections of status aspirations. Anil Seal, *Emergence of Indian Nationalism*, p. 34.

[101] R.E. Pahl and J.T. Winkler, 'The Economic Elite: Theory and Practice', in A. Giddens and P. Stanworth, eds., *Elites and Power in British Society* (Cambridge: Cambridge University Press, 1974), p. 114.

[102] Sharma, *Keranipuran*, p. 8.

[103] Sarkar, *Writing Social History*, p. 227.

[104] See Vidyasagar's letter to Prasannakumar Sarbadhikari regarding one such applicant, a 'gentleman's son' in Prafulla Kumar Patra, ed., *Vidyasagar Rachanabali* (Calcutta: Patra's Publication, 1991), pp. 656–7.

the several mentioned by Sarkar, as the principal of the Sanskrit College and a member of the Board of Examiners, Vidyasagar was responsible for the Brahmo scholar Akshaykumar Datta being appointed the head teacher in the Normal school that he established in 1854.[105] Besides this he was also invested with limited control over the hiring and firing of subordinates.[106] Other prominent members of this class had a similar role in the colonial bureaucracy.[107] This, following Wright's definition, was operational control as all the decisions had to be finally ratified by a British official higher up in the rung. Indeed, an embittered and frustrated Vidyasagar's resignation from all official posts in 1857 due to the various restraints put on him by the same bureaucracy of which he was a part, is a point that can bear out large generalizations about the limited nature of indigenous middle class control.[108]

The second important feature of this class was that it lacked both the material and ideological resources to become a nascent bourgeoisie. The main reason for this has been argued very well in a recent article by Amiya Bagchi, where he shows how colonialism generated a political economy which both created market forces and structures that ensured their failures.[109] Political oppression that systematically prevents the natural expansion of the economy and its corollary class forces evokes a political response. The

[105] Ibid., p. 700.

[106] An emphatic example is the case of a bellman Madhusudan who (in a manner reminiscent of James Scott's *Weapons of the Weak* [1985]) had hit upon a scheme of combining two jobs, one at the Sanskrit College, where Vidyasagar was then Principal, and one at Fort William, and covering the former by getting someone else to work on his behalf. Given that his salary at the college was Rs 4 a month, this was a perfectly understandable act. Vidyasagar found out about this 'deception' and reckoning it to be 'highly improper' summarily dismissed Madhusudan. See Arabinda Guha, ed., *Unpublished Letters of Vidyasagar* (Calcutta: Ananda, 1971), pp. 14–15.

[107] Rajendralal Mitra for example wrote a letter of recommendation for Haraprasad Shastri, but which was unfortunately not accepted. See Satyajit Chaudhuri et al., eds, *Haraprasad Shastri*, pp. 72–3.

[108] For an illuminating study of this particular aspect see Asok Sen, *Iswarchandra Vidyasagar*.

[109] Amiya Bagchi, 'Markets, Market Failures, and the Transformation of Authority, Property and Bondage in Colonial India', in B. Stein and S. Subrahmanyam, eds., *Institutions and Economic Change in South Asia* (Delhi: Oxford University Press, 1996), pp. 48–70.

only barrier that, for example, impeded the entry of Indians into deserving posts in the social and economic system was the unavoidable fact of their Indianness.[110] It is this situation of engineered backwardness that created the social and political significance for the new middle class or the intelligentsia. In this respect a historic analogy, if not parallel, maybe drawn with the Czarist Russia and the exaggerated social significance of the Narodniks as the only group capable of articulating the desires of the many. To put it differently: the fetters on the productive forces were *felt* by all the social classes, but bourgeois property relations being weak, and the proletariat too young, the traditional role of a liberal bourgeois *class*, fell on the shoulders of our new middle class.

Placed in a contradictory class location, where its own position in the political economy was severely confused, which classes could it lead or guarantee liberation for? As some theoreticians have argued, as the 'only non-specialised section of society (because it was not locked into a particular class role within the relations of production) the intelligentsia ... appeared to represent the interests of the 'nation' as against conflicting sectional and class interests'.[111] Thus Aswinikumar Banerjee in his disputation with Pearymohan Mukherjee confidently affirmed that it was 'the middle class gentry' and not the 'mushroom aristocracy' that formed the 'backbone of the Congress'.[112] We must remind ourselves that during the Swadeshi Movement (1905), the first articulate expression of organized nationalism, the majority of the industrial bourgeoisie remained unconcerned.[113] The category of the bhadralok, including the struggling actuality of the clerk, the individual reforms of Vidyasagar, and the landed interests of the Tagores, provided the only ideological basis for dismantling existing differences of class realities. Only from the pen of a bhadralok could come the evocative imagery of *Bande Mataram*.

Partha Chatterjee repudiates Benedict Anderson's thesis by arguing that the 'elite' in colonial countries did not follow the modular forms of bourgeois

---

[110] Ibid., pp. 65–70.

[111] Tony Cliff, 'Deflected Permanent Revolution', in *Trotskyism After Trotsky* (London: Bookmarks, 1999), pp. 60–9; see especially pp. 67–8.

[112] *Indian Mirror*, 23 September 1898.

[113] See Sumit Sarkar, *The Swadeshi Movement in Bengal: 1903–1908* (New Delhi: People's Publishing House, 1973).

development of the advanced world. Half a century before Chatterjee, Trotsky drew a similar conclusion along Marxist lines:

A backward country assimilates the material and intellectual conquests of the advanced countries. But this does not mean that it follows them slavishly, reproduces all the stages of their past.... A certain repetition of cultural stages in ever new settlements was in fact bound up with the provincial and episodic character of that whole process. Capitalism means, however, an overcoming of those conditions. It prepares and in a certain sense realises the universality and permanence of man's development. By this a repetition of forms of development by different nations is ruled out ... historic backwardness ... compels the adoption of whatever is ready in advance of any specified date, skipping a whole series of intermediate stages.[114]

The combined and uneven nature of development and assimilation produced the bhadralok as an ethic and a sentiment. This was to come to fruition in 1905 when zamindars, petty tenure holders, print and railway workers, and our historically neglected kerani, were to come together to give political shape to the battle cry of *Bande Mataram*. The nation was brought into being, not in the private world of the 'elite' as Chatterjee has argued, but in the ideological dissolution of class conflicts. This process of ideological disaggregation forms the focus of the next chapter.

---

[114] Leon Trotsky, *The History of the Russian Revolution* (London: Pluto Press, 1977) pp. 26–7.

2

Ideologies and Practices

Its object was 'the moral, social, intellectual and physical advancement of young men'. Its programme comprised classes of Philosophy, History, Political Economy, and opportunities for meetings, lectures, discussion, musical entertainments and indoor and outdoor games. The monthly subscription was Rs. 1 and the entrance fee was Rs. 2. The Maharaja of Cooch Behar was the patron, W.W. Hunter the president, and Nandalal Sen the honorary secretary. Among the members we find the cream of European and Indian society—five judges of the High Court, the President of the Bengal Chamber of Commerce, members of the Legislative Council, professors, lawyers, doctors and zamindars.[1]

In the previous chapter we devoted much time to classes. Classes and nations are indeed the most important instances of collectivities in the modern world. One, as we have argued previously, is an objective social relation, while the latter a purely subjective notion. Similarly, the fundamental difference between a collectivity and an organization is that the former need not subscribe to any structure or rules of operation. Organizations are premised upon some mechanism determining both its structure and the action of its members. A sense of collective identity by contrast does not involve any such procedure.[2] Collectivities exist, if and only if, their members

---

[1] Brahmabandhab Upadhyaya writing about the Concord Club (1886) quoted in Julius L. Lipner, *Brahmabandhab Upadhyaya: The Life and Thought of a Revolutionary* (Delhi: Oxford University Press, 1999), p. 68.

[2] For an elaboaration of this argument see Callinicos, *Making History: Agency, Structure and Change in Social Theory* (Ithaca: Cornell University Press, 1988). Callinicos supports this formulation with the following example. A worker may refuse to cross a picket line because she believes in class solidarity without there having been any collective decision by the proletariat as a whole to support the strike.

coordinate their actions in view of the identity they believe themselves to share. This brings us to the question of the beliefs agents have about society, in other words, the question of ideology.

There can be two ways of determining ideology. First, as a clear cut political doctrine, or creed, whose concepts are logically linked to form a 'system' which has achieved internal consistency and has been subject to some amount of formal philosophical elaboration. The second way is to define ideology as a whole range of concepts, ideas, and images which provide the frameworks of interpretation and meaning for social and political thought in society, whether they exist at the high systematic philosophical level or at the level of casual, everyday, contradictory, common sense explanation.[3] Gramsci, once more, is of use to us here. He argues that there are always two distinct arenas in ideology: philosophy and common sense. The two arenas fuse when an ideology becomes 'organic' to the mainstream of historical development. That ideology then is widely dispersed through society and forms the basis, not only of philosophical reasoning but also of the 'naïve' and spontaneous conceptions of the world held by ordinary people and thus becomes part of the common sense of the age.[4] It is only when a current of ideas has become, in this way, 'a cultural movement, a religion, a faith' that it is capable of performing its organic role, 'that of preserving the ideological unity of the entire social block which that ideology serves to cement and to unify'.[5]

While this maybe so, we are still left with another problem about ideology. There are usually in society several ideologies in simultaneous existence, both at the level of common sense and in the sense of doctrines. What then explains the acceptance of individuals of certain ideologies? In other words, what informs the choice of individuals to be, say a Marxist, or to believe that the sun goes round the earth? Seen in this way, ideologies are connected to human consciousness and the study of ideology has to take this into account. 'Understood in this way', says Eric Olin Wright, 'to study "consciousness" is to study particular aspects of the mental life of individuals, namely those elements of a person's subjectivity which are discursively accessible to the individual's own awareness'.[6] In the final reckoning it is

---

[3] I am grateful to David Arnold for pointing out this crucial distinction.

[4] Antonio Gramsci, *Selections from the Prison Notebooks*, pp. 323–43.

[5] Ibid., p. 328.

[6] Eric Olin Wright, *Classes* (London: Verso, 1985), p. 244.

persons who hold ideological beliefs. But they do so due to social processes. Explaining why an individual or a group holds such beliefs, is thus a matter of analysing social mechanisms and historical developments, not of locating intellectual preferences or individual psychology.

It is this sense of ideology being social consciousness that we shall use in this chapter. Accordingly, we are concerned with understanding the ideology, or ideologies, that made the bhadralok, even though they were a composite of varying class positions, appear to be a coherent social whole. Previous historians have all commented on the importance of education and literary values to the constitution of the bhadralok identity. In fact, most scholars have used that to determine the homogeneity of the group as well as claim the invalidity of Marxist concepts in trying to analyse them. In this chapter we shall try to focus on this general problem of the ideological moorings of the bhadralok and the more specific problem of education.

Vidya: The Emergence of a Concept

A significant aspect about the writings on vidya, or knowledge, in the mid-nineteenth century was the association of knowledge with private property. This is most evident in the textbooks and homilies published by minor textbook writers, some of them from Battala. The great advantage of vidya, as viewed by these writers, was that it could be owned as property without risking the negative effects of ownership. According to one rhyming couplet on the subject, vidya was the perfect property. Relatives and kin could not cheat one out of it, as it could not be distributed. It could not be stolen by thieves, and donations could not lessen its quantity, or quality. Vidya is hence referred to as *mahadhan*, or supreme wealth.[7] In an era when access to education was increasingly being determined by wealth it is not surprising that the discourse would try and seek some comfort in the intrinsic qualities of knowledge. A more popular version of this poem further illustrates for us some of the other concerns of the authors.

Gopalchandra Bandyopadhyay was one of the better selling textbook authors of the time. More than one edition of his books were published

---

[7] This poem appears in several forms in many textbooks. See for instance, Woomesh Chandra Bhattacharjea, *The New Infant Teacher* Part III (Calcutta, 1877), p. 27; Gopalchandra Bandyopadhyay, *Hita Shiksha*, Part I (Calcutta: Hitaishi Press, 1869), pp. 31–2; A prose version of the same theme is found in Kalikrishna Bhattacharya's *Naba Niti Sara*, Part I (Calcutta: Subharnab Press, 1858), pp. 32–3).

regularly and at least one of his works was published by the prestigious Stanhope Press. The poem on vidya formed a part of his *Hita Shiksha* (1868), which itself had three editions. This was a veritable achievement given the deluge of similar moral lesson books at the time including Vidyasgar's *Akhyanmanjari* (1863) and *Bodhodoy* (1851). In Bandhopadhyay's version, the poem on vidya, acquires a veneer of enlightenment. It begins with the usual disquisition on how vidya was a unique property that nobody could steal, borrow, or denigrate. It then goes on to elaborate on the singular achievements of vidya, which included the railways, telegraph, and the microscope. There was nothing as powerful as vidya and Bandyopadhyay declares it to be the one *dhan* (material possession, wealth) that could buy heaven for man. The poem ends with a direct bourgeois exhortation: a call to *shram*, or industrious labour, in order to acquire vidya.[8]

Recently Brian Hatcher has outlined a very useful way of looking at the nineteenth-century pedagogy. He has argued that contemporary instructional manuals should be seen as a fusion of Hindu moral pedagogy and Victorian bourgeois values. His excellent discussion of the *nitisastra* tradition which accords a 'fundamental importance [to] learning, or vidya' is of vital importance to our argument. Hatcher has shown how specific aspects of the Hindu moral tradition were reinvented to fit modern bourgeois parameters.[9]

The poems and homilies on vidya by the lesser-known authors clearly follow this model. On the one hand, the language in which these poems are written aspire to be a Sansikritized Bengali. They contain more *tatsama* words (that is, words unchanged from Sanskrit) than *tatbhava* words (that is, words derived from Sanskrit but changed) and *desaja* words (that is, words derived from or of non-Sanskrit roots). The verse form also gives an illusion of it being an actual Sanskrit *shloka*. On the other hand, due to the already extant tradition of *nitisastra*, the poem intensifies the fantasy of being a part of 'traditional' Brahminical learning. Simply put, these writers were trying to approximate in their own way the legitimizing powers of upper-caste pedagogy. They were also trying valiantly to marry this tradition successfully to the new bourgeois values of industry, science, and rationality. In other words, here we see the unfolding of some of the fundamental constituents of a bhadralok modernity: upper-caste Hindu tradition

[8] Bandyopadhyay, *Hita Shiksha*, Part I, pp. 31–2.
[9] Brian Hatcher, *Idioms of Improvement*, pp. 117–37.

redesigned within a Victorian bourgeois garb. Vidya, or learning was going to be one of the most important aspects of this rhetoric.[10]

By the mid-nineteenth century books were available cheaply and in abundance at least within the boundaries of Calcutta. However, Battala, the source of cheap publications, had changed considerably in its importance. The publications from the presses of Battala in this period were aimed specifically at the layer of 'less successful educated men' and the non-English educated populace, and were markedly disassociated from other educational publications. They concentrated on scriptures, mythologies, and the so-called 'obscene' tales. Gurudas Chattopadhyay, one of the noted publishers of this period, pointed out the anomalies of prices of the publications produced in Battala and other presses, as he acknowledged that the books published in Battala, in sheer volume, sold twenty times more than other 'good' books of Bengal.[11] This being the case, however, it cannot be deduced that Battala was furthering the cause of education by making available for the general public cheap and accessible books. We will see later how books published in Battala were being pushed out of the circuit of what was being increasingly considered as 'good' or educational. The condemnation of the Battala presses by Chattopadhyay signified that even though print was democratizing the availability of books in terms of both price and accessibility, there had already developed a hierarchy within printed literature that negated such developments.

Let us go back to our pensioner Tarakrishna Haldar who had the rare visitation from Vidya. A notable point about his proselytizing mission is his realization that communicating individually to people was no longer possible. Hence his dependence on the printed medium. If we recall our remarks about the concept of the videshi in Bhabanicharan's *Kalikata*, spatial boundaries for our zealous pensioner had clearly changed. Space was no longer a repository of known people and their individual lives but an abstraction which could be filled by any number of people. In other words,

---

[10] Ranajit Guha also discusses this assimilative process of the two hierarchical traditions in his 'Dominance Without Hegemony and its Historiography' in Ranajit Guha, ed., *Subaltern Studies VI* (New Delhi: Oxford University Press, 1992), pp. 240–56.

[11] Quoted in Gopalchandra Ray, 'Bangla Bayer Byabsa', in Chittaranjan Bandyopadhyay, ed., *Dui Shataker Bangla Mudran O Prakashan* (Calcutta: Ananda Publishers, 1981), p. 360. Gurudas Chattopadhyay was the first publisher of the young Rabindranth's work.

a nameless people had been born and his book was addressed to this collectivity. Suddenly, the horizons of the individual had been widened indefinitely changing all conceptual parameters of communication. A contemporary textbook for schools puts this very well in its discussion of printing. Of all the machines invented by man, it claimed the printing press to be the most important and useful. The role that printing played in the spread of vidya was virtually unmatched and it could even be said that it played a crucial role in the very process of civilization. In the dark days 'before print', when a book was written, 'even people nearby remained ignorant of its existence, let alone people in other countries or distant lands'.[12]

The idea of and need for communication is an important issue and needs to be taken seriously. The intense penetration of everyday life by institutions and social disciplines is so much a part of the modern reality that we often fail to notice its importance. Michel Foucault has illustrated the surveillance aspect of this development, whereby institutions acquire in modernity the power to regulate and systematically supervise individual behaviour 'down to the finest grain of the social body'.[13] The reason for this shift, though not clear in Foucault, is not hard to construe. Since the mode of surplus appropriation under capitalism is directly related to the level of labour productivity, the systematic supervision of producers both inside and outside the process of production becomes a necessity. The life of the agent outside the work place thus comes under focus in such an intense manner only under capitalism. Thus, only with the advent of modernity that the ruling class acquires the need, and consequently the means, to penetrate the daily lives of the masses. Print and printing must be seen as one such artefact of modernity, like the railways, that simultaneously creates an anonymous collective as well as permeates its everyday life. It is in this more fundamental sense that one may use the term 'print-capitalism'.

These theoretical concepts in place, an attempt can now be made to make sense of the central thesis of Haldar's dream. Education, as we have argued in the previous chapter, was the only source of sustenance for a significant layer of salaried men. Knowledge, or vidya, acquired an obsessive focus for all contemporary writing. Most books were said to be disseminators of vidya, and would often devote entire chapters to its significance. A *vidyan*

---

[12] Jadunath Raya, *Shikshabichar* (Calcutta: The New Sanskrit Press, 1870), p. 11.

[13] M. Foucault, *Discipline and Punish: The Birth of the Prison* (Harmondsworth: Penguin, 1977), pp. 57, 80–1.

(a man who possessed vidya) looked handsome even if he was physically ugly; became genteel, bhadra, even if he was not so by birth; and was respected even if he was not a *kulin*.[14] The distinguishing attribute of vidya was that it was disassociated from material wealth, being a form of wealth itself. Material wealth and riches would not follow men in the afterlife, but vidya would; riches could disintegrate, but vidya once attained was permanent.[15]

The association of the bhadralok with education and intellectual labour had become generalized to a common sense by the end of the century. Memorable anecdotes about great men were almost always on the basis of their proficiency in knowledge or intelligence. Thus, it was said of Harishchandra Mukherjee, the renowned editor of the *Hindoo Patriot*, that in five months he had read over fifty-seven volumes of *The Edinburgh Review* two or three times and learnt their contents by heart. He was also reputed for his ability to recite passages from Kant and Gibbon's *Rise and Fall of the Roman Empire*.[16] In 1873, Lal Behari Dey (1824–94) on return from his travels in north-west India proudly catalogued the achievements of the Bengalis:

By far the most interesting portion of the population of Calcutta are those hundreds of young Bengalis who have received a liberal education, and thereby divested themselves of the prejudices of their countrymen. You will find scores of intelligent natives in every public office in Calcutta .... The head writer of every public office in the North West is invariably a Bengali. The Deputy Post Master of every *tapal* office is a Bengali. The head masters of most English schools are Bengali. Most of the business connected with the Railway and Electric telegraph departments of the North West is managed by Bengalis. In Bengal we employ men of the North west as our porters and gate-keepers, and in every other post requiring muscular strength; and in the North west they employ Bengalis in every situation requiring mental exertion. I have never yet met a man or heard of a man who has denied that the Bengalis are a highly intelligent race.[17]

[14] Nabakumar Gupta, *Niti Kaumudi* (Dhaka: Nandakumar Guha and Co., 1867), pp. 1–2.

[15] Nandakumar Kabiratna Bhattacharya, *Gyan Saudamini* (Calcutta: Vidyaratna Press, 1863), pp. 11–13.

[16] Roper Lethbridge, ed., *A History of the Renaissance*, p. 161. The fascinating story of Vidyasagar's learning of the Arabic numerals from milestones is another famous and oft-quoted example.

[17] Lalbehari Dey, 'Calcutta and Those that Live in it', *Bengali Magazine* (November, 1873), pp. 183–4.

One should not draw a mechanical connection between the needs of the political economy and the discursive importance of knowledge. Printing and an educational drive were a part of capitalist 'progress' in most countries, and Bengal was no exception, particularly given the moral responsibility of a 'civilizing mission'. Needs of the state (Fort William College, 1800), private British initiative (Calcutta School Society, 1818), and the advances of the missionaries coalesced in the unique context of colonialism.

The books published by the School Book Society first articulated the need for educational works. The Society's antecedents lay in contemporary developments in England, where the first few decades of the nineteenth century formed the age of 'Philanthropy in Education'. Under *laissez faire* and 'free enterprise', mass education was delegated to a matter of private charity, outside state control. The result was the formation of a number of denominational societies, which ardently took up the work of popular education as a part of social and religious service to the community, and as a safeguard against 'vice, irreligion and subversive tendencies among the poor'.[18] As can be imagined from its historical precedence, the School Book Society was hardly a politically independent agent of education, its politics of reform and guidance were intrinsically tied up with the prevalent colonialist ideals. The earlier form of education current in the several indigenous *pathshalas*, were sought to be remodelled to suit the new axes of the ideology of education. The new books, as a result, did not introduce new ideas in totally unrecognizable form, but used the older structures for a new effectivity. The content material was generally culled from the texts employed in the native vernacular pathshalas, and then reformulated to produce an 'improved' version.[19] Reformulation, as an inscription and description, served as a device of textual control.

Books published on edifying subjects from the mid-nineteenth century bring into focus the pervasiveness of this education ideology across Bengal. We must remind ourselves that a majority of the consumers of these books,

[18] H.C. Barnard, *A Short History of Education in England 1760–1944* (London: University of London Press, 1961), pp. 156–69.

[19] The first publications of the Society were two sets of Bengali tables selected by the Rev. May of Chinsurah from the syllabi of the native schools, collections of Bengali lessons drawn up on the plan of the National School Society of England and the model of one Mr Dufief of Philadelphia, a set of fables by Bengali members of the Society, and a sizable number of publications purchased from the Serampore Press. See *First Report*, pp. 1–8.

the clerks and white collared employees, had strong links with the mofussil, having their families there.[20] Also the institutional infrastructure of Western education had developed considerably by this period, and schools and colleges teaching the liberal arts had mushroomed not only in and around Calcutta, but also in certain key areas of the province as a whole. In 1875, there were roughly 2,064 students studying for a BA (bachelor of arts) degree. The number of students in government and aided schools was higher still. An approximate account for the Presidency was provided in the annual report of the Governor-General (see Table 2.1).

TABLE 2.1   Number of students in government and aided schools

	Muslims	Hindus
Burdwan Division	5,770	93,371
Calcutta	774	5,876
Presidency Division	19,136	59,605
Rajshahye Division	25,145	30,927
Cooch Behar Division	855	1,338
Dacca Division	12,633	34,244
Chittagong Division	9,931	12,295
Patna Division	5,127	40,490

Source: Report on the Administration of Bengal 1974–75 (Calcutta, 1876), p. 471.

The need for printed books was inscribed in this structure from the very bottom level upwards. Students desirous of any sort of state funding from the basic elementary level had to be proficient in 'writing the vernacular of the district and reading it in printed books as well as in manuscripts'.[21] Newspapers were being read, according to official estimates (which were bound to be understated), by around 30,000 people in 1875; of these eight were published in Dacca, three in Assam, two in Burdwan, three in Patna, eight in Rajshahi, one in Bhagalpur, eight in the Presidency division, two

[20] The Brahmos were the foremost in the educational zeal in the mofussil. According to one reformer it seems that by 1863 people like Theodore Parker were being read widely among Western-educated Brahmos in Dacca. Bangachandra Ray, *Amar Jibanalekshya* (Dacca: Umeshchandra Sen, 1913), p. 21.

[21] *Report on the Administration of Bengal 1874–75*, p. 81.

in Chinsurah, and twenty-one in Calcutta.[22] It seems that one-third of Bengal's government clerks came from the Bikrampur region around Dacca.[23] The breadth and spread of the education ideology was thus impressive but unsurprising.

The texts published both by the great and the good like Vidyasagar, or by lesser known authors like our pensioner had a shared admixture of priorities. First, a unique feature that all the texts had in common was the form in which their subject matter was organized. They were all compact conspectuses of information on various subjects ranging from the utility of education to the railways. Certain issues were, however, common to all, and these were: (i) thoughts on education, diversely codified as the aim in life or self-edification; (ii) directives on chakri; (iii) the importance of physical fitness and hence a balanced diet; (iv) the social location of wealth in relation to knowledge; (v) the state of the Bengali language and possible methods for its improvement; and usually a chapter on (vi) morals or religion. The other important attribute of these books was the fluidity of their subject positions. They could simultaneously pass as didactic textbooks for institutions or as homilies for the individual reader. Their advertisements would declare that they were fulfilling the desideratum of subjects in the Bengali language, and all uniformly had moral titles like *Upadesh Manjari* (1868), *Nitiratnahar* (1870), and *Nitiranamala* (1871). They were not written for the express purpose of any school syllabi, but would often, judging by their popularity, be included in them. What they all taught, without fail, was the importance of education as both an intellectual and social qualification, and the differences between the educated and the uneducated.

Culture Strikes Back

The dominant system of spectacular representation of wealth, which had augmented the cock-fights of the first half of the century, had echoed in the glittering parties of the 'Prince', Dwarkanath Tagore, had been publicized in the weddings of the cats and dogs of the rich, came under the scathing criticism of the next generation. Hutom inaugurated his *naksha* with a blinding satirization of the babu whose present-day vulgar pomposity owed its origin to his great-grandfather's fortunes, made as a dewan to a salt

---

[22] Ibid., pp. 94, 480,

[23] Sarkar, *Writing Social History*, p. 170.

agent.[24] Pearychand Mitra, whose grandfather had married the shipping
magnate Madanmohan Datta's daughter and inherited his fortunes, and
who himself, as we have mentioned before, was on the board for several
companies, had a similar position on wealth and spending, as exemplified
in Baburam in his *Alaler Gharer Dulal*. The most dramatic and
confrontational account of this ideological shift was, however, between
Dwarkanath Tagore, entrepreneur and merchant, whose lavish parties had
impressed even the Queen, and his scholarly, sagely, son Debendranath.

The Tagore family of Jorasanko bears in its genealogy one of the most
concrete instances of the triumphal progress of culture, with members of
the family incorporating an almost spectacular abundance of talent and
literary accomplishment. If the dominion of culture needed a ruler it would
certainly have found one in the charismatic singularity of this family. The
family's fortunes, as we have seen, were built upon joint business ventures
with the East India Company, first initiated by Gopimohan Tagore, which
later reached commanding heights at the hands of his illustrious son,
Dwarkanath. The public life of the Tagores begins with Dwarkanath who
strides across every contemporary newspaper and journal as the 'prince' of
Calcutta society, in his shrewdness, benevolence, business speculations, and
private scandals. The inner life of 'culture' that Chatterjee's argument rests
upon, was almost, if not totally, absent from the procedures of articulation
of Dwarkanath's life—in biographies, in reports, or private correspondence.
The focus, rather, is on the very public achievements of Tagore, particularly
in areas of contestation with the Company. On the eve of his trip to England
in 1838, *Gyananweshan* tells us that the prince had done all that befits the
rich. The list does not include, as it would in the next decade, a catalogue
of his literary achievements, but relates instead Tagore's achievements as a

---

[24] Arun Nag, ed., *Satik Hutom Penchar Naksha*, pp. 30–3. The Company had
acquired its monopoly over salt in 1772 under Warren Hastings, which not proving as
profitable as was imagined, was leased over to private agents in 1776. When even this
failed, an agent was recruited for an entire salt producing area, and it was decided that
the salt would be sold at a pre-determined fixed rate. The agent was always British while
the next in position, the dewan, was an Indian. Lacking knowledge of the intricacies of
transactions the agent would usually leave most of the dealings to the dewan who made
enormous profits. Many prominent men from the earlier half of the century owed their
family fortunes to this enterprise. Foremost among them were, Dwarkanath Tagore,
Ramhari Biswas, and Krishnachandra Palchaudhuri.

superb host of huge parties he threw for Europeans and natives alike, and the wonderful buildings he erected as a memorial to his wealth.[25]

A sharp break in the self-portrayal of the family comes with Dwarkanath's son, Debendarnath. The appellations that the two figures gained in contemporary society was illustrative of this break: while the father was known as the 'prince' both at home and abroad, the son engrossed in his non-monetary and spiritual undertakings earned the nickname of 'Maharshi'.[26]

Debendranath's autobiography takes off within a renunciatory framework. He begins his autobiography not in the usual manner with his birth and family history, but rather with the beginning of his second life, that is, the beginning of his spiritual life. The narrative mode is significant in its conflation of the two beginnings, that of the text itself and his spiritual life. Due to the specificities of its genre as an autobiography, it thus appears to the reader that his life begins at the age of eighteen when he experiences his spiritual awakening. What stands out as the most significant register of this disjuncture between his past and the present is his orientation towards material wealth. The first two chapters are replete with guilt-ridden sentiments about his past luxuries and their embodiment as the real obstruction to spirituality.[27]

The analytical categories of private and public which form the fundamental parameters in theorizing nationalism for the recent historians of Bengal, find perfect correspondence in the life of Debendranath. He forms the point of departure for the cultural achievements of the later Tagores. He has to his credit the consolidation and institutionalization of the Brahmo religion, which become under him not merely a private faith but a part of public lifestyle. The new Western-educated professionals either were members of the Brahmo Samaj or identified strongly with its progressive

---

[25] *Gyananweshan*, 17 February 1838.

[26] It is worth reproducing here a letter from the 'Prince' to the 'Maharshi' highlighting the intense nature of the ideological/personal conflict between the two men. Dwarkanath wrote to his son from London in 1846: 'It is only a source of wonder to me that all my estates are not ruined. Your time, I am sure, being taken up in writing for the newspapers and in fighting with the missionaries than in watching over and protecting these important matters.' Cited in Satyendranath Tagore, *Amar Balyakatha O Bomabai Prabash* (Calcutta: Kantik Press, 1915), p. 7.

[27] Priyonath Shastri, ed., *Pujyapad Srimanmaharshi Debendranath Thakurer Swarachita Jivan-charit O Parishishta* (Calcutta: Bannerjee Press, 1898), pp. 1–21.

values of widow remarriage, regeneration of the Bengali language, and the more directly nationalist projects like the *jatiya mela* (1867).[28] It is also no surprise that the more famous of the literary giants of the nineteenth century, Rabindranath Tagore and Michael Madhusudan Dutt made their first forays into the literary world in the pages of the Brahmo journal, the *Tattobodhini Patrika*.[29]

This was definitely a new development as Debendranath's previous generation did not share the latter's cultural attributes nor did it forge a conscious rhetoric against wealth and money. From an aggressive display of wealth by Dwarkanath, who had no compunctions in his choice of making it, his enterprises ranging from indigo, silk, to prostitution, we have the renunciatory rhetoric of his son, moving the terms of social appraisal from money to non-monetary registers of culture and taste.[30]

'How shall I describe the physical appearance of the babu?' asks Shibnath Shastri, the Brahmo reformer in his social history of the nineteenth century. 'Their face, forehead and eyes are darkened with the excesses of the night. The head bears a wavy mantle of hair, the teeth are fashionably coloured with *mishi*, and a feather-light dhoti graces the body.... In the daytime these babus either slept or flew kites, watched cock-fights, or whiled away their time in playing musical instruments, and listening to obscene *panchali*s or half-*akhrai* songs. Come night-time they would gather at the whorehouses and immerse themselves in the pleasures therein'.[31] This portrait of gross physical pleasures was then the exact antonym of a bhadralok. But how does one recognize a bhadralok?

Etymologically bhadralok is an almost exact translation of gentleman. Already in the second quarter of the century there appeared in the *Bangadoot*

---

[28] Shibnath Shastri, himself a prominent Brahmo writes in his *History of the Brahmo Samaj*: 'the first adherents ... were mostly high officers under Government; and the movement was entirely a movement of the leaders of the educated community of the time'. Quoted in Benoy Ghosh, ed., *Samayikpatre Banglar Samajchitra*, p. 41.

[29] See Debipada Bhattacharya, 'Bangla Samayikpatra', in Chittaranjan Bandyopadhyay, ed., *Dui Shataker Bangla Mudran O Prakashan*, pp. 283–300; Rabindranath Tagore, *Jiban Smriti* (Calcutta: Vishwabharati, 1970), pp. 189–90.

[30] The House Assessment Books of the Corporation of Calcutta in 1806 lists a brothel in 235 and 236 Bow Bazar Street owned by a member of Dwarkanath's family. It had forty-three rooms for prostitutes and its rental value was Rs 140. See S.N. Mukherjee, *Calcutta: Myths and History* (Calcutta: Subarnarekha, 1977), p. 101.

[31] Shibnath Shastri, *Ramtanu Lahiri* pp. 55–6.

an article comparing the new Bengali middle class to its European counterpart.[32] A leading student in the Hindu College, Kailashchandra Dutta, wrote an interesting article for the *Hindu Pioneer* in 1836 entitled 'What is a Gentleman?' Gentlemen, the author was once informed by a lady friend, were 'a people of a particular sort with whom one likes to associate'. This delightful and vacuous remark is then concretized by the author himself. He begins with the rejection of certain common assumptions about the word; 'most people' he says 'will exclaim that birth dubs a man a gentleman'. Of course by this he certainly does not mean to imply 'every kind of birth, because then a tinker or tailor would be one'. Thus the 'adjective *respectable* preceding "ancient family", may complete the sense'. Now comes the real twist in his argument. All preceding registers of eminence had been challenged by colonialism. Caste or rank no longer had their previous relevance, as was demonstrated by the meteoric rise of the *banias*. Dutta asks: 'Who will swear (except perhaps the present writer) that the long train of his ancestors has maintained an unspotted character, has been undisgraced by pickpockets or murderers?' Thus a new illustration for the gentleman is provided:

Universal respect for certain individuals, not necessarily of the brightest genius nor favoured by fortune's smile, is owing to some qualities which constitute a good man. It matters little whether such men have smooth complexions, scarlet uniforms or fringed gloves.... If one of these men wears a plain dress, a leathern belt, a waistcoat not lined with silk, he is not the less esteemed. He has not been guilty of leading a sorry matrimonial life and running away with another man's wife.... In company he neither talks flippantly nor impudently, has not the air of a bravo or a beau, does not swagger or bully, or unnecessarily offer his gold snuff box with a looking glass under the lid, nor bows to the company before he takes his seat.[33]

There are a few things distinctive about this definition. The first and the most obvious is the discarding of older marks of status, that is, caste, birth, etc. Dutta's own surname (kayastha) suggests a social mobility which was unthinkable in pre-colonial times. The Tagores were a plebeian version of Brahmins who would not have had the previous economic and later cultural dominance if not for the generalization of resources by colonialism.[34] The

[32] *Bangadoot*, 13 June 1829.

[33] *Hindu Pioneer*, 1, 5 (January, 1836), pp. 69–71.

[34] Rabindranath was married to a poor and undistinguished family as not many from the Brahmin community were willing to marry their daughter to one from the

second characteristic of the gentleman is his undisputed individuality. Ancestry, heredity, and even profession are disregarded in this passage in favour of inner marks of breeding, in other words, culture. The soul of the gentleman thus lay in liberal education and the rarefied life of the mind. There was a uniform critique of excess in all forms and a privileging of education over material wealth.[35]

This critique of wealth should not be seen as pure conspiracy on the part of a section of the bhadralok to secure consensus amongst the more unfortunate ones. The tedium of a salaried job and constant humiliation at the hands of British superiors were sources of angst for even the well established bhadralok. Bankimchandra's brother Sanjibchandra was demoted for his (alleged) impertinence to a British judge.[36] In a telling anecdote about Rajendralal Mitra, his wife was reputed to have asked first whether his Ll. D. epithet would bring any extra income, and when explained it would not, she was supposed to have lost all interest in the honorific title.[37] Rajnarayan Basu, in his popular lecture *Sekal ar Ekal*, laments about chakri.[38] There was hence a constant underlying anxiety about material life amongst all sections of the bhadralok which made the critique of wealth an acceptable common sense.

But while a critique of wealth and conspicuous spending was a dominant sentiment among all classes of the bhadralok, it was also ironically a problem as some of the major bhadralok figures did command substantial wealth. Debendranath despite his disavowal of material pleasures and wealth, never wore a set of clothes more than a few times. His entire wardrobe was frequently handed down to servants and replacements made. He also never

Pirali caste. Also certain prominent figures of the nineteenth century were from non-Brahmin, even non-Kayastha, backgrounds, like Matilal Seal, Rasikkrishna Mallik, Mahendralal Sarkar, and others. Recent studies on caste validates this view in greater detail. See for instance, Hitesranjan Sanyal, *Social Mobility in Bengal* (Calcutta: Papyrus, 1981) and S. Taniguchi et al., eds., *Economic Changes and Social Transformation in Modern and Contemporary South Asia* (Tokyo: Hitotsubashi University Press, 1994).

[35] From pedagogic aphorisms to serious philosophical disputations this theme was widely prevalent: See for example, Kalikrishna Bhattacharya, *Naba Niti Sara*, pp. 63–4; Gopalchandra Bandyopadhyay, *Hita Shiksha*, pp. 31–2; Woomeshchandra Banerjee, *The New Infant Teacher*, Part 3 (Calcutta, 1877), p. 27.

[36] Satyajit Chaudhuri et al., eds, *Haraprasad Shastri*, pp. 21–2.

[37] Ibid., pp. 63–4.

[38] Rajnarayan Basu, *Sekal ar Ekal*, pp. 81–6.

used towels because their rough texture; muslin was bought especially for him to dry himself.[39]

The discourse about material wealth was hence not a simple one. There was a delinking of wealth from money, as a distinction, whereby wealth became denotative of a whole world of culture, politeness, and respectability, bhadra as it were, and though these dispersed fragments were constituted through money, money was exterior to the semiotics of the discourse itself. In certain instances money could represent wealth; but it did not define it completely. Wealth had a series of other representations in which money played only a minor part. Status came to be constituted anteriorly to wealth which money as a material substance could not buy. Consider, for example, yet another incident from the life of the Maharshi. Once he was invited to a performance at the Shovabazar palace. It was a grand occasion where all the wealthy and big names of Calcutta gathered. This was at the time when the Carr, Tagore and Company had just been declared bankrupt and Debendranath had to sell a substantial portion of the family property to keep his debtors at bay. The situation created intense speculation amongst the rich in the city as to what Debendranath would wear to the party. This was how the Maharshi presented himself in the words of his grandson:

Kartadadamashai [grandfather] was probably aware of such speculations. He called for the jeweller Karamchand and asked him to make a pair of velvet shoes encrusted with pearls ... now there remained the question of clothes, what was to be the attire for the evening? The sarkars and dewans began to worry as to what they would be asked to make ready, expensive shawls, silk robes or what! Kartadadamashai ordered: none of that, I shall go in white .... On the appointed day he was all in white ... no hint or trace of zari or velvet in his entire costume ... except for the shoes. Everyone at court was in their best colourful clothes with jewels and ornaments glittering about their bodies ... therein entered Debendranath. The entire assembly fell silent as he sat on a couch only slightly extending his feet.... The Raja of Shovabazar was a friend of Kartadadamashai [Radhakanta Deb], he then turned to all and pointed to his feet and said 'look at that, that is what is called taste, what we have adorned our bodies with, he has considered to be only worthy of his feet'.[40]

It is understandable why it was the attributes of richness and not wealth itself, that came under scrutiny. The 1850s saw a generation of men for

---

[39] Abanindranath Tagore, 'Gharoa', in *Abanindra Rachanabali*, Vol. 1 (Calcutta: Prakash Bhaban, 1975), p. 83.

[40] Ibid., pp. 87–8.

whom the commercial dreams were a very recent past. The changes in the economy made independent business even more attractive. The complaint of the age was not that the Bengalis were rich but that they were not rich enough to take on the English. The criticism of wealth was on the basis of squandering it in a distasteful way, not on the grounds of actual possession of it. The experiments of Jyotirindranath, Debendranath's son, with business was illustrative of this.

Around 1883–4, Jyotirindranath, an extremely cultured man of his time and one of the chief intellectual influences on the formative period of Rabindranath's life, bought a steel hulk at an auction sale for Rs 7000, with the intention of starting his own steamer business. Rabindranath reports in his autobiography that his brother 'must have thought it a great shame that our countrymen should have their tongues and pens going but not a single line of steamers'. Previously he had also, rather unsuccessfully, tried his hand at starting a match factory and at manufacturing power looms. No doubt his close friend Nabagopal Mitra had a profound effect upon the young zamindar. This ambitious nationalist project brought ruin to Jyotirindranath:

On one side was the European Flotilla Company all capped up, on the other my brother ... alone; and how tremendous waxed that battle of the mercantile fleets, the people of Khulna and Barisal may still remember. Under the stress of competition steamer was added to steamer, loss piled on loss, while the income dwindled till it ceased to be worthwhile to print tickets. The golden age dawned on the steamer service between Khulna and Barisal. Not only were the passengers carried free of charge, but they were offered light refreshments *gratis* as well! There was formed a band of volunteers who, with flags and patriotic songs, marched passengers in procession to the Indian line of steamers. So while there was no want of passengers to carry, every other kind of want began to multiply apace.[41]

Jyotirindranath never recovered from this failed enterprise. His younger, more famous brother's comment on this venture was nevertheless one of hope. He said one should remember that 'all the loss and hardship due to his endeavours fell on him alone, while the gain of experience remained in reserve for the whole country'.[42]

All the moral tracts, whether by the lesser known or the more famous authors, usually had a chapter on wealth and its successful and effective

[41] Rabindranath Tagore, *My Reminiscences* (London: Macmillan, 1917), p. 252–4.
[42] Ibid., p. 252.

utilization. *Artha*, or wealth, was defined by one author as 'that which made exchange possible'. This particular book went into three successive editions, because of its popularity. The chapter on *artha* was absent when the book was originally published, but was added to the second edition and formed the largest chapter (fourteen pages) of the book:

Artha is a fundamental necessity of human beings. Whether it be the care of the body, the welfare of the family, the propagation of *dharma*, or the earning of *vidya*, nothing can be accomplished without *artha*. Without it man can neither earn the jewel of *vidya* nor fulfil his duties to god.

The illiterate and the poor eat indiscriminately, live in unorganised and dirty houses and lead slovenly lives without *artha*, only which can open the doors to the world of *vidya*.[43]

Vidya, or education, was hence not only knowledge, but the mark of privilege. It was carefully disassociated from wealth and hierarchized above it. Thus, the only way that vidya could be made to sit uncontradictorily within the discourse was by changing the boundaries of material wealth itself, such that both vidya and artha came to become natural prerogatives of a particular group.

Mobilizing Culture: Similitude and Difference

The sharpest and most coherent critique of wealth and conspicuous consumption came from the pens of the rentier class. Kaliprasanna Sinha published his *Hutom Penchar Naksha* in 1861. A collection of sketches depicting the urban life of Calcutta, the *Naksha* remains one of the best social documents of its time. Bawdy, bold, and scathingly bitter in places, it plumbed the social mood without sparing either man or social institution. Its popularity lay in part precisely in this pitiless criticism of all that was considered to be above critique. *Kalikata Kamalalaya* and *Nababubilash* have sometimes been portrayed as precursors to this mode of cavilling of wealth and material riches. While this may be so, it is unlikely that *Hutom* or Pearychand Mitra drew their inspiration from these texts. *Kalikata Kamalalaya*, in particular, is quite indulgent of the display of wealth by the

---

[43] Becharam Chattopadhyay, *Griha Karma* (Calcutta: Presidency Press, 1864), pp. 38–52.

section of the bhadralok referred to as *bhagyaban*.[44] Pearychand Mitra, was a much stronger influence on *Hutom*, indeed some his sketches are direct reproductions of some earlier writings of the former.[45] The relevance and acceptance of the new ideology espoused in *Hutom* can partly be judged by the vast numbers of tracts that were published soon after.[46] The majority of them were published from Battala and written by upper-caste men possibly pursuing the treadmill life of a kerani. *Hutom's* criticism of wealth and riches struck an immediate reverberating note. Here was a validation of their material reality conspicuously bereft of bright lights, flowing wine, or caprices with prostitutes. Not only that: here was someone saying loudly and clearly all that was wrong and not to be aspired for. All of a sudden the city which had seemed a collage of unattainable luxuries was represented within a recognizable dichotomy of the useless and indolent rich and the hard working, unhappy keranis, *shipsarkars*, and headwriters.

Alas! those who were counted on to mitigate the woes of Bengal, those who are in possession of immense wealth and could care for the welfare of the *jati* and the motherland are the ones who indulge in the worst of vices and are the walking embodiments of sin. What could be more lamentable! It is nearly a hundred years since the British have come to this country and how has our situation changed? the same flaunting behaviour from the Nawabi days still prevail, the same fancy attires, and lavish hairstyles can still be seen; there has been some change amongst ordinary *madhyastha* people, but our lords refuse to change.[47]

Hutom's text constitutes one of the first acknowledgments of the change in society from the days of the *bania* to that of the salaried masses. Its popularity

---

[44] Bhabanicharan Bandyopadhyay, *Kalikata Kamalalaya*, pp. 118–20. Patronage by the rich was still quite an important social function in Bandyopadhyay's time, and the rich *bania* was known for his support for Brahmins and artists in his court. A strong critique of these activities was thus unlikely to have come from Bandyopadhyay.

[45] Characters such as 'nakal Singi', 'Keshto', and 'Tepi Pishi' are all from Pearychand Mitra's *Mad Khaoa Bara Dai Jat Thakar Ki Upaya* (1859). See Nag, ed., *Satik Hutom*, pp. 93, 95, 147.

[46] It is impossible to give a comprehensive list of such tracts, but some of them are: *Byomchand Bangal* (Harishchandra Mitra), *Ghar Thakte Babui Bheje* (Dhaka: Girish Press, 1872); Bholanath Mukhopadhyay, *Koner Ma Kande Ar Takar Puntli Bandhe* (Calcutta: Hindu Press, 1863); *Apnar Mukh Apni Dekho* (Calcutta: Hindu Press, 1863); Dwarkanath Mitra, *Mushalang Kul Nashanang* (Calcutta: Bhaskar Press, 1864); and Nabinchandra Chattopadhyay, *Baruni Bilash* (Calcutta: School Book Press, 1867).

[47] Arun Nag, ed., *Satik Hutom*, pp. 201–2.

was based on two things: one, the articulation of anger and frustration of a significant majority and second, its language. Although a seminal text in establishing a moral point about wealth and riches being subordinate to culture, taste, and education, *Hutom's* text is produced in the everyday, earthy language of the street. It was, in this sense, a truly mobilizing book, more so when one thinks of the efforts that a section of the intelligentsia was putting in at that very time to 'purify' the Bengali language. Kaliprasanna himself could not resist the urge to authenticate his true qualifications in the text, just so that it might not be confused with the work of someone truly obscure.[48]

There are no apparent heroes in *Hutom*. Unlike *Alaler Gharer Dulal*, where in a clear story-line the reader is meant to identify with Benibabu, the teacher and the younger studious and pious son of the rich babu, Ram. There is no such clear cut story in *Hutom*, being a collection of sketches of everyday social life in Calcutta. The structure of the text captures the unconscious fragmentation of urban life with its almost conscious refusal of, or resistance to, the presentation of an overarching, integrated, coherent view of the city as a whole. Its imagistic and episodic approach highlights the spirit of a new urban existence: the fleeting fluidity of metropolitan life. Diverse and apparently incongruent elements are rudely dragged from their moorings to be reassembled in the glaring light of criticism. This shock-like character of the text matches its language and its harsh, unrefined critique. Historians of print have commented upon the disjuncture between the production and reception of printed texts. Kaliprasanna's own purpose in writing *Hutom* may have been a tangential acknowledgement of the need to move on from the luxuries of a previous era. There certainly was an element of settling accounts with particular immoral individuals.[49] But *Hutom* became a social text for a whole class of people far beyond Kaliprasanna's own life or known circles.

Despite the apparent absence of heroes in *Hutom*, the sympathies of this strange cantankerous voice were not hard to discern. All through the description of the city are scattered stray references to the common bhadralok, the not-so-rich layer of society. In one place he is unable to

---

[48] In the preface to his second edition in 1868 he thus mentions his achievements as the scholarly translator of the Mahabharat. Arun Nag, ed., *Satik Hutom*, pp. 22–3.

[49] Kaliprasanna's men were instructed to distribute copies of the text, early in the morning to selected households. Arun Nag, ed., *Satik Hutom*, p. 3.

afford a carriage to go to work and is ridiculed by the coachman; elsewhere he is harassed by the police or some minion of the colonial order. Indeed, the attitude towards the colonial order is one of gentle derision. The police and various functionaries of the law are represented as ruin for the poor. Missionaries are ridiculed.[50] In all of this, our common bhadralok is easily located in his conspicuous absence. *Hutom's* criticisms are quite specifically aimed at two aspects of the social order: one, the renegade rich and two, the lower castes who have used their ill-gotten wealth to rise in society. In many cases the two points of derision are combined in the same person:

As the Brahmins and Kayasthas started on their trek to civilization, all the Nabasak [lower caste], Harisak, Muchisaks of the city started to crawl as well, eventually we saw the rise of second Rammohans, Debendranath Tagores, Vidyasagars and Kesab Sens among the lower castes. Instead of the usual two chapattis and a bit of vegetable at dinner, 'fowl curry' and 'rolls' were introduced.... Seeing that carrying a bunch of keys to the shop and wearing the ubiquitous dhoti was no longer seeming, carriages and Broughams were procured ... Slowly through double-dealing and low cunning and investing money as *bania*s, some really *chotolok*s of the city became rich.[51]

Herein lies another crucial mobilizing determinant of *Hutom*. Sumit Sarkar has made an important point about the social denudation of the traditional rural literati in the context of colonialism in general, and the rise of Calcutta as a metropolis in particular.[52] The change in land arrangement settlements and the demise of traditional crafts had forced the Brahmins, *jajmans* and *purohits* to move from their native villages to Calcutta where until the 1830s, two sources of income were open to them. One was as *sabhapandits* to the affluent *bania*s of the time, and the other as teachers, either in small *tols* of their own or, if exceptionally lucky, in the Fort William College.

From the 1840s, however, Sanskrit and the concomitant culture of traditional learning was definitely on the wane, and graduates of the Sanskrit College were finding it increasingly difficult to find a job.[53] Sarkar cites the example of Ramkrishna and his brother Ramkumar. The former was finding life very hard as a pundit in one of Calcutta's tols and both brothers had to take up jobs, with considerable self-abnegation, as temple purohits to their

[50] Ibid., pp. 39–49.

[51] Ibid., p. 53.

[52] See Sarkar, *Writing Social History*, pp. 216–81.

[53] Subolchandra Mitra, *Life of Pundit Iswar Chandra Vidyasagar* (New Delhi: Ashish Publishers, 1975), p. 113.

lower caste Kaibarta patron, Rani Rasmoni.[54] The changes in social structure spelt disaster for most of our petty bourgeois layer, whose memories of caste superiority and land ties with the native village, made the humiliating drudgery of office work all the more unbearable. The caustic remarks of *Hutom* at lower castes who had made their money through either deception or favours, thus evoked a powerful response. The moral content of the text, the scathing criticisms of the rich, and the compassion for the madhyastha, or the middle class, combined with the unique accessible and humorous language, made *Hutom* stand out from all the straight-laced didactic literature of the times. It was an infallible invitation to the kerani to join the ranks of the bhadralok ethic.

Identity can be established both as identification and/or as difference. One of the ways in which the differential realities within the bhadralok could be disregarded was, as we saw earlier, through categorizing the areas of similitude. Another potent way was by pointing out difference. The availability of education, and more significantly, books, could not be regulated in the light of the widespread usage of cheap printing. Also, for all its problems, the colonial education system managed to establish, for the first time, at least the *principle* that education was a right and prerogative of all, irrespective of caste or creed. Thus, the Lieutenant-Governor, Richard Temple said with some pride in 1875 that the scholarship system in education carried out 'the true catholic principle that everybody of superior ability and character, to whatsoever creed, tribe, race, or class ... shall have his chance of rising from the lowest to the highest place in the educational roles'.[55] But if education and culture were constitutive of being a bhadralok, then there had to be some mechanism by which the bhadra could be distinguished from the non-bhadra. If books signified an undifferentiated enlightenment for all, then what would happen to the distinctiveness of a few?

From the publication of the Adam's Report onwards, there was a growing concern in the administrative circles regarding the efficacy of the Filtration Theory. In 1863–4, the policy makers lamented that the great masses of the people of Bengal, including the labouring and the agricultural classes, were 'in reality scarcely touched as yet by our educational operations'. 'Various plans', as the Director of Public Instruction wrote in that year, 'have

[54] Sarkar, *Writing Social History*, p. 226.

[55] *Report on the Administration of Bengal*, pp. 78–9.

been devised and tried for bringing school instruction to bear upon them
... but the result has almost uniformly been that the schools which have been
organized or improved for their benefit have been at once taken possession
of and monopolized by classes who stand higher in the social scale'.[56]

There is a note of democratic impulse in this concern that deserves
attention. The colonial authorities displayed the fundamental contradiction
inherent in any capitalist ethos. One of the foundational difference between
the bourgeois and the pre-bourgeois social structure pointed out by Marx
is the levelling out of *visible* hierarchies 'veiled by religious and political
illusions'.[57] For the colonial authorities, the specific privileging of individuals
on the basis of customary authority or rank was thus the most backward
manifestation of the indigenous social order. Coming from a social world
which had already cut off the heads of kings, and had entrenched a firm
rhetoric against feudal privileges, the British found all institutions which
bore such marks, from the caste system to the indigenous educational
network, most repugnant.[58] As far as education was concerned, thus, the
primary impulse was to remove all such traces. Poromesh Acharya has noted
this change in his study of the indigenous pathshalas, whence he comments
that all 'separate classes of institutions without any link or relation of any
kind between them, each catering to a distinct class or community' were
replaced by a 'complete and continuous Western system'.[59] The ideology of

[56] 'Note on the State of Education in India, 1855–66' in *Selections from the Records
of the Government of India*, No. 54, (Home Department, June 1867).

[57] K. Marx and F. Engels, 'Manifesto of the Communist Party', in *Selected Works*,
p. 38.

[58] This is, by no means, a validation of the 'progressive' views of the colonial state.
It is a well-documented fact that the British had no qualms in fostering feudal practices
and premodern values when it came to the political or economic needs of colonialism.
The relationship of the colonial state with the Indian princes bears vivid testimony to
this opportune privileging of 'traditional' values. For details on the princely states, see
Michael Fisher, *Indirect Rule in India: Residents and the Residency System 1757–1857*
(Delhi: Oxford University Press, 1991); for a classic study of the British adopting Mughal
symbols of authority, see Bernard S. Cohn, "Representing Authority in British India" in
E. Hobsbawm and T. Ranger eds., *The Invention of Tradition* (Cambridge: Cambridge
University Press, 1992).

[59] Poromesh Acharya, 'Indigenous Education and Brahminical Hegemony in Bengal',
in Nigel Crook, ed., *The Transmission of Knowledge in South Asia* (New Delhi: Oxford
University Press, 1996), pp. 98–118; see especially pp. 98–99.

freedom, a necessary corollary to the freeing of labour power and the worker from his/her means of production, was used as a constant polemic against the natives.

For the bhadralok, however, this was not the case, and one needs to dissociate moral indignation and social critique from historical judgement. Caste and privileges of rank were registers of both political and social life, which all classes in the bhadralok conglomeration were used to. These were factors that marked them out from the peasants in their native villages and the new workers in the towns. The loss of these privileges was thus understandably treated with panic and despondency. Even contemporary British commentators noticed this, albeit with adequate irony:

The priests are a very ill-paid class, and the Brahmin priest has fallen on very evil days; formerly he lived in comfort in the odour of sanctity, now he struggles along in an atmosphere which is little removed from contempt.[60]

One can see why *Hutom's* stringent opprobrium of lower castes found such sympathy amongst all classes of the bhadralok. The major worry for the kerani was, as we have seen, 'mass education'. Thus Bengali tracts on education, from the high culture of Vidyasagar to the cheap tracts by unknown authors were united in their difference against those lower classes, who might as a result of education be unwilling to follow the callings of their fathers. One such tract thus worriedly speculates:

It has come to pass that people are leaving their hereditary professions to learn English. Why? In order to secure a job [....] Soon it will be impossible to live in this land. If the peasant does not plough the field but starts looking for an office job, either we shall all starve to death or horror of horrors, have to take up cultivation ourselves [....] In this possibility of impending doom the only option is for people to stick to their traditional professions or to witness the dismantling of society altogether.[61]

This was the ideological basis for much of the fears around the *Kaliyuga* myth. Between 1853 and 1867 more than thirty books had been catalogued on this subject, all uniformly published from either the outskirts of Calcutta, or in Calcutta from the Battala region.[62] This does not, of course, include

---

[60] J.C. Jack, *The Economic Life*, p. 90.

[61] Chandrasekhar Sen, *Ki Holo*, pp. 46–7.

[62] Jatindramohan Bhattacharya, *Mudrita Bangla Granther Panji 1853–1867* (Calcutta: Paschim Bangla Academy, 1993).

the countless tracts that must have escaped formal cataloguing. Among 505 plays published between 1858 and 1899, thirty-one had 'Kali' as their titles.[63] As Sarkar has elegantly demonstrated, most of these tracts were the reworking of the apocalyptic myth of *Kaliyuga* with their specific focus on the tedium of chakri, and opposition to the common folk posing as bhadra with a distinct misogynist slant. A fairly typical representative would be Shailendranath Haldar's *Kalir Sang* (1880). In this the servants outline the various features of *Kaliyuga*: the Brahmins have been rendered stupid and the peasants read the Vedas. Charlatans and cheats lounge under the loving care of the rulers while the pundit goes hungry. Honest people earn no good will and swindlers are accepted approvingly. Alcoholism is rampant and women of virtue are derided in favour of harlots.[64]

It was relatively easy for this ideology to arrive at a satisfactory conclusion as far as their women were concerned, for the state view on womens' education favoured a 'womanly tendency' in their course structures for female schools.[65] It was possible that the book could import to the Hindu homes, 'the evils of suffragetism, or the spirit of revolutionary and rationalistic iconoclasm, condemning all ... ancient institutions that [were] ... the outcome of a long past'.[66] Hence a separate system of education stressing the virtues of *stridharma*, obedience, and companionship to men, found full support in both colonial and bhadralok discourse. It is well known how the 'novel reading woman' emerges in this period as the anti-thesis to the 'good wife', whose greed, sloth, and sexuality broke up many a peaceful home in the literature of the late nineteenth-century.[67] And as far as mass

[63] Cited in Sarkar, *Writing Social History*, p. 205.

[64] Reprinted in Jayanta Goswami, *Samjchitre Unabingsa Satabdir Bangla Prahasan* (Calcutta: Sahityashree, 1974), p. 194.

[65] The education report of 1919, emphasizes that the character of education given to the girls, ignores their needs and the kind of life that they will lead in the future. It omitted what ought to be the essential elements in their short and precious period of training, namely the teaching of domestic duties and the implantation of the best Hindu ideals of womanhood. *Report of the Commission Appointed by the Government of India to Inquire into the Condition and Prospects of the University of Calcutta*, Vol. 2, Part 1 (Calcutta, 1919), pp. 5–35.

[66] Ibid.

[67] See for example, Asutosh Basu, *Samaj Kalanka* (Calcutta, 1885); Ambikacharan Gupta, *Kalir Maye Choto Bou Orofe Ghor Murkho* (Calcutta: Cornwallis Press, 1881); Batabihari Chakrabarti, *Kalir Kulta Prahasan* (Calcutta: Kar Press, 1877); Anonymous, *Hemantakumari* (Calcutta, 1868).

education was concerned, the answer lay in the practical employment of the conceptual strategies of the educational ideology—limited and particularized education for the many, and once again, on this the bhadralok was united in their difference from the non-bhadra.

One of the essential agreements secured between the bhadralok and the colonial state was that the education of the lower classes had to be effected with minimum resort to the printed book. For British discourse, both official and unofficial, this tacit understanding had two incentives. One was the cost involved in educating a whole population and the second more serious cause was what education would entail. Major Lees, the acting Director of Public Instruction, made the state's position very clear on this issue. He pointed pragmatically to the high price of elementary school books, and how the government should instead invest in a more practical educational approach for the peasant, with a telling comment about the fears around mass education:

Some caution and foresight are necessary, lest in our well intentioned zeal ... we do not deluge the country with a large class of discontented men, dissatisfied with their position in society and in life, and disgusted with the ... government that took them from what they were, to make them what they are. This would fill our bazars with socialism, and red republicanism instead of contentment and prosperity....[68]

Gordon Young, writing on the need for training schools for teachers of the ryots, specifically emphasized that 'the study of *things*' was more important for the ryot than the 'study of *words*'. Raising the curiosity and developing the various faculties, he felt, was more important than 'book cram'.[69] As a result, writing at the end of our period of study, the missionary John Murdoch found the vernacular schools starved of books and printed literature:

A large proportion of the children in vernacular schools are *homo unius libri*, 'a man of one book'. A 'Reader' is often the only book in the actual possession of the child, constituting his entire library [....] It is granted that the personal example of the teacher and his oral instruction are the most influential factors in a school. The

[68] James Long, ed., *Adam's Report on Vernacular Education in Bengal and Behar, With a Brief View of its Past and Present Conditions* (Calcutta: Home Secretariat Press, 1868), p. 22.

[69] William Gordon Young, *Tracts on the Rural Population of Bengal and Behar* (Calcutta: Sanders, Cones and Co., 1858), p. 10.

training of teachers, however, is a slow and expensive process. On the other hand, books may be multiplied at once in any required number.[70]

Books were the site of combination of the substance of European knowledge with native forms of thought and sentiment and its adaptation to the feelings, sympathies, and histories of the people.[71] In a graphic description of the teaching methods employed in teaching peasant boys the tales of the Bible, James Long referred to the parables and the poetic form, essential in his opinion to the Orient, by which he had transformed knowledge 'in a way suited to their capacity and modes of thought'. Prose and its ancillary textuality were obviously considered unsuitable for the peasant.[72]

What the peasant was to learn was, however, clearly marked out. The complete exclusion from education was not a viable alternative, so a controlled participation was actively encouraged. 'Useful' knowledge, which would help the labouring classes to integrate more fruitfully to their labour, was the organizing principle behind mass education as practiced in this period. Seton-Kerr remarked that education should enable the ryot to write a letter of business, to draw out a bond, to understand the terms of a mortgage, to cast up his accounts, and to know if his receipts for rent were correctly signed.[73] Pearychand Mitra qualified such statements by stating that what the village schools pupils should learn must be 'practically and not from books'. Nothing should be guarded against more carefully, felt Radhakant Deb, than the 'insensible introduction of a system whereby, with a smattering knowledge of English, youths are weaned from the plow [sic], the ax [sic], the loom, to render them ambitious only for the clerkship'.[74] It is important to note in this context, that the opposition to English education for the non-bhadralok did not merely signify a vernacular education for them. It is precisely in this period that the bhadralok was trying to restructure the Bengali language and strong claims were being

[70] John Murdoch, *India's Greatest Educational Need: The Adequate Recognition of Ethics in her Present Transition State* (London and Madras: Christian Literature Society for India, 1904), p. 9.

[71] Second Report of the General Council of Education, p. 33.

[72] James Long, *How I Taught the Bible to Bengal Peasant Boys* (Christian Vernacular Society for India, n.d.), pp. 1–3.

[73] James Long, ed., *Adam's Report*, p. 21.

[74] James Long, ed., *Adam's Report*, pp. 21–2.

made by them about the language being the key to national awakening.[75] The point of contention was the notion of a 'liberal education' of the sciences and arts of Europe, imparted whether in English or Bengali. As the School Book Society put forward in its twelfth report, that the idea was to make English and the vernacular interact harmoniously together, and this could be achieved by English imparting the 'ideas which elevate the mind, and improve the moral condition', and the vernacular communicating those ideas through the country. It was, they claimed 'by the combination of both, that all important ends of education can be attained'.[76] Thus, it was ultimately the *content* of mass education rather than the medium of instruction that was under debate.

In 1860, J. Peter Grant, the Lieutenant-Governor of Bengal submitted a plan to the government which declared that the education imparted to the rural population 'should range no higher' than that which was already being afforded by the indigenous pathshalas. The books to be supplied to these schools, according to this plan, were to contain in a compact form, all that had hitherto been taught at such places by dictation, namely arithmetic, agricultural, and commercial accounts, forms of agreements and so on.[77] Accordingly in 1872, the Lieutenant-Governor directed the Director of Public Instruction to give especial attention to the suggestion that book-keeping and zamindari management after the native methods should be taught in the lower and middle class schools. He particularly insisted that a prize be offered as an incentive, for the best handbook for school use on zamindari accounts and management, shop accounts, and farm business.[78] It is worth pointing out in this context, that the radical peasant upsurges of the Indigo Rebellion and the Santhal Uprisings of this period, gave the state a rationale for educating the peasantry in land accounts such that they would not be cheated by the land and plantation owners.[79] From the 1860s

---

[75] See among others Haraprasad Shastri, 'Kaleji Shiksha', in *Haraprasad Granthabali* (Calcutta, Basumati Sahitya Mandir, n.d.), pp. 321–4; and Rajanikanta Gupta, *Amader Vishwavidyalaya* (Calcutta, n.d.), pp. 17–30.

[76] *Twelfth Report of the Calcutta School Book Society* (Calcutta, 1840), pp. 32.

[77] James Long, ed., *Adam's Report*, p. 23.

[78] General Proceedings, Education Department, February 1872, No. 52.

[79] Also the state saw the relationship between a 'civilizing' education for the masses and the interests of the Empire. The report on general or mass education of 1883 traced the causes of the Deccan riots to the 'ignorance of the peasantry' and their inability to read the documents that they signed. The report stated clearly that the condition of the

onwards there was a marked rise in the number of books on zamindari and *mahajani* accounts. The noteworthy point of these publications was that they were issued from mainly outside Calcutta, and within Calcutta from the Battala area.[80] Even works by the bhadralok, on this subject were published from presses of Battala, which they generally avoided in the case of other educational and discursive works.[81]

Gramsci noted an almost similar process at work in Italy under backward capitalist development. There was a 'fundamental division' in education between classical and vocational schools under the rational formula: 'the vocational school for the instrumental classes, the classical school for the dominant classes and the intellectuals'.[82] The attitude of the rentier bhadraloks on the education of their peasants was along identical principles. In 1870, the government was toying with the idea of an additional land cess to fund popular education from the taxes of the landholders. The controversy that the plan unleashed in this class corresponded to their anxiety about mass dissemination of books and learning. Couched within a perspective of rights over land of the landholder, this debate clarified the agenda for what the nature of education in the countryside ought to be. First, a tax on land was considered entirely insupportable, instead a tax on salt was suggested, which was payable by all. From the funds thus raised, a plan for the elevation of the masses was proposed. The money could be used to establish higher and lower agricultural schools in every sixth village, where these schools would be attached to high and low lands for agricultural and horticultural purposes, where the children would learn their trade. The produce of the land would pay for stipends for each child in order to induce

masses was 'dangerous to the tranquillity of the empire'. See the *Second Report of the General Council of Education in India Formed With a View to the Promotion of the General Education of the People on a National Basis as Laid Down in the Education Despatch of 1854* (London, 1883), pp. 3–11.

[80] See for example, Prasanna Chandra Sen, *Krishi Karjer Mat* (Dhaka: Sulabh Press, 1867); Dinanath Mukhopadhyay, *Jamidari Bigyan* (Hooghly: Budhodoy Press, 1866); Kaliprasanna Sengupta, *Jamidari Darshan* (Hooghly: Budhodoy Press, 1863); Tarinicharan Basu Chaudhury, *Jamidari Mahajani Hishab* (Dhaka: Sulabh Press, 1875), this ran into five successful editions; Harimohan Mukhopadhyay, *Krishi Darpan* (Calcutta: Chanpatala Bangla Press, 1859), this was issued from the Chanpatala Bangla Jantra at Battala.

[81] Prasanna Kumar Tagore published one such work from the Vidyaratna Press at Battala under the assumed name of Parashar titled *Krishi Sangraha* in 1862.

[82] A. Gramsci, *Selections from Prison Notebooks*, p. 26.

parents to part with their labour as well as to minimize investment. The higher schools were to conduct lectures in botany, physiology, and the physical sciences in Bengali:

In these agricultural schools, instructions should be combined with amusements and physical exercise, and the utmost attention should be paid to moral training. Lessons should be pictured out to the boys by questions and ellipses mixed. Starting points are merely to be taken from text books, but knowledge should be communicated to the students by oral gallery lessons. It should be kept in view that the students learn things rather than words, and that memory be not cultivated at the sacrifice of higher faculties.[83]

The position of the non-bhadra thus was perpetually linked to an organic orality, within the culture of print but distanced significantly from it. The potency of the differentiation between the bhadra and non-bhadra on the basis of education was great. Powered by the fear of peasants and the low folks taking over their jobs, the lower rungs of the bhadralok were only too happy to concur to this ideology.

The Thorny Problem of Class

No ideology is ever wholly logical or consistent. All great ideologies bring together discordant elements and have to struggle to make contradictory ideas fit the scheme. There are always breaks in the logic, loose ends, and internal contradictions. The ideology of education was no exception. First of all there was the problem of making it appear as an organic ideology of the bhadralok as a whole because the bhadralok socially was far from being a consistent and coherent class. One had to settle on how to suture the discordant realities of, say the Tagores, with that of the clerk on his meagre salary of Rs 30.

An ideology prefiguring national mobilization was hence bound by its very logic to show elements of class tensions. Vertical realities of class could be incorporated within the horizontal mobilization of a national identity, but they could hardly be erased. Colonialism in Bengal created a disproportionately large urban petty bourgeoisie. For Marx, the term included pre-eminently the mass of peasant small-holders, the shopkeepers, independent artisans, or small businessmen in small towns. By the nature

<hr>

[83] Takoordass Chuckerbutty, *Thoughts on Popular Education* (Calcutta: City Press, 1870), pp. 18–19.

of its mode of production, such a stratum was incapable of collective political leadership and, as a result, oscillated between the two major classes, the proletariat and the bourgeoisie. By contrast, in Bengal, a large section of the urban bourgeoisie in this period was *propertyless* and pre-eminently engaged in bureaucratic employment, especially in the agencies of the state. Their material condition of life was often extremely poor, particularly in comparison with their aspirations to a fully bhadralok way of life. The kerani, despite his low income, hence had to have a newspaper to read, his watch to keep time by and his wife had to occasionally have some 'hair oil'.[84] Also the majority of them were from the two upper castes of the Brahmin and Kayastha.[85]

This strain in the maintenance of a lifestyle by the less fortunate, under the twin imperatives of a colonial work-discipline and the need and pressure of distinction from the lower orders, formed the theme of several tracts of this period. Nanda, in the popular farce *Kerani Charit* (1885), is a typical example. He has some land in his native village but refuses to settle there; 'there is a certain status to a chakri', he says, 'that status is essential to be a part of 'civilized society', irrespective of how much property one has in the village'. But life in the city is hard and Nanda could not make ends meet and so managed to survive by petty embezzlements and through bribes.[86] Contemporary British observers held only contempt for this class. One such commentator, while admitting that the clerks were extremely ill-paid and that they had fairly miserable lives, said that this class had 'from time immemorial supplemented its pay by exactions on a generous scale', and that any prosperity of this group of people was 'ill-deserved' as they were 'as a whole ignorant, disloyal to its employers, prone to swindling, selfish and rapacious to an incredible extent'.[87]

Their differences with the upper rungs of the bhadralok have been stressed elsewhere in this book, but it is worth restating. Bankimchandra Chattopadhyay made his brother Sanjibchandra leave his job because he

[84] Taran Sharma, *Keranipuran*, pp. 7–8.

[85] James Long, *Five Hundred Questions on the Social Condition of the Natives of India* (London: Trübner and Co., 1865), pp. 24–5.

[86] See Goswami, *Bangla Prahasan*, pp. 647–8.

[87] J.C. Jack, *Economic Life*, p. 90.

could not 'bear to see him employed as a little kerani'.[88] The first day of work is described by a bhadralok in the following terms:

> Mr. Pigeon made me over to his head Baboo, Kinooram Chuckerbutty, to make of me what he could; and with supercilious contempt the Baboo told me to mend his pens. Was Young Bengal to submit to this? Shades of Bacon, Addison, and Johnson came over me, was the student who kept company with you so long and pored over your pages night and morning, now to mend the pens of an old kerani?[89]

This particular gentleman was later to be titled a Rai Bahadoor.

The members of this class were thus not acquainted with the luminous edifications of Bacon or Johnson. The aided schools, started from the middle of the century, were the means of education for this class. The Committee for the Improvement of Schools observed that these schools were the result of the 'increasing desire ... among the middle classes' for an English education for their children. These people were, the Committee stated, 'of comparatively humble means' and hence unable to afford the high fees of the more renowned institutions in the *zillah* schools or the metropolis itself. The people whose children resorted to these schools were found to be mainly tradesmen, petty talukdars, and *amlah*s, ones who could afford the monthly fees of eight annas. The government records accredit them with two objectives:

> Either to enable their children to prepare themselves for entering the higher English schools ... and so to avoid the necessity of sending them to the Sudder station ... or ... to enable them to obtain as much knowledge of English, and no more, as is sufficient for becoming inferior clerks, copyists, salesmen, hawkers, & c. without resorting to the Zillah School at all.[90]

Printing strategies followed this division in status of the upper and lower layers of the bhadralok. The case of the publication of the *Shishubodhak* is a demonstration of this.

The *Shishubodhak*, in sharp contrast to the primers written by the bhadralok like *Bodhodoy* (written by Vidyasagar) (1851) or *Charupath* (by

---

[88] Bankimchandra Chattopadhyay, 'Sanjibchandra Chattopadhyay', in Asitkumar Bandyopadhyay, ed., *Sanjib Rachanabali* (Calcutta: Mandal Book House, 1973), p. 513.

[89] Shoshee Chunder Dutt, *Bengaliana: A Dish of Rice and Curry, and other Indigestible Ingredients* (Calcutta: Thacker, Spink and Co., 1858), p 4.

[90] A.M. Monteath and A.P. Howell, *Selections from Education Reports of the Government of India* (Delhi: National Archives of India, 1960), pp. 79–80.

Akshaykumar Datta) (1854), embodied in it the syllabus of the pathshalas which had remained unchanged despite English education. Its contents reflected the traditional methods of learning in its emphasis on oral mathematics, *Chanakya Shlokas* and methods on how to write personal and village names. Most lessons were in the verse form, including instructions on letter writing.[91] In 1857, when Long was preparing his returns of presses, almost all the presses at Battala had published several copies of this work.[92] But while the Vidyaratna Press at Ahiritola Street had issued 10,000 copies in that one year, not a single copy of this work had been published by any of the other presses which were not situated at Battala. This was an indicator of the actual readership of Battala, which was composed of people like Nanda of our story, and the innumerous and ubiquitous kerani, who never contributed to the Bengal 'renaissance'.

They were not, however, without literary aspirations. A list of vernacular newspapers published in 1851, show that although among twenty editors, more than half were Brahmins, this was not so when it came to the actual ownership of the presses. In fact among press owners, only one-third were Brahmins, while an almost equal proportion were from the lower castes.[93] The lower rungs of the bhadralok thus produced, throughout the latter half of the century, a steady stream of farces, moral tracts, dramas, and poems from the cheap presses. They also, it appears, contributed copiously to the minor vernacular newspapers. The *Grambartaprakashika* (1863–84) started by Harinath Majumdar, from Kumarkahali in the Nadia district is a case in point. Majumdar who had Brahmo connections in his youth, started the journal to expose the exploitation of peasants by the triumvirate of

[91] The verse form was considered more appropriate for children, women, and peasants. In a letter to the poet Iswarchandra Gupta, J.E.D. Bethune urged him to write poetry which would be suitable for schools for girls as the verse form was one 'which is both more attractive to children ... and more easy for them to remember', quoted in Asit Kumar Bandyopadhyay, *Unabingsha Satabdir Prathamardha O Bangla Sahitya* (Calcutta, 1959), p. 215.

[92] Of the Battala presses listed in Long's Returns, the Gyanoday Press had issued 6,000 copies, the Kamalalaya Press had 9,00 copies, the Kamalasan Press 1,500 copies, the Lakshmivilas Press had 3,000 copies, the Nistarini Press 2,000 copies, the Sudha Sindhu Press 1,500 copies, and the Vidyaratna Press had the largest number at 10,000 copies. See Long, 'Returns Related to Publication in the Bengali Language', in *Selections from the Records of the Bengal Government*, No. XXXIII (Calcutta, 1859), pp. 24–62.

[93] *Friend of India*, 1 May 1859, cited in Ranu Basu, 'Some Aspects', p. 113.

colonial officials, the Indigo planters and the zamindars, in this case the Tagores. All through his life he struggled against dire poverty and earned the wrath of the Tagores, and the journal finally had to be discontinued.[94] Several other similar journals published from the outskirts of the capital bore the marks of this untrained literati.[95] The postal statistics of the period bear some evidence of the rapid spread of books and newspapers around the Presidency:

TABLE 2.2   Postal records for the years 1861–71

	1861–2	1865–6	1870–1
Newspapers Received	24,265	25,639	32,881
Books Received	1,419	2,164	5,201
Newspapers Despatched	6,113	11,776	–
Books Despatched	781	1,140	–

Source: W.W. Hunter, *A Statistical Account*, p. 221.

Though the bulk of the bhadralok appeared to be a part of the ideology of learning and education, its seams were frayed around the edges. Occasional glimpses of insight into the actual nature of education and literary artifices comes through in the satirical tracts. One text thus comments:

Actual learning and the accompanying qualities of true knowledge are hard to come by these days. Reading eight pages here and three and a half chapters there, a man is made out like a much decorated flower basket with five different kinds of flowers. The Calcutta University and safety matches (which ignites on box) are made of the same stuff. Rub the stick against the box and it bursts into flame, parrot some of the stuff learned by rote and a pass degree is allotted. *Punthigata Vidya* (*vidya* solely dependent on the book) and other people's money is the same thing: totally useless to oneself.[96]

[94] See the biography of Kangal Harinath, Brajendranath Bandyopadhyay and Sajanikanta Das, eds, *Sahitya Sadhak Charitmala: Kangal Harinath* (Calcutta: Bangiya Sahitya Parishad, 1947).

[95] Some well known examples are *Murshidabad Patrika* (1856), *Uttarpara Pakshik Patrika* (1856), *Rajpur Patrika* (1860), *Dhaka Prakash* (1861), and *Majilpur Patrika* (1856).

[96] Anonymous, *Hak Katha* (Calcutta, 1873), p. 29.

The Western-educated babu was seldom spared in these cheap tracts. The rhetoric against the indulgence of the *bania* was used to mercilessly mock the bhadralok of high learning. The fathers in these tracts scrimp and save to give their sons an 'English education'. Consequently, the sons turn to the bottle and to prostitutes, leaving their chaste wives, and repay their fathers' kindness by referring to them as 'old fools'.[97] Even the Brahmos were not spared. In one farce, Rajababu, a member of the rural gentry is the object of ridicule who funds aided schools, medical dispensaries, and all such approved social projects but is addicted to women and wine. He is assisted in all such adventures by the local doctor and the school teacher: the two social categories who in the high literature were the embodiments of morality. The trio are depicted to be avid patrons of the Brahmo Samaj.[98]

It is crucial to understand that these critiques of 'Westernization' or the 'modern Babu' were not coming from the same social imperatives of the high bhadralok, who themselves had developed such critiques. Michael Madhusudan Dutt's *Ekei Ki Bole Sabhyata* (1860) or Dinabandhu Mitra's *Sadhabar Ekadashi* (1866) and Bankimchandra's essay on the Babu that appeared in the *Bangadarshan* in 1872, stand out as prominent examples.[99] These, besides being strong moral dictums on education and learning, incorporated strong nationalist messages. Criticism of Western ways was conducted within a strong polemic in favour of all that was truly Bengali, particularly, the Bengali language.

The British, however, did not distinguish between the kerani and the high bhadralok when it came to defending Imperial privileges. Following the Ilbert Bill, racism had become much more rampant and open in the social life of Calcutta. Incidents of humiliating treatment towards Indians irrespective of caste or class were becoming more frequent. To the rulers, the babu's primary identity was his nationality, class identities came later and in more intimate dealings. Thus, the same treatment was meted out to keranis and the new middle class alike. In fact, due to the majority of the

[97] Harishchandra Mitra, *Ghar Thakte Babui Bheje* (Dhaka: Sulabh Press, 1863).

[98] Nemaichand Sheel, *Erai Abar Borolok* (Calcutta: Stanhope Press, 1867).

[99] See, Michael Madhusudan Dutt, 'Ekei Ki Bole Sabhyata' in Brajendranath Bandyopadhya and Sajanikanta Das, eds., *Madhusudan Rachanabali* (Calcutta, 1954); Dinabandhu Mitra, 'Sadhabar Ekadashi' in Gopal Haldar, ed., *Dinabandhu Rachanasangraha* (Calcutta, 1973) pp. 161–214, and Bankimchandra Chattopadhyay, 'Babu' in *Bankim Rachanabali* Vol. 2 (Calcutta, 1969), pp. 10–12.

former, the term 'babu' when used in a derogatory sense by the British usually insinuated a kerani. As early as in 1852, an arrogant strain of this attitude could be evinced in a response in the *Calcutta Review* to a petition of the British India Society:

[The] modest wish ... that one-half of the best appointments in India be made over to natives, the desire for enhanced salaries, the dexterous confusion of complaints of maladministration, of proposals of reform ... sink into nothing when we remember that all this combination of puerility and ignorance, and this clumsy attempt at patriotism, are declared to express the feelings of the most intelligent of the native community ... The spectacle of a set of Babus ... who have obtained ... ten times more than they would have obtained under any other Government ... pretending to represent the old Hindu and Mussulman families, and the hard working agriculturists ... is, we think, rather too much of a good thing.[100]

The babus on their end, likewise were united as bhadralok under the shadow of oppression. In this rhetoric of defence the kerani was not distinguished from the deputy magistrate. The *Som Prakash* in 1874, for example, ratified that the rulers 'do not look on them [the babus] with favourable eyes'. When 'every way of progress ... (was) closed to them' what was to become of the 'hundreds of natives educated and turned out from Government institutions every year?' The babus had become an 'eye-sore' to the British 'because they cannot and do not honour them by taking of [sic] their shoes in their presence; nor are they able to keep standing like cranes before their rulers'. The babus were a threat to the British, according to the writer, because the 'example held out by these men may destroy their long enjoyed supremacy'.[101]

This, however, did not expunge class realities. The farces and tracts from the latter half of the century, particularly in the popular press, used the rhetoric against indolence and leisure that *Hutom* used, but for an entirely different target. The butt of ridicule for this genre of writing was usually, as mentioned earlier, the English-educated babu who had acquired along with his education, its corollary evils of drinking, mocking his own heritage and to top it all, subservient to his newly-educated wife. These tracts also had very little sympathy for reform, in the name of the nation or otherwise. In

[100] W.S. Seton-Kerr, 'Charters and Patriots', *Calcutta Review*, 18, 36 (July–Dcember, 1852), pp. 422–3.

[101] *Som Prakash*, 28 March 1874, reprinted in P.T. Nair, ed., *Calcutta Gazette: Introductory Volume* (Calcutta: Bibhash Gupta, 1989), pp. 68–9.

Gangadhar Chattopadhyay's *Ekei Ki Bole Bangali Saheb* (1874) the author detected the root of all the evils of the *Kaliyuga* in Rammohan and his anti-Sati movements, which were carried forward by Ramgopal Ghosh and his band of Brandy-drinking youths and finally consolidated by Kesab Sen who robbed the high castes of all purity and gave the washerwoman the same status as that of a *Brahmani*. One could always read these signs as social conservatism, which they no doubt were. But perhaps there was more to it than that.

The appeal to the nation till 1905 at least, was articulated in a language and social setting that was practically alien to most. The various associations, both literary and political, where such themes were rehearsed were extremely select in their membership. Inclusion in the ranks of the new middle class was not based on processes of bureaucratic appointment, but rather on previously existing power. Inherited wealth and marital alliances continued to play a large and fairly exclusive role. Pearychand Mitra's grandfather, for instance, married into the millionaire family of the Duttas of Hatkhola. Ramkamal Mukhopadhyay, principal clerk at Fort William's Engineering Department commanded substantial wealth and bought a huge property at Khidirpur and called it 'Bara Bari' (big house). His nephew, Yogweshwar Mukhopadhyay, who later became a deputy magistrate, was Bankim's classmate and married Bankim's niece. Their daughter was to marry the famous poet Hemchandra Bandyopadhyay's son. Hemchandra, Bankim, and Sanjibchandra Chattopadhyay all met at Bara Bari to discuss the arts.[102] Rajnarayan Basu, the famous Brahmo reformer also married into the Dutta family of Hatkhola.[103] He was also related by marriage to the Young Bengal icon Ramgopal Ghosh.[104] Haragopal Sarkar another diligent reformer was married to Ramtanu Lahiri's niece.[105] The Tagores were related by marriage to the leading men of the age like Asutosh Chaudhuri, Pramatha Chaudhuri, Janakinath Ghoshal, and so on. The various educational institutions like the Sanskrit College and Hindu College, and later Presidency College served as key areas of class mobilization.[106]

[102] Shibendranarayan Shastri, *Banglar Paribarik Itihas* Vol. 2, p. 88.

[103] Rajnarayan Basu, *Atmacharit*, p. 60.

[104] Ibid., p. 111.

[105] Shibnath Shastri, *Atmacharit* (Calcutta: Paschimbanga Niraksharata Durikaran Samiti, 1979), p. 75.

[106] Consider the graduates of the Sanskrit College between 1867 and 1876: Umeshchandra Batabyal (Premchand Raichand student, Statutory Civilian), Bireshwar

Compounded with this inner circle of marriages and relations were the various associations started by this class which proved to be another mark of exclusivity. This list is fairly long so we shall quote only a few representative examples. Rammohan's Atmya Sabha (1815) is probably the first of its kind. Its members included: Darpanarayan Tagore's son Gopimohan Tagore and his son Prasannakumar Tagore, Anandaprasad Bandyopadhyay, zamindar of Telenipara, Kalinath Roy, zamindar of Taki, Nandakishor Basu, father of Rajnarayan Basu, Dwarkanath Tagore, Brindaban Mitra, grandfather of Rajendralal Mitra, the famous scholar, Kalishankar Ghoshal, Raja of Bhukailash, and others. The Gouriya Samaj (1823) was a platform for the so called 'conservatives' and 'liberals' alike. Among its members were: Dwarkanath and Prasannnakumar Tagore, Tarachand Chakrabarty the radical Young Bengal, Radhakant Deb, Ramdulal Dey, and others. The Anglo-Indian Hindu Association (1830) established by the students of Rammohan's Anglo Hindu School, Hare School, and Hindu College discussed only secular matters, primarily vidya.[107] Another similar secular association which only discussed the liberal arts was the Gyansandipan Sabha (1830) established at Umananda Tagore's house at Pathuriaghata.[108] The Debating Club was set up in the same period at Lakshinarayan Datta's house at Chorbagan to assist the spread of Western education.[109] The Sarbatattadipika Sabha (1832) with Debendranath Tagore as its secretary and Ramaprasad, Ramohan Roy's son, as the president was devoted to the improvement of the Bengali language.[110] The Vidyotsahini Sabha (1853) started by Kaliprasanna Singha had a similar aim. The Young Bengal's Society for the Acquisition of General Knowledge (1838) was a landmark institutions of its day. The Suhrid Samiti (1854) with members like Debendranath, Harishchandra Mukherjee, Kishorichand Mitra, and others pledged to 'fight for social progress and against superstitions'.[111]

Chattopadhyay (English lecturer at the same college) Gopalchandra Sarkar (Lawyer, Calcutta High Court), Shibnath Shastri, Haraprasad Shastri, Haridas Bhattacharya (Principal, Jaipur Raj college and Director of Public Instructions, Jaipur) and so on. See Shyamacharan Gangopadhyay, 'Amar Jibaner Kataguli Katha', *Prabashi* (1927), cited in *Haraprasad Shastri Rachana Sangraha*, pp. 50–51.

[107] Brajendranath Bandyopadhyay, ed., *Sambad Patre Sekaler Katha* Vol. 2, pp. 121–2.

[108] Ibid., p. 122.

[109] Ibid., pp. 122–3.

[110] Ibid., pp. 124–5.

[111] Benoy Ghosh, *Banglar Bidyotsamaj* (Calcutta: Prakash Bhaban, 1979), p. 87.

As some of their names eloquently suggest (Atmya, Suhrid, Family Literary Club (1857)), most of these associations were in-house affairs of the rich rentier bhadralok and the new middle class. Most of them started off from homely discussions within these houses amongst friends and associates. Of the Academic Association formed by the Derozians in 1828, Lal Behari Dey observed that 'Derozio's drawing room proving too confined a place for these discussions' the young friends decided to formalize them by starting an association.[112] Rabindranath in his autobiography gives us an idea of this social phenomenon:

The more I think of that period the more I realise that we have no longer the thing called a *mujlis*. In our boyhood we beheld the dying rays of that intimate sociability which was characteristic of the last generation. Neighbourly feelings were then so strong that the *mujlis* was a necessity, and those who could contribute to its amenities were in great request .... What goings and comings we used to see, how merry were the rooms and verandahs with the hum of conversation and the snatches of laughter![113]

Satyendranath Tagore writing about these gatherings in his father's time, refers to them humorously as 'Debendra Sabha': which had its *aamdarbar* for the common folk and the *khasdarbar* for the select.[114] In the latter darbar Raja Kalikumar, the poet Nabinchandra Bandyopadhyay, Akshaykumar Dutta, Rajnarayan Basu, and others had privileged entry. From the glittering parties and sabhas of the *bania*, the new generation had moved to a new social space of books, knowledge, and culture.

The common kerani, as this social picture indicates, was hardly the centre of attention in these reforms and literary discussions. For him, there was little time and even fewer gains to be had from such projects: the threat of losing a job for sedition was much more real to him than to Sanjibchandra. Much more real and closer to home were the teachings of the mad saint of Dakshineswar who was more or less rejected by the upper classes. Ramkrishna's critiques of modern life, Western education, and the values fostered by colonialism found far greater empathy with this section. They could thus confidently use Western sources to ridicule the Western educated. Issac Watt's *Improvement of the Mind* (1751) was transliterated to emphasize the superficiality of a 'college education':

---

[112] Lal Behari Dey, *Recollections of Alexander Duff* (London: T. Nelson and Sons, 1879) pp. 44–5.

[113] R. Tagore, *My Reminiscences*, p. 123.

[114] Satyendranath Tagore, *Amar Balyakal*, pp. 62–3.

Some boys with a strong memory can recite all the chapters of Euclid, but fail to explain a simple geometry problem. Memory may help to retain all the written words of the shastras, but the memorizing reader would still be in the dark about their deep ideas [....] Reading books, collected from all over the world may be one way of being literate, but if other people's words are examined by your own criticality, you would be like a load-bearing ox. If through memory you can recite your chemistry, moral sciences, or botany, you may be called literate; but gyani, never![115]

The rebuffing of Western values, whether in the earthy metaphors of Ramkrishna, or in ridiculing the upper layers of the Western educated, was for the kerani and the petty bhadralok the only available, but nevertheless potent, language of the nation. Despite the ideological unity that recognized all as bhadralok, class realities thus remained.

George Campbell in a letter about certain writings in the *Halishahar Patrika*, to the Viceroy Northbrook, voiced a major worry in 1873. He wrote: 'What really means nothing in Bengal may be read and copied by others in other parts of India, in whose hands and before whose eyes such matters would really be inflammatory and dangerous'. 'All the boys in Calcutta' he feared, 'may read and not rebel, but what would a frontier Pathan think if he reads a translation of such things and finds that such things are published with impunity?'[116] Campbell, unaware of the modern theorizations on print, nevertheless put his finger on an important and significant question. Lord Ellenborough thought that it was 'contrary to all reason' that 'at a time when the press and increasing railways and electric telegraph will enable them [Indians] to communicate and co-operate' the British would be able to 'retain ... [their] hold over ... [the] country'.[117] The press and its products were, needlessly to say deserving of attention. Books united the bhadralok, reinvented for them a social identity, and books again expressed the resentment of the kerani. An understanding of the role of print is thus crucial to penetrate this world of books. The next chapter investigates this world and tries to discover the actual channels through which the ideology of the bhadralok was established.

---

[115] Hiralall Mookerjee, *Watt's Improvement of Mind or Nitirutnahara* Part 1, (Calcutta, Nuton Bangla Press, 1870), p. 21.

[116] S.C. Saniyal, 'History of the Press', *Calcutta Review*, 132, 236 (January, 1911), pp. 145–7.

[117] Cited in C.H. Cameron, *An Address to Parliament on the Duties of Great Britain to India in Respect of the Education of the Natives and their Official Employment* (London: Longman, Brown, Green and Longmans, 1853), p. 20.

3

The Forms and Uses of Print

See patient Wilkins to the world unfold
Whate'er discovered Sanskrit relics hold,
But he performed a yet more noble part
He gave to Asia typographic art.[1]

In the introduction to his history of books in pre-revolutionary France, Robert Darnton makes two important points. First, he argues that the history of print in general and books in particular makes it possible to 'gain a broader view of literature and cultural history'. Second, that the study of books read by the people of an epoch gives a clue into the 'articulations of ideologies and the formations of public opinions' and thus helps to show how the culture of print can shape 'reality itself' and help 'determine the course of events'.[2] There are, in general, two schools of thought on the import of print and printing. One tends to see print primarily as an innovative technology which by its very specificity can become an agent of change, and Darnton clearly sides implicitly with this trend.[3] There is a major theoretical problem with this position. Undoubtedly certain books, tracts, or ideas ensconced in them, can give impetus to major world historical events. Thomas Paine's *The Rights of Man* (1792) is an oft-quoted but nevertheless good example. The question, however, remains as to what informs the writing of such books, or in other words where do new ideas

---

[1] 'Extracts from Government Records', *Bengal Past and Present*, Vol. XXIX, 1925, pp. 214–15.

[2] Robert Darnton, *The Forbidden Best-Sellers of Pre-Revolutionary France* (London: Harper Collins, 1997), pp. xvii–xxiii.

[3] See for example, E. Eisenstein, *The Printing Press as an Agent of Change: Communication and Cultural Transformation in Early Modern Europe* (Cambridge: Cambridge University Press, 1979).

come from? If we go with this first school of thought on printing, then the answer seems to lie in other books and more books ad infinitum. We are then forever caught in this introspective textual world which, while helpful in certain ways, does not answer our more fundamental question, as Brecht famously put it, 'who teaches the teacher?'

There is another way of looking at print. There are those who argue print to be the handmaiden of capitalism and hence attach more importance to larger social processes which account for the rise of print and its reception.[4] We tend to agree more with this latter view than with the former. Having said this there remains, however, a few issues that need clarification on the sole basis of print itself as a new technology. We can approach it with the rather obvious question as to what makes print specifically suited to capitalist social relations? The answer to this question forms the basis of this chapter.

One of the primary criterion of capitalism is that it requires labour power to be 'free'. This being the basic impulse of its relations of production, capitalism requires the political forms of democracy and equality which has its own homogenizing and autonomous responses in the polity. We shall find these reflected in a not too distant manner in the technological form of print. First, print creates an abstractness in its communication. A printed document may be meant for a specific purpose, or even a specific readership, but its form dictates that it remains available to all. It is worth noting the contrast that this has with earlier forms of communication.

Kasiram's Mahabharat, the first Bengali rendition of the epic, hinted very clearly at how it had been composed: *Mahabharater katha amrita saman/ Kasiramdas bhane sone punyaban.* (The tale of the Mahabharat is like the food of the gods/told by Kasiramdas it is for the ears of the good and holy.) Obviously, Kasiram had not *written* the Mahabharat, to be *read* by the good and holy, but it was *told* by him for the *hearing* of an audience. Ramgati Nayaratna, in one of the first histories of the Bengali language in 1872, attributed both the epics to the traditional bards, or *kathaks*, from whose word of mouth, according to him, both Kasiram and Krittibas had organized their texts.[5] Stories, histories, scriptures, all the forms of knowledge that the

---

[4] Benedict Anderson's now famous phrase print-capitalism is about this relationship between print as a technology and capitalism as a mode of production. B. Anderson, *Imagined Communities: Reflections on the Origin and Spread of Nationalism* (London: Verso, 1994), pp. 33–45.

[5] Ramgati Nayaratna, *Banglabhasha O Sahitya Bishayak Prostab: A Treatise on the Bengali Language and Literative* (Hooghly: Budhodoy Press, 1872–3), pp. 81, 134.

manuscript, or *punthi*, held was not interiorized in the text itself; they had to be transmitted, either taught to the students or read out by bards at community gatherings. There was an in-built limitation to how far the particular version of any tale could be carried. The community to which this knowledge was transmitted was very specific and known. The specificity of a printed book, however, is always mitigated by its abstract receptivity. It is impossible to predict, once a book is printed, who will read it and how. Printing as a technological form thus calls for an anonymous audience.

The second register of printed literature is that it is by its very nature democratic. Reproduction demystifies any singular uniqueness of handwritten literature and mass reproduction allows the circle of books to be expanded endlessly. Just as generalized commodity production destroys the specificity of handicrafts, printing destroys localized understanding and receptions of texts and creates broad audiences. The investigation of this process of destruction of earlier modes of transmission and creation of new ones forms the basis of this chapter. Within a discussion of its historical origins, and its various negotiations with earlier forms of information, we will argue that printing in Bengal, particularly from the middle of the nineteenth century, constituted and assisted in, the formation of the ideology of the new middle class. This chapter will mobilize some of the basic constituents of the acts of reading and writing and seek to demonstrate how these primary functions of knowledge production were altered to fit new social imperatives.

From *Punthi* to Print

Though the first Bengali book was published in 1778, the year 1800 can really be regarded as a watershed of Bengali printing and publishing, with the establishment of the Fort William College. The College initiated the beginning of a concerted effort on the part of the state to align the Indian languages to the administrative machinery by way of training its officials. A number of Bengali books were printed during this period to assist in this project. As a point of historical coincidence, one of the doyens of Bengali printing, William Carey, arrived at Serampore in January of 1800 along with William Ward and Joshua Marshman, where they succeeded in buying a house and setting up a press. Between 1800 and 1818[6] the twin institutions

[6] 1800 to 1818 is usually considered the first phase of print in Bengal. Print and printing entered a new phase with the establishment of the Hindu College and the Calcutta School Book Society in 1817.

of the Serampore Press and the Fort William College published twenty books in Arabic, seventeen in Bengali, thirty-six in Urdu and Hindi, seventeen in Persian, twenty-four in Sanskrit, and several others in Burmese, Chinese, Marathi, Telegu, Oriya, and Kannada.[7] Among the Bengali books were Carey's *Dialogues Intended to Facilitate the Acquiring of the Bengali Language* (1801), *A Grammar of the Bengali Language* (1801), *Raja Pratapaditya Charita* (1801) by Ramram Basu, *The Butrisha Singhasun* (1802) by Mrityunjay Vidyalankar, *Hitopodesh* (1802) by Golaknath Sharma, the same by Mrityunjay Vidyalankar and Ramkishor Tarkachuramani, *Lipimala* (1802) by Ramram Basu, *Maharaj Krishnachandra Rayasya Charitam* (1805) by Rajib Lochan Mukhopadhyay, *Tota Itihas* (1805) by Chandi Charan Munshi, *Purush Pariksa* (1815) by Haraprasad Ray, *A Vocabulary of Bengalee and English* (1810) by Mohan Prasad Thakur, and the *Itihasmala* (1812) and *The Bengalee English Dictionary* (1815) by Carey. The first Mahabharata was printed in Serampore in 1802 and the Ramayana in 1801.[8]

These books, along with several copies of the Bible produced in Serampore, cannot be said to be indicative of any independent direction in publishing, except in a marginal way, as they were either commissioned for the syllabus of the College, or printed for the avowed purpose of the spread of Christianity. Even then the list given earlier provides a fair idea of what were considered to be the primary sources for print to work with. Barring the dictionaries and grammars, most of the books printed were translations from Sanskrit or Persian. It was not as if new vistas of literature and literary forms were being opened by print; but rather it was the slow accommodation of print within older paradigms.[9] According to James Long, of the thirty books printed in 1820, five were on Krishna, four on Durga, three were tales, five were 'obscene', and there was one work each on dreams, music, astrology, and medicine. Rammohan's translations and almanacs made up

[7] Sisir Kumar Das, *Sahibs and Munshis: An Account of the College of Fort William* (New Delhi: Orion Publications, 1978), appendix E.

[8] The Mahabharat and the Ramayana were not sponsored by the College of Fort William, but it bought 100 copies each of the two works to encourage the undertaking. See James Long, 'Early Bengali Literature and Newspapers', *Calcutta Review*, 13, 25 (January–June, 1850), pp. 138–9.

[9] These texts were, however, the first experiments with the prose form in Bengali, and early histories of the Bengali language considered them to be the forerunners of the novel.

the rest. 'From 1822 to 1826', remarked Long, 'appeared 28 works, all with three exceptions, mythology or fiction. Matters proceeded in this train till about 1850, when the tide turned in favour of useful works'.[10] Not only in its content but also in its form print appeared to be unadventurous before 1850. In 1827, Bhabanicharan Bandyopadhyay, advertised in the *Samachar Darpan* that he was about to publish the Bhagwat Gita in the form of a punthi. It was to be printed by Brahmins only, on handmade paper, and the types were to be washed in the sacred waters of the Ganga.[11] Bhabanicharan had, in fact, undertaken various similar projects with other Shastric texts.[12] There was a large number of printed books which imitated the punthi in both form and content. Also, several punthis were rewritten from printed texts. This interplay of forms naturally posed the question of the survival of the traditional media of the manuscript, and/or the contestation of the new, that is, print. Did the two exist in complementality, tension, or mutual exclusion? There was a far more complex relationship between the forms concerned; print did not simply hegemonize the earlier forms. An interrogation of the sites of production of both is necessary to arrive at any satisfactory conclusion. Where were the manuscripts being produced in the nineteenth century?

The vast printing and publishing complex at Battala, spread over both sides of Chitpur Road in north Calcutta, was making available printed versions of the punthis to the readers of Calcutta and elsewhere at very low prices.[13] In order to maintain the vital link between Calcutta and the adjacent

[10] James Long, 'Returns Related to Publication in the Bengali Language', in *Selections from the Records of the Bengal Government, No. XXXIII* (Calcutta, 1859), p. VII.

[11] Quoted in Brajendranath Bandyopadhyay, ed., *Sambad Patre Sekaler Katha*, Vol. 1 (Calcutta: Bongiya Sahitya Parishad, 1970), p. 78.

[12] See the preface by Bishnu Basu, ed., in Bhabanicharan Bandhopadhyay *Kalikata Kamalalaya and Kalikata Kalpalata* (Calcutta: Pratibhash, 1986). There is, however, a distinctly revivalist intent behind these particular works. This being the era of the Young Bengal, Bhabanicharan, who wrote scathing editorials against the Derozian culture of the Hindu College, was perhaps trying to re-enact some of the older 'Hindu' values. Nevertheless, it is interesting that he would choose this particular reverse printing strategy as one of the ways to do so.

[13] For a detailed account of Battala see Sukumar Sen, *Battalar Chapa O Chabi* (Calcutta: Ananda, 1984); 'Battalar Besati', *Visva Bharati Patrika* (Shravan, 1948), pp. 16–25; 'Early printers and Publishers in Calcutta', *Bengal Past and Present*, 87 (January–June, 1968), pp. 59–66; Nikhil Sarkar, *Jokhon Chapakhana Elo* (Calcutta, 1977); Chittaranjan Bandyopadhyay, ed., *Dui Shataker Bangla Mudran O Prakashan* (Calcutta, 1981), pp. 21–34, 269–83, 332–67.

towns, hawkers were employed who bought the books themselves at wholesale price and sold them at a profit. They also served another function. They would buy up manuscripts from families and households and bring them back for publication to Battala. In this process, as early as the 1820s, the printers amassed a significant horde of old manuscripts which they then published at a very low price.[14] These printed books had the additional attraction of several plates of illustration, cut from metal blocks. According to Sukumar Sen, these were older than the Kalighat *pat* paintings, and the former had a strong impact on the latter in terms of iconography.[15]

The enormous publishing industry of Battala must be taken seriously not only in terms of its publishing strategies, but also as a point of departure for our discussion on the dialogue between the new and the old. Punthis, recovered from all over Bengal, were being printed here into books. This practice at one level demonstrated the resilience of tradition, in the sense that print had been unable, at least at this point, to introduce new subjects for its discourse. At another level, however, these printed books altered the perceptual significance of the punthi. The knowledge of the punthi, normally the preserve of a select few connected with the channels of education, were now available at Battala, to anybody, irrespective of caste or gender, at a nominal price. A contemporary source commented ironically that Saraswati herself had her seat at Battala, where everything from *Sambhog Ratnakar*, (obviously a 'licentious' copy) to the Vedantas, Patanjali, and books on Samkhya philosophy were available. One could, it asserted, buy the Mahabharat for only a paisa.[16] For its part, print was not only representing the function of the punthi, but was changing its social component. The manuscript, as it existed before print, was not solely an objective storehouse for knowledge. It was surrounded by an intricate network of attributes which

---

[14] Kabikankan Mukundadas' *Chandimangal*, edited by Ramjay Vidyasagar was published by Visvambhar Dev, the first printer at Battala in 1823–4. He also printed *Karunanidhivilas* compiled by Jayanarayan Ghosh in 1820. Ramchandra Kavikesari's *Haraparvati Mangal*, was printed in all probability by another pioneer at Battala, Harachandra Roy at the Bengali Press. Bharatchandra's *Annadamangal*, a specific favourite with the printers, had several editions till as late as 1874–5. For a fuller discussion on the number of manuscripts reprinted, see Sukumar Sen, *Battalar Chapa O Chabi*, pp. 11–17.

[15] Sukumar Sen, *Battalar Chapa O Chabi*, p. 20.

[16] Jaharlal Dhar, *Kalikata Rahasya, Adhunik Kalikatar Jibanta Pratibha* (Calcutta, 1896), pp. 51, 124.

were part of the knowledge that it contained. For example, the paper used for writing the punthi, and the curvilinear style of writing were as fundamental as the actual contents. This is why Bhabanicharan and others had to reproduce the punthi in its entirety, its form as well as its content, in order to appear convincing. Battala was, however, reproducing merely what the punthis contained in the form of the modern book, which altered the very status of the punthi.

Once the punthi had been extracted from its original position and surroundings, its content too could be made to serve different purposes. The printing history of Bharatchandra's Annadamangal serves to demonstrate this. Bharatchandra Roy (born 1712), a Brahmin poet in the court of Krishnachandra Roy of Nadia, wrote his Annadamangal around 1753. It was a trilogy which consisted of three practically independent parts: (i) *Annadamangal* proper being the story of how Parvati became Annada or the goddess of food and plenitude; (ii) *Kalikamangal,* which contained the famous tale of *Vidyasundar,* a romance recounting the love of Vidya, the daughter of king Virsimha, and Sundar, the son of king Gunasindhu; and (iii) the *Annapurnamangal,* containing *Mansimha,* a tale set in the Mughal court.[17] *Sachitra Annadamangal,* with six illustrations, was first printed in 1816 by Gangakishor Bhattacharya, who, it is believed, had been a compositor at the Serampore Press during an earlier part of his life.[18] The *Friend of India* listed it as 'Exploits of several of the Gods' and apparently did not find anything morally offensive about it.[19] There is no way to compile exact information on all the editions that this text went through after 1816, or who published them. But one thing was clear, that *Vidyasundar* was the only part chosen by the printers for endless re-editions. In 1825, it was priced at Rs 1, and by 1857 it was selling at between 1 and 2 annas.[20] In 1850, the Rev. Wenger called it 'probably [...] the greatest favourite with

[17] For biographical details of the poet see Sukumar Sen, *History of Bengali Literature* (Delhi: Sahitya Akademi, 1960), pp. 20–22; Dinesh Chandra Sen, *History of Bengali Language and Literature* (Calcutta: Calcutta University Press, 1911), p. 34–7; Manomohan Ghosh, *Bangla Gadyer Char Jug* (Calcutta: Dosgupta and Co., 1942), p. 18–21; and other regular histories of the Bengali language.

[18] See B.S. Kesavan, *History of Printing and Publishing in India, A Story of Cultural Reawakening, South Indian Origins of Printing and its Efflorescence in Bengal* (New Delhi: National Book Trust, 1985), pp. 271–96.

[19] Quoted in Long, 'Early Bengali Literature and Newspapers', pp. 148–9.

[20] Long, 'Returns', pp. 12–13.

the middle and upper classes, especially with the fairer sex'.[21] In 1857, there were at least three presses, all at Battala, which published a total of 7,000 copies of the work, and one of them, the Lakshmibilas Press had sold 3,750 copies of it in four months only.[22] What is perhaps important for us, is not only its obvious popularity, but the fact that the original *Annadamangal* text had more or less receded into the background in order to make room for the tale of *Vidyasundar.* Though *Annadamangal* remained in some of the texts, as a sort of invocative preface, *Manasimha* was not printed until 1854.[23] The number of plates of illustrations, in all its various editions up to 1860, were six. In the 1816 edition, all six were on *Vidyasundar.* In the 1845 edition from the Sindhu Yantra Press, only one out of the six, depicted Shiva and Parvati. Benimadhab De's *Bharatchandra Granthavali* (1873–4) had twenty-two illustrations, out of which seven pertained to this tale.[24] Print had thus not reproduced the punthi of *Annadamangal.* It had created a new text, that is, *Vidyasundar,* in its own right. This book was so popular that it was not uncommon to see the protagonist, Sundar in the costume of Young Bengal in some versions.[25] Even Vidyasagar had printed a copy of it in his Sanskrit Press. Due to the variety of editions and interpretations that the presses of Battala had generated of the original work, Vidyasagar went to the length of checking the original punthi preserved at the Krishnanagar royal palace, and modelled his copy on it.[26] It was supposed to have been critically edited, for Wenger found 'some of its readings to be widely different from those of older editions'.[27]

It is perhaps not enough to say that print transformed the *Annadamangal* punthi into the new book of *Vidyasundar.* The whole tenor of its reception changed as well. The punthi of *Annadamangal,* like all punthis, was valued for its literary merits. *Vidyasundar,* in its new form, however, was created for the express purpose of sensationalism, to ensure steady sales. Previously,

[21] J. Wenger, 'Popular Literature of Bengal', *Calcutta Review,* 13, 26 (January–June, 1850), p. 261.

[22] Long, 'Returns', pp. 2–3, 31–2, 35–6.

[23] It was printed at Battala by the Kabita Ratnakar Press, see Jatindramohan Bhattacharya, ed., *Mudrita Bangla Granther Panji 1853–1867* (Calcutta, 1993), p. 109.

[24] Sukumar Sen, *Battalar Chapa O Chabi,* Appendix.

[25] Wenger, 'Popular Literature', p. 262.

[26] Asit Kumar Bandyopadhyay, *Bangla Sahityer Itibritta,* Vol. 3, Part 2 (Calcutta: Modern Book Agency, 1993), p. 124.

[27] Wenger, 'Popular Literature', p. 262.

it had been contained within the other texts which being about the exploits of Shiva and Parvati, to a large extent mitigated its sensuality. On its own, it related only the love story of the protagonists, and their erotic love games on the night of their secret wedding, which previously a minor part of a larger text, grew conspicuous in its isolation. It was dubbed by Wenger as a book 'the study of which must destroy all purity of mind; and yet it cannot be doubted, that if any book is read by, and to, respectable Bengali females, this is it'.[28] It is noteworthy that it first appeared in Battala, not within the folds of the *Annadamangal*, but as *Vidyasundar* only.[29] Its wide dissemination, as opposed to the selective accessibility of the punthi, and the fact that it was readily available for money, when combined with its sensationalism, expressed its purely commercial enterprise. Hence, even though it might superficially appear that print was, in its early days, suffused in the older manuscript tradition, it was in actually doing different ideological work, by altering the terms of the traditional discourse.

The articulations of print, within the social formation, could not have been possible without other structures of legitimization: the new emphases on reading and education, the colonial network of schools and colleges and the rise of new classes and their ideologies. Haraprasad Shastri, one of the avid manuscript collectors of the nineteenth century, excellently grounded the transition from the punthi to the book in the contemporary social context. He used the example of an imaginary 'Bhattacharya Pundit' who owed his repertoire of knowledge to his punthis, and held his family inheritance of manuscripts dearer than his own life, constantly dusting them and keeping them tightly bound in thick cloth. The full sun of *Bhadra* delighted him; he would spread his dear possessions in the sun and sit guard over them all day, lest they be damaged by a sudden shower.

His son went to an English school, and later went on to get a job (chakri). Valuing the sentiments of his father, he preserved his punthis, even though they were practically useless to him. Bhattacharya's grandson learnt very little English but secured a job nevertheless. He had no notion about the meaning of the punthis, and did not care much either. His wife, thinking them to be rubbish, threw them out.[30]

[28] Ibid., p. 266.

[29] *The Third Report of the Proceedings of the School Book Society, Third Year, 1819* (Calcutta, 1820–21), Appendix II.

[30] Haraprasad Shastri, 'Presidential Address at the Annual conference of the Bangiya Sahitya Parishad, 1914' in Satyajit Chaudhuri et al., eds, *Harprasad Shastri*, pp. 311–12.

From one generation to the next, the punthi steadily lost its social relevance. The genealogy of the punthi and its incontestable relation to the larger changes in the nineteenth century society, prompts an investigation into the other facets of knowledge production that print may have displaced or reoriented.

Ways of Reading: Print and Orality

John Wenger gave an overview of the popular literature of Bengal in 1850. According to him:

Compared with the middle and lower classes of other countries [...] those of Bengal may be said to be fond of reading, or at least listening to the readings of others. The sight of a man poring over his book is not uncommon, even in the meanest village. When the crew of a boat is permitted [...] to congregate on the poop [...] the hardy rowers almost invariably form a group of listeners around a man, who professes to read to them [....] The reader, sitting on his haunches, with his book laid on the floor before him, spells out couplet after couplet; for all popular books are in verse, or are read, as if they were in verse [....] Reading, to a common native, is not the easy task that it is to an European. It is always carried on aloud, and according to sing-song tune, the modulations of which are not readily acquired. To this music the head beats time [....] This is the orthodox method of reading among the lower classes of Hindus [....] We have seen the youthful scribe of a darogah, singing aloud to his Superior and to ourselves a report of a robbery, containing an enumeration of stolen articles, according to the approved tune [....] with as great solemnity, as if it had been the most affecting story of the *Ramayana*, or the *Mahabharat*.[31]

Intoning and reading, so derisively conflated by Wenger, was in reality an important composite even after the arrival of print, because there was no history as yet of reading silently to oneself. We are not rehearsing here any essential position about the unchanging and eternal pre-modern orality versus the new modern print. We have seen in the case of the manuscripts how there was a radical refoundation of that tradition with the coming of print. Similarly reading, as a contingent element of orality, acquired certain concrete contents, in order to make itself commensurable to the new form.

By the mid-nineteenth century, silent reading had grown privileged enough over reading aloud, to the extent that the latter was associated only with a specific readership. The contemporary literary evidence points largely towards the audience community being that of women. Manomohan Basu's

---

[31] Wenger, 'Popular Literature', p. 258.

reading skills were utilized by the 'old, middle aged and one or two young women of the neighbourhood'.[32] Long knew of a man 'who was for years employed by a rich Babu to read 2 hours daily to 40 or 50 females in his house'.[33] Within the royal household of the Raja of Burdwan, the zamindar's wife would hold reading sessions, where young incumbents of the family read to the gathering of women.[34] It was not as if men were not being read out to. Wenger's observations, in fact, bear such a testimony. In the small towns and villages there were gatherings, where a mixed audience for readings was not uncommon. But hearing had acquired the connotation of *inability to read*, and aurality was no longer a constitutive part of the text itself. Prior to the coming of print, the culture of community reading did not bear any *necessary* correspondence to literacy. The missionary William Ward encountered several men from varied castes—weavers, barbers, peasants, oil pressers, goldsmiths, and so on—who could read the Puranas expertly.[35] Even then they would employ Brahmin readers to read out to them. It was highly unlikely that Gadadhar Shiromoni, Ramdhan Tarkabagish, or Sridhar Bhattacharya, the famous kathaks of the eighteenth and nineteenth century, who were regularly commissioned to read for the foremost families of Bengal, were reading to an illiterate audience.[36] Reading was more of a performance than a mark of literacy. The predominance of the poetic form in Bengali literature further helped to dramatize and syntactically organize reading situations.

[32] Manomohan Basu, *Samajchitra, Purba O Bartaman Athaba Kereler Jiban* (Calcutta: Nepalchandra Ghosh, 1981), p. 103.

[33] Long, 'Returns', p. 15.

[34] Benoychandra Mitra, *Rajarampur Srikrishnapur Mitrabangsha* (Burdwan, 1942), pp. 116–17, 163. We find a number of instances of this custom of regular reading sessions or permanently employed readers within prominent households. The Tagore family had one such reader, a Vaishnavi, who would come every morning to read to the women, and also supervise their education. See Swarnakumari Devi, 'Sekele Katha' in *Swarnakumari Devi Granthabali* (Calcutta, n.d.), pp. 199–200.

[35] William Ward, *View of the History*, p. 70.

[36] Gadadhar Shiromoni was a permanent kathak of the Raja of Burdwan. His reading of the Gita, had earned him a fortune in his lifetime. For a history of the kathaks in contemporary sources, see Durgadas Lahiri, *Bangalir Gaan* (Calcutta: Bangabasi Electro-Machine Press, 1905), pp. 277–9; Bholanath Chakravarty, *Sei Ekdin ar Ei Ekdin, Arthath Banger Purba o Bartaman Abastha* (Calcutta: Cornwallis Press, 1875), pp. 13–14; Rajnarayan Basu, *Bangla Bhasha O Sahitya Bishayak Baktrita* (Calcutta: Nuton Bangla Press, 1878), pp. 62–4.

Printed books that structured the insistence on a silent reading culture, invested reading, as a cultural practice, with the *ability* to read, or literacy. From the mid-nineteenth century, reading aloud was indicative of illiteracy, its agents being either women or lower class men. An official report in 1879, indicated this shift very clearly:

> Frequently in this very town of Calcutta, an observant passer-by sees a large knot of natives collected round a Tailor or native grocers' shop to hear a man (the most prominent person for the time being) reading a tale in Mussalmani-Bengali, in which the auditors appear to take the most lively interest, whilst the crowd observes the utmost decorum and order, and would resent any approach to interruption; and the reader is looked upon as a prodigy of learning; the only gift perhaps which he has being a ready knowledge of the alphabet and words and fluency of reading, which is always rapid, sonorous, and musical, and must be accompanied with rapid motions of the head and body, without which he could not go on.[37]

So literacy was not even the ability to read: it was the invocation of knowledge of which literacy formed the primary but only a very partial element. This is perhaps why reading aloud was retained in the cultural legacy of the nineteenth century within a very specific location, that of pedagogy, where it remained as an essential part of the educational methodology.

First, there was the custom of *ghoshano* (probably a derivation of *ghoshona*, meaning announcement in Bengali). This was a method by which a head boy was chosen in a class who would loudly recite a subject, stringing words together in a rhythmic tune, and the other boys would follow.[38] It was certainly nothing like the *kathakatha*, in either its function or content, but the echoes of that tradition would appear at interesting junctures. 'I remember', wrote Manomohan Basu, 'before I was five, the household Gurumahashay, would, stripping me naked, tie my dhoti around my head like the headgear of the *Ramayana* singer, and then, making the other students stand in a row, he would ask me to *ghoshao*'.[39] Adam's report on the Rajshahi District had a graphic description of this practice:

---

[37] 'Reports on Publications Issued and Registered in the Several Provinces of British India during the year 1878', in *Selections from the Records of the Government of India, Home Revenue and Agricultural Department*, No. LIX (Calcutta, 1879), p. 159.

[38] Rajnarayan Basu said it was the *payar* meter, or that in which Krittibas and Kasiram wrote their respective epics. See Rajnarayan Basu, *Sekal Ar Ekal*, pp. 24–6.

[39] Manomohan Basu, *Samajchitra*, pp. 101–2.

Not only are printed books not used in these schools, but even manuscript textbook are unknown. All that the scholars learn is from the oral dictation of the master [....] The principal written composition which they learn in this way is the *Saraswati Bandana* [...] which is committed to memory by frequent repetitions and is daily recited by the scholars in a body before they leave school, all kneeling with their heads bent to the ground, and following a leader or monitor in the pronunciation of the successive lines or couplets.[40]

Without either written or printed media, the only means of preserving knowledge was by memorizing it. But as orality gradually became fixed as an index of knowledge fit only for the lower classes, women, and children, memory and memorizing became inferior forms of knowledge. The 'memorizing native' formed a powerful negative image in the discourse of the missionaries and early educationists. In the orientation of the indigenous forms of knowledge, the written word had no primacy over either seeing it on the page, reciting, or hearing it. In fact, it carried no meaning in itself unless recited or heard. Memory was directly related to knowledge, since the notion of retention of the written word on paper or parchment was at best the passive principle of knowledge. If not spoken, recited or performed, it was knowledge insofar as it remained active in memory—individual, communitarian, or generational.

With the rapid advance of the printed book, however, this position of memory was reversed. Memory became an erratic medium compared to the permanence of print. More importantly, memory came to be conceptualized only as a retentive tool having lost its organic relation to knowledge. The textuality of print was not organized for memory to function. Thus, in the initial decades of the nineteenth century, when printed books were just making their appearance, the function of memory itself grew to be displaced and arbitrary. There were instances of people memorizing entire dictionaries.[41] Jagannath Tarkapanchanan, the acclaimed Sanskrit scholar from Tribeni, was rumoured to have given testimony in court, reproducing exactly a quarrel between two Englishmen, without knowing a word of the English language.[42] There were several guidebooks written on how to increase one's memorizing capacities, a rather ironic

[40] Long, ed., *Adam's Report*, p. 97.

[41] Rajnarayan Basu, *Sekal Ar Ekal*, p. 24.

[42] Bishnuchandra Maitra, *Apachay O Unnati* (Calcutta: Nabakrishna Press, 1890), p. 43.

enterprise from a culture which was once founded upon *smriti* (memory) and *shruti* (aurality). These books endorsed the trajectory that memory had taken within the discourse of print. While agreeing on the utility of memory, they recommended memorizing only if accompanied by the right amount of critical thinking. Memory became a mere tool for organizing facts, which, unless assisted by individual rational thinking, would not amount to being knowledge at all. Further the texts corroborated the logic of textual culture to its full potential. Among the things that killed memory, one text listed child-marriage, masturbation, being in debt, procrastination, and having too much milk or ghee in one's diet. In other words, it reproduced the type of reformative axioms of an English education.[43] The essential relation between reading, memory, and knowledge being severed, they functioned uncoordinated in the margins of the new knowledge.

The relationship between print and orality was thus one of rearticulation rather than of direct displacement. The social context for orality was hollowed out by print, and its form was used in the transmission of the new knowledge. Small town reformers, eager to disseminate the tales of the new printed books, would write them out as small couplets in English, and sing them with musical accompaniments in the streets.[44] Actual practices of the oral tradition, however, found no favour in the new discourse. The kathaks, for example, plying a dwindling trade, had fallen from the grace of the educated middle class. *Hutom* was scathing about the contemporary kathaks. The bards, it claimed, had no Shastric knowledge to speak of. Mere possessors of mellifluous voices, they memorized words from the Chanakya Slokas or some couplets of some *padabali*, and then, in their eagerness to earn money, sat on stools to 'kill Vyasdev'.[45] Krishnakumar Mitra, a noted Bramho

[43] Nibaranchandra Ghosh, *Smritividya Ba Swaranshakti Bardhaner Upay* (Calcutta: Samya Press, 1898), pp. 72–3.

[44] Rajnarayan Basu has spoken of the Arabian Nights being sung in payar as 'the chronicles of the Sassanians/that extended their dominions ... etc'. See *Sekal Ar Ekal*, pp. 24–6.

[45] Kaliprasanna, himself having undertaken the encyclopedic project of translating the Mahabharat from Sanskrit, prided himself on his command over the shastras. One of his pet idiosyncrasies was cutting off the tuft of hair on Brahmin pundits, the mark of their caste and education, who failed to meet his exacting standards. He had a formidable collection of fifty-one such hair pieces at the time of his death. In the passage quoted he referred to the misreading of Vyasa's Mahabharat by the kathaks. See Arun Nag, *Satik Hutom Penchar Naksha* (Calcutta, 1991), pp. 81, 147.

reformer of the period, documented in his autobiography the cheap tricks played by illiterate kathaks.[46] Both accuse the bards of lack of education and avarice.

But while the essential components of orality were attacked by the new middle class, their critique was not a general one. Nabinchandra Sen lamented the waning of this culture from a different perspective. The kathaks of his ancestral village had recounted to him how they were fast losing their profession because women no longer liked to listen to them. From this Sen sensed the arrival in Bengal of the new subject of the 'novel reading' woman. Thus, he wrote ruefully that the novel had taken the place of the punthi. Sita's place was occupied by Suryamukhi, Ramchandra's place by Sitaram, in Sabitri's place there was Kundannandini, and Bipula had abdicated in favour of Bimala.[47] Clearly the shift of women from orality was not considered praiseworthy.

Lekha Para: Writing as a Social Category

What we have termed so far as the 'oral' or 'aural' tradition was not in any sense purely oral. Written words and writing played a large role in it, though not in the way writing is focused upon in the present sense. The manuscript culture, which depended to a certain extent on writing, was, however, made meaningful only with the intervention of orality. But although hearing, rather than sight, had dominated the older noetic world in significant ways, writing was nevertheless an important constituent of this world.

As a necessary adjunct to the punthi tradition, good handwriting had a place of merit before the coming of print. Copying punthis was a serious occupation, and if able to write a good hand, even women, children, or old men, without any distinction of caste or creed, would take it up. Pens were usually made from reeds, vulture feathers, or iron. Works of poetry or literature were written on tulot, punthis on religious rites on palm leaves, and written charms to be worn as amulets, were inscribed on bhurjapatra.[48]

[46] Krishnakumar Mitra, Atmacharit (Calcutta: Bharat Mihir Press, 1937), p. 51.

[47] Nabinchandra Sen, Amar Jiban, Vol. 1 (Calcutta: Prabasi Press, 1907), p. 94. Suryamukhi, Sitaram, Kundannandini et al., are all characters from the various novels of Bankimchandra Bandhopadhyay.

[48] Panchanan Mandal, Punthi Parichay, Vol. 1(Calcutta: Vishwasharati, 1951), pp. 7–9.

Writing was not, in this tradition, the sole expression of literary production. It was an interim constituent, a medium in the actual process of creativity, that is, reading and hearing. But even as an intermediary agent writing had a strong cultural standing. One very functional reason for the importance of writing was the necessity to maintain the records of the medieval state. The Muslim state employed *nakal nabish* or copyists to document governmental proceedings. According to their skills at writing, they were given titles of *zarin rakm*, or golden writer, *shireen rakm*, or sweet writer, *roushan rakm*, bright writer, *maskn rakm*, or perfumed writer, and so on.[49] The combined imperatives of statecraft and the existing manuscript tradition maintained the need for writing and writers.

One of the most important mediaeval rituals associated with education that survived till the end of the nineteenth century, concerned writing. *Hatekhari*, literally meaning chalk-in-hand, was the ceremony by which every Hindu child began his or her education.[50] There are descriptions of this custom in the *Mangal Kavyas* and other literary sources of the sixteenth century.[51] Basanta Kumar Bose, has a vivid description of this ceremony:

When the boy is five years old, the ceremony of *hatekhari* takes place and a *yajna* is performed by the family priest, but no *pindas* are necessarily offered to the ancestors [....] The young boy wears a red silk dhoti and chaddar and is seated on a painted wooden plank (*piri*). A piece of chalk (*khari*) is placed in his right hand by the priest, and he asked to go over, with the chalk, some characters which the priest had written on a black stone dish. Rich people invite their kinsmen and relatives on this occasion, but it is not compulsory to do so.[52]

[49] Narendranath Laha, *Ashtadash Satabdi Porjonto Europeogan Kartrik Bharate Shiksha Bistar* (Calcutta: Oriental Press, 1923) trans. Ajarchandra Sarkar, p. 85.

[50] We have in our period study, instances of girls going through the ritual. It was rare, but not totally absent. See Prasannamayi Devi, *Purba Katha* (Calcutta: Adi Brohmo Samaj Press, 1917), p. 156.

[51] See Asutosh Bhattacharya, ed., *Baish Kabir Manasamangal Ba Baisha* (Calcutta: Calcutta University Press, 1962), p. 59; Surendranath Bhattacharya, ed., *Jagajjiban Birachita Manasamangal* (Calcutta: Calcutta University Press, 1960), p. 159; Bijitkumar Dutta and Sunanda Dutta, eds, *Manikram Ganguli: Dharmamangal* (Calcutta: Calcutta University Press, 1960), p. 115.

[52] Quoted in Muhammad Abdul Jalil, *Madhyajuger Bangla Sahitye Bangla O Bangali Samaj* (Dhaka: Bangla Academy, 1986), p. 127.

In the nineteenth century the yajna was mostly dispensed with, but offerings were made to either the family idol or Saraswati.[53] Adam puts it down as something 'expressly prescribed by the authorities of Hindu law', but there is no mention of it either in the Manusmriti or in the tenets of the sixteenth-century law maker, Raghunandan.[54] Perhaps it was the adoption of the custom of *bismillah*, by which Muslim children began their education under a munshi or a maulavi.[55] There were instances in the nineteenth century of Hindu children performing the bismillah, with an offering of *sinni* (a sweet dish) to the Maulavi, and pronouncing the bismillah before learning the Persian alphabet.[56]

Whatever may have been the genesis of hatekhari, it was one of the practices which confirmed the incorporation of writing within the culture of reading and listening. The structural uncertainty that writing might otherwise have had was dispelled by prioritizing it as a part of the genealogy of reading itself. Adam's report was excellent proof of this. 'The hand of the child', he observed, 'is guided by the priest to form the letters of the alphabet, and he is also then taught for the first time to pronounce them'.[57] This positioning of writing, accounted for the fact that the manuscript culture remained largely oral–aural even in the retrieval of the material preserved

[53] Several autobiographies have mention of *hatekhari*, as a widely spread custom. See Debaprasad Sarbadhikari, *Smritirekha* (Calcutta: Nikhilchandra Sarbadhikari, 1933), p. 18; *Krishnakumar Mitra Atmacharit*, p. 18; Manomohan Basu, *Samajchitra*, p. 101, and others.

[54] Long, ed., *Adam's Report*, p. 93. For the nineteenth-century reception of Manu, see Manomohan Basu, *Hindu Achar Byabahar* (Calcutta: Madhyastha Press, 1876), pp. 16–17; for the ideas and prescriptions of Raghunandan, see Bani Chakrabarti, *Samaj Sanskarak Raghunandan* (Calcutta: Bani Chakrabarti, 1970), pp. 105–10. Both Manu and Raghunandan marked the *upanayan* as the start of the process of the education for the Hindu male child, whereby the guru initiated him into *Bramhacharya*, by the recitation of the *gayatri* hymn, and then the so baptized student left for his ashram. His return home after the completion of his formal education was marked by another ritual, the *Samabartan*. Interestingly the graduation ceremony of the Calcutta University was, and still is, called the Samabartan.

[55] See S.M. Jaffar, *Education in Muslim India: Being an Inquiry into the State of Education during the Muslim Period of Indian History, 1000–1800 AC* (Delhi: Idarah-iAdabiyat-iDelli, 1973), p. 151.

[56] *Atmajibani, Arthath Bhai Girish Chandra Sen Kartrik Bibrito Atma Jibanbrittanta*, (Calcutta, 1906), pp. 1–2.

[57] Long, ed., *Adam's Report*, p. 93.

in the texts. Manuscripts were not easy to read, and what readers found in manuscripts they tended to memorize. The verbalization of the written texts also often continued the oral mnemonic patterning that made it easy to recall. There was an easy composite of reading, listening, and writing, which made possible the existence of both the manuscript and the oral tradition within the pre-print order.

But writing had a very specific relation to the manuscript tradition. It did not resort to composition via writing as the defining mark of intellectual activity. The nature of manuscript writing was more transcriptive than compository. It always required the intervention of some form of orality, either verbally when read or aurally when transcribed. The primary requisite of a modern sense of authorship, the direct association of a piece of work in unaltered form with the person who produced it, was not a strong priority before print. That is not to say that such associations were non-existent. Poetical compositions such as the *Annadamangal*, or *Chandimangal*, were associated with particular, individual authors like Bharatchandra and Mukundadas. But due to their modality of transmission, primarily through the interlocution of several generations of bards, readers, and listeners, it was never considered important to adhere strictly to what any individual author had *originally* written. Print, on the other hand, prioritized writing as the only medium of literary composition. The permanence of the printed page oriented writing as the only visible referent to knowledge and the indelible printer's ink fixed the content of the written word in such a way that the author was fixed to each word of his writing forever. The inextricability of the writer and his writing had two important consequences: first, it gave the writer ultimate individual possession over his writing. There existed no other agency but his own, which could alter, appropriate, or erase what he had written. This unique responsibility over individual production and the strong association between the author and his work would in turn give rise to individual styles and specificities of writing. Second, since a piece of writing could be traced to its producer, in constant form, writing itself acquired a different ontology. Within the precepts of nineteenth-century notions of selfhood, composition replaced writing as a simple copying practice, and turned writing inwards as a deep meaningful act. The complete anonymity of the reader, as a disjuncted portion of the act of writing, concentrated more than ever the selfhood of the author and gave authorship itself a novel omnipotence.

Most Bengali books written in the early decades of the century carried
no indication of who their authors were. Most of Rammohan's important
works between 1815 and 1833 were published anonymously. In view of
the fact that these were laying out the foundations of his philosophical
principles, and were the primary disputations of Bramhoism, it can hardly
be supposed that in their case anonymity was a form of disguise. It is
noteworthy, however, that while Ramomhan's Bengali publishers did not
have a problem with this form, his contemporary and adversary, Mrityunjay
Vidyalankar's *Vedantachandrika* (1817), printed by a European, not only
carried his name, but had two title pages (one in English and one in Bengali),
while Rammohan's works lacked any.[58] It was the School Book Society that,
in its third report, for the first time documented his works in his name.[59]

As several contemporary sources complained, the first spate of books
from the Bengali press were either the re-writing of old traditional stories
or mythologies, or at best translations from English. Before the establishment
of the Hindu College and the School Book Society, that is, between 1801
and 1817, the total number of books produced did not exceed thirty in any
single year. Of these, 44.25 per cent were on scripture and mythology.
They were followed by dictionaries and grammar (16.09 per cent), moral
tales (9.77 per cent), and Christian tracts (a mere 8.62 per cent). Books on
history accounted for 5.17 per cent of the total production, and tracts in
Mussalmani Bengali 3.45 per cent. A total of seventy-seven scriptural and
mythological books were printed over this period, an average of 4.53 books
each year; dictionaries and grammars stood second with twenty-eight books,
at an annual average of 1.65 books, followed by seventeen moral tales, at an
average of one book per year. In the other categories an average of less than
one book was published each year.[60]

[58] Rammohan's *Vedanta Grantha* (1815), *Vedanta Sar* (1815), and *Dayabhag* (1816–
17), were published by Ganga Kishor Bhattacharya from the press of Ferris and Co. His
Utsabananda Bidyabagisher Sahit Bichar (1816) and others were published by Lallulal,
who was once a teacher of the Hindustani language at the Fort William College.

[59] *The Third Report of the Proceedings of the School Book Society, Third Year, 1819*
(Calcutta, 1820–1), pp. 38–9.

[60] All statistical data has been computed by Tapti Roy, 'Disciplining the Printed
Text: Colonial and Nationalist Surveillance of Bengali Literature', in Partha Chatterjee,
ed., *Texts of Power, Emerging Disciplines in Colonial Bengal* (Calcutta: Samya, 1996),
pp. 38–40.

Between 1818 and 1843, a period associated with rising missionary activity, Christian tracts increased from the low average of 0.88 books per year to 6.50. This category now exceeded the Hindu scripture and mythology, which contributed an average of 6.11 books per year, to be closely followed by grammars and dictionaries (6.04). Natural Science and moral tales claimed far less—3.92 and 3.15 book per year receptively. In terms of their representative shares in the total number of books, Christian tracts accounted for 16.54 per cent, scriptures and mythologies 15.56 per cent, dictionaries and grammars 15.36 per cent, natural science 9.98 per cent, and moral tales 8.02 per cent. Books on law claimed 6.75 per cent and history 4.79 per cent. The fact that 40.70 per cent of all books were reprints, denoted that a major part of publishing was still the printing of older works, rather than the commissioning of 'original' writing. The reprint figures also reflect the great demand, compared with other categories, for dictionaries and grammars.[61]

The scriptures and mythologies, which were considered repetitive by Europeans, were not so perceived by their producers. They had quite simply not relinquished as yet the traditional position of writing in literary production. Also they were bound by the tastes of their readers, long trained to enjoy those very tales, which assured them their rapid sales. It must also be remembered that the prose form was not the norm in pre-print Bengali writing. So, when the transition was made from rewriting to 'original' authorship from the middle of the century, the early phase registered a remarkable rise in books of poetry. Between 1844 and 1852, 7.22 books of poetry were being produced every year, comprising 7.86 per cent of all the books, from an average of 0.18 books per year before 1817.[62]

It has been argued forcefully by historians of orality, that print makes for more tightly closed verbal art forms.[63] The emergence of Bengali prose was also largely attributed to the coming of print, among other things. But 'original' prose, that is, novels or prose pieces other than translations or religious and/or social reformative disputations, did not begin before our period of study. There were, however, certain distinct developments, which

[61] Ibid., pp. 40–1.

[62] Ibid., p. 41.

[63] Walter J. Ong, *Orality and Literacy: The Technologizing of the Word* (London: Routledge, 1990), pp. 132–3.

when collated together appear as a preparatory phase of print compared with what the nineteenth century dubbed as 'original' writing.

First, as we have noted earlier, there was a noticeable rise in the number of grammars and dictionaries issued from the press. Bengali grammar, or rather the lack of it, was an insurmountable problem for the early European experiments with the language. The several grammars for Bengali produced by Europeans like Manoel da Assumpcam (1743), Halhed (1778), Lebedev (1801), Carey (1801), Keith (1820), and Haughton (1821), can be seen as a base line in the history of the colonial encounters with the Bengali language as a medium of communication.[64] As Halhed explained in the preface to his Grammar with due solemnity:

The wisdom of the British Parliament has within these few years taken a decisive part in the internal policy and civil administration of its Asiatic territories; and more particularly in the kingdom of Bengal, which by the most formal act of authority in the establishment of a supreme Court of Justice, it has professedly incorporated within the British Empire. Much however still remains for the completion of this grand work; and we may reasonably presume, that one of its most important desiderata is the cultivation of a right understanding and of a general medium of intercourse between the Government, and its subjects; between the natives of Europe who are to rule, and the Inhabitants of India who are to obey.[65]

The grammars were not merely a linguist's contribution to serve directly the purposes of the colonial state. Each book was designed to reveal Bengali as an artificial and deficient 'jargon', and organize it within the rules of stable grammatical laws and orthography. Further, given the fact that they denied even the existence of any recognizable language called Bengali, the grammars were the foundational move to formulate one. This call for 'correctness' of language was taken up by the Bengalis themselves from the turn of the century. In 1789, right after the publication of Halhed's book, the Calcutta Gazette carried a letter requesting a 'bhadralok' to write a

[64] For a history of Bengali grammars see, Mohammad Abdul Kaium, A Critical Study of the Early Bengali Grammars. Halhed to Haughton (Dhaka, 1982), and Suniti Kumar Chattopadhyay and Priyaranjan Sen, eds., Manoel da Assumpcam's Bengali Grammar. Facsimile reprint of the original Portuguese, with Bengali translation and selection from his Bengali–Portuguese Vocabulary (Calcutta: Calcutta University Press, 1931).

[65] Nathaniel Brassey Halhed, A Grammar of the Bengali Language (Calcutta: Ananda, 1980), pp. i–ii.

grammar of Bengali for the general well-being of the people.[66] The *Bangadoot* in 1830 repeated the same appeal to its 'learned readers' for the uplift of the 'general masses'.[67] Rammohan's *Sambad Kaumudi* emphasized in its seventh issue that it was important for a Hindu to know the grammar of his own mother tongue before learning a foreign language.[68] The urgency for a grammar underlined in fact the urgency for a standardized prose form. It is perhaps worth pointing out that there was not a single book published in the early nineteenth century on prosody, or on any issue around the verse form. Print was only concerned with prose, that is, a form that could sustain the contemporary notions of 'original' writing. Early educationists ceaselessly emphasized writing as the approved means of learning lessons. As opposed to the traditional method of committing lessons to memory, early lesson books were provided with blank sheets of paper, on which the reader was to practice his or her writing.[69] The insertion of writing in the place of reading and memorizing was a step forward in the process of composition, but what was to be written?

Transliteration from English prose works was a common practice for early Bengali prose writers, consolidated no doubt by encouragement from institutions like the School Book Society and the Vernacular Literature Society. One of the first books published by the former was *Nitikatha* (1817), a collection of thirty-one fables, translated from English and Arabic, by Tarinicharan Mitra, Radhakanta Deb, and Ramkamal Sen. Within the same year three editions of the work had to be printed, resulting in a total of 6,000 copies.[70] Akshaykumar Dutta, considered one of the pioneers of Bengali prose, based the most important of his works on English texts.[71]

[66] Quoted in Sushil Kumar De, *Bengali Literature in the Nineteenth Century* (Calcutta: Firma KLM, 2nd edn 1962), p. 72.

[67] Brajendranath Bandyopadhyay, *Sambad Patre* Vol. 1 (Calcutta, 1946), p. 56.

[68] From the subject index of *Sambad Kaumudi* published in the *Calcutta Journal* (31 January, 1822), quoted in J.K. Majumdar, *Raja Rammohan Roy*, p. 288.

[69] See *The First Report of the Institution for the Encouragement of Native Schools in India* (Serampore, 1817), p. 9.

[70] *The First Report of the Proceedings of the Calcutta School Book Society, Read at the Annual General Meeting of the Subscribers, held at the Town Hall of Calcutta, July 4, 1818* (Calcutta, 1818), p. 4.

[71] The two volumes of his *Bahyabastur Sange Manab Prakritir Bichar* (1851, 1853), were based on George Coomb's *The Constitution of Man* (1828), while the two volumes of his *Bharatbarsher Upasak Sampraday* (1870, 1883) on Horace Wilson's *Sketch of the*

Both the *Akhyanmanjai* (1863) and the *Bodhodoy* (1852) of Vidyasagar were similarly modelled on English texts.

The Vernacular Literature Society, established in 1851, had a policy of distributing prize money for 'original' work. Its report outlined its modus operandi thus:

One main feature of novelty in the Society's operation in the past year and a half has been the partial development of their long cherished plan of stimulating the production of original composition, instead of depending on translations which can never at their best wear anything but a stiff and foreign aspect. For some years the Society appealed in vain; the premium, the amount of which was necessarily fixed by a prudent regard to their financial position, may have been too low to induce the better class of writers to come forward....[72]

The tale in verse, *Padmini Upakhyan* (1858), by the eminent poet Rangalal Bandyopadhyay, was considered by the Society to be the 'first original composition of real merit', but due to its verse form did not receive, the prize. The prize was ultimately awarded to Madhusudan Mukherjee's prose work *Sushilar Upakhyan*.[73]

Diffusion of the idea of 'original' writing, and its built-in inevitability of publication, was institutionalized in more than one way. Such examination scripts of students as were considered meritorious were published in dailies like the *Bengal Herald* and *Hurkaru*. There was also a formal ceremony held at the Town Hall, where students read out their pieces in the presence of the Governor-General himself, who then distributed prizes for the best composition.[74] Contemporary journals declared prizes for 'original' articles on issues ranging from 'self reflection' to 'social reform'. The best essay would be rewarded with money and consequently be published.[75] As a result

---

Religious Sects of the Hindus (1846). For details see Akshay Kumar Datta, *Bahya Bastur Sange Manab Prakritir Bichar* (Calcutta, 1851–1853), Horace Hayman Wilson, *The Religious Sects of the Hindus. Based on the "Sketch" by H.H. Wilson ... with additions from later sources of information*, Compiled by J. Murdoch (London and Madras, 1904) and George Combe, *The Constitution of Man* (Hartford, 1854).

[72] *Report of the Transactions of the Vernacular Literature Society From July 1st. 1858 to December 31st. 1859* (Calcutta, 1860), p. 10.

[73] *Report of the Transaction of the Vernacular Literature Society*, p. 10.

[74] Rajnarayan Basu, *Atmacharit*, pp. 17–20.

[75] See for instance, Saratchandra Chaudhuri, ed., *Shiksha Parichar*, Vol. 1, (Baishakh, 1297), p. 24. The most popular of them was the Kuntalin prize, offered by the Kuntalin House of H. Bose, which claimed to have helped establish several writers. One such prize-winner was a short story by the scientist Jagadishchandra Bose.

of such concerted efforts, from the middle of the century, there arose in Bengal, the independent, and very specific, category of the 'author'. He was no longer masked in anonymity, as in the days of the Battala, but rather his name extended the power of his individual word. Long noted in 1859 that the new Bengali works were rather high priced when they were 'copy wright' [sic], as 'various natives now find the composition of Bengali books profitable, and some authors draw a regular income from them'.[76] There was a regular hierarchy of prices. In 1864, Bhudev Mukhopadhyay's ninety-one page *Shikshabishayak Prostab* was sold for a whole rupee, while lesser known authors like Umeshchandra Chattopadhyay's *Ashusambidayini* (1865), which consisted of 275 pages, was priced at only 8 annas.[77] The difference was an acknowledged one, as a contemporary book on female education lamented, that people valued books only if written by a famous man.[78] In 1855, Long listed 515 men connected with Bengali literature. In just four years he wrote:

That the Bengali mind has been roused from the torpor of ages is pretty clear from the increase of the number of Bengali authors. I have before me a list of them which I have drawn up, and which gives the names of more than 700, and at the present time there is great ambition to be a writer in his own language. The supply is equal to the demand and were there a larger reading population, authors would multiply still more rapidly.[79]

Writing was no longer anterior to the writer, but the writer to his penmanship. Print individuated writing and bound the author in the specificity of his work.[80] It is no surprise then, that a catalogue of Bengali books available for sale in 1865, showed a total of 901 books, quite a substantial leap from the 322 books recorded for sale by Long, in 1857. In this list there was a striking increase in works of prose fiction and drama:

[76] Long, 'Returns', p. 12.

[77] Jatindramohan Bhattacharya, *Panji*, pp. 14, 112.

[78] See advertisement to, Ramsundar Roy, *Stridharma Bishayak* (Calcutta: Chaitanya Chandrodoy Press, 1859).

[79] Quoted in Sripantha, *Jokhon Chapakhana Elo* (Calcutta: Banga Sanskriti Sammelan, 1977), pp. 118–19.

[80] In one of the numerous satirical pieces of this period, there is an incident related, where a young wife had refused to change her clothes because she was in the 'presence' of one of Bankim's novels. Obviously a contrived situation though it may be, it gives us an idea of the personalization of writing.

114 prose fiction works, amounting to 12.65 per cent of the total, and 112 dramas (12.43 per cent). By comparison, in 1857 there were only eight dramas and twenty-eight fiction works, and in the nine years from 1844 to 1852, there were only twenty-four prose works and twenty-two works of fiction. Scriptures and mythologies plummeted in 1865 to only sixty titles; Christian tracts to a mere ten, and the vocabularies and dictionaries having served their immediate purpose, fell to thirty-one titles.[81] The Bengali language was ready for the lone horseman, who was soon to stop before the closed doors of a temple.[82]

Educating Print: Fonts, Compositions, and Typographic Errors

Once the fundamental relationship between authorship and print had been established, attention was turned to the other requisites of the printed page, of which one of the primary requirements was a system of disciplined fonts. 'That the Bengali letter is very difficult to be imitated in steel', complained Halhed, 'will readily be allowed by every person who shall examine the intricacies of the strokes, the unequal length and size of the characters, the variety of their positions and combinations'. 'It was no easy task', he claimed, 'to procure a writer accurate enough to prepare an alphabet of a similar and proportionate body throughout, and with the symmetrical exactness which is necessary to the regularity and neatness of a fount [sic]'.[83]

The 'symmetry', 'exactness', or 'regularity', the much coveted ordering of the Bengali script that Halhed desired, was not, however, achieved by him. Instead what marked his work was a conscious attempt to justify his particular choice of lettering within all the forms that existed in the various strands of the manuscript tradition.[84] In his opinion, the many forms of the

---

[81] Tapti Roy, 'Disciplining the Printed Text', p. 47.

[82] The opening lines of Bankim's *Durgeshnandini* (1881), which was hailed as the first novel of true literary merit.

[83] Halhed, *A Grammar*, p. xxiii.

[84] He made a distinction among the two prevalent forms of the letter 'ra': 'র', 'ব': "ব র ro, is distinguished from ব bo either by a stroke across or a dot beneath it; as রাখন raakhon to place." And in the case of 'la': "ল ন lo, two forms of l, as বল bol strength. This letter in the common corrupted writing of modern Bengalese is usually confounded with ন no in shape ..." *Grammar*, p. 13.

Bengali alphabet and the complexity of compound letters presented a major obstacle in the effort to standardize their form. He argued that many 'disfigured' alphabets established their positions in the manuscript permanently, which he gave examples of in the appendix to his book.[85]

The fifty-two letter Bengali alphabet, with its equally varied permutations in the punthis, was a formidable resistance to European notions of regular print. Different representations of the same letter, which the fluid textuality of the manuscripts could allow, posed a veritable threat to the notion of order which was a correlative to print. The tension was so distinct in Bengal, perhaps due to the role that print had assumed in the province. Not only was it equated with 'science' and 'modernity' but was very much invested with educational efforts. In the words of William Carey:

One grand step towards imparting instruction to our Indian neighbours with due effect, will be that of *improving them in their own language*. To secure this, two or three things are necessary. The various Characters of the language, with their numerous combinations, should be given to them printed with the utmost accuracy, that by frequently reading and copying them, they may become fully acquainted with the powers of their own language.[86]

Also, in the case of early print, used as it was for proselytization, the printed word was also carrying the word of God. There was, therefore, a distinct anxiety to secure management over the unruly alphabetical system. In a long letter to Vidyasagar in 1865, John Murdoch, an agent of the Christian Vernacular Education Society of Madras, graphically enumerated his woes over the Bengali typography:

[85] Before Halhed's work, William Bolts, a rather colourful figure of eighteenth-century Calcutta, had cut the types of the Bengali alphabet. Halhed mentioned this in his Preface, as a failure to execute 'even the easiest part, or primary alphabet' and that the project if completed 'would not have advanced beyond the usual state of imperfection' Halhed, *A Grammar* pp. xxiii–iv. Later historians like Chittaranjan Bandyopadhyay, however, hailed Bolts as the father of primary ideas about Bengali printing. He compared Bolts' type with that of Wilkins, cut after five years, and found the former virtually free of the influence of the patterns of writing of the munshis, on which Wilkins, after five years, could not achieve any appreciable improvement. See Chittaranjan Bandyopadhyay, 'Boltser Bichal Haraf', in *Dui Shataker*, pp. 367–75.

[86] William Carey, *Hints Relative to Native Schools, together with the outline of An Institution for their Extension and Management* (Serampore: Mission Press, 1816), pp. 11–12.

In addition to about 50 simple letters of the alphabet and a dozen vowel symbols, I had master upwards of 120 joined consonants. I found them united in all sorts of ways. Some were written after or below each other, like ক topsy-turvy and impaled as in ক্ত, sometimes two heads were stuck on one body as in ক্ষ, in other cases, as the letters were so compressed, altered or mutilated that it was impossible from inspection to recognize them. Nor was this all. When I had gone over the whole of the second part of your Borniporichoy, I cherished the vain hope that the dreary task was ended. On taking up, however, the Gospel of St.Mark, printed last year, I found there a variety of new forms. Again, on examining another edition of the same Gospel, printed at the same press, in the same year, I came across as many same combinations. Lastly, on turning to the 'Introduction to the Bengali Language', by Dr. Yates, I met with the very consolatory remark, 'The forms of them (the compound consonants) differ more or less in every fount [sic] of type'.[87]

Murdoch's exaggerations may seem somewhat violent, but the remedies that he suggested were very much a part of the discourse on the standardization of typography. He forwarded a scheme for using the *biram* (stop mark) to denote the suppression of the inherent vowel which had troubled him greatly, that is, in the place of ক, he proposed breaking it up as ক্‍ক, which would do away with the joined consonants in the script. This, he argued, would save trouble for the printers, by enabling much smaller and hence less expensive fonts, and reducing by almost one half the variety of types required in a composing case. Also, comparing the Bengali with the Roman characters, he pointed out the advantages of the latter, due mainly to the clarity of its script.[88]

The projection of the Roman type as a 'standard' for printed works was a theme that found constant refrain throughout the nineteenth century. The missionaries, never known for their love of the Bengali language, even in the heydays of Orientalism, were for the rejection the Bengali script altogether in favour of the Roman.[89] They had, where the public sphere had not been resistant to such attempts, very deftly inserted the Roman script as the only script suited to the spoken language, as in the case of Santhali.[90] The logic given for this obliteration of the vernacular script was

[87] John Murdoch, *Letter to Babu Iswarchandra Bidyasagar on Bengali Typography* (Calcutta: Christian Vernacular Education Society, 1865), pp. 2–3.

[88] Ibid., pp. 3–6.

[89] See *The Fifteenth Report of the Proceedings of the School Book Society, Thirty-first to Thirty-fourth Year, 1848–1851* (Calcutta, 1852), pp. 34–35.

[90] Ibid., Minute by Cecil Beadon, p. 35.

that it was still sufficiently malleable to be directed towards a better end. The indistinctness that so marked Bengali writing in European eyes was attributed to the carelessness and inaccuracy of the human agents involved, and also the 'corrupt' form of the letters, which of course would vanish once the script itself had been ordered.[91] The adoption of the Roman script, felt C.E. Trevelyan, would reduce the cost of printing and 'make knowledge cheap and bring books down to the level of the means even of the poorest class of people'.[92] The *Christian Observer* rejoiced in the possibility of the native characters wholly vanishing.[93] Others with less hopeful views wanted to at least introduce italics and capitals in the script, to approximate the Roman script as much as possible.[94] The dialogue between technology and subject matter was never clearer. Both demanded the restructuring and complete overhauling of the language. The new printed script of Bengali was thus to bear both the 'truth effect' of science and the edification of knowledge.

By the 1850s this was, more or less, a part of the general common sense amongst the new middle class. As an educationist, Bhudev Mukhopadhyay preferred the printed character to the handwritten form in the first exposure to learning.[95] In a speech delivered at the fourth session of the *Jatiya Mela* in 1870, Jogendranath Ghosh urged his countrymen to dedicate themselves to 'the development of the Bengali type and case', for on it depended 'the actual prosperity of Bengal and the Bengali language'.[96] Perceiving this intimate connection between print and knowledge, the new middle class experimented with types and cases. Vidyasagar had invented a new method of arrangement of the types in their cases to facilitate

[91] See Carey's comments on the issue in, *The First Report of the Institution for the Encouragement of Native Schools in India*, pp. 21–2.

[92] 'The Application of the Roman Alphabet to All the Oriental Languages', *Contained in a Series of Papers written by Messrs. Trevelyan, J. Prinsep, and Tytler, Rev. A. Duff, and Mr. H.T. Prinsep. And published in various Calcutta periodicals in the year 1834* (Serampore, 1834), pp. 11–12.

[93] 'The Application of the Roman Alphabet', p. 117.

[94] See Note by E.S. Montagu in *The Third Report of the Proceedings of the School Book Society, Third Year, 1819* (Calcutta, 1820–1), p. 50.

[95] Bhudev Mukhopadhyay, *Shikshabidhayak Prostab*, p. 35.

[96] Jogendranath Ghosh, *Bangla Mudrankaner Itibritta O Samalochana* (Calcutta: Nutan Bangla Press, 1870), p. 33.

composition: it was called the 'Vidyasagar Sort.'[97] As printing gradually coincided with the paradigms of education, the technology became co-terminus to the product of technology. From the mid-nineteenth century onwards, greater care was consequently taken of the details of printing, and spelling, punctuation and typographic errors were sought to be minimized. In the late eighteenth and early nineteenth century, auditory processing continued for some time to dominate the visible printed text. It could be seen strikingly in the early printed pages, which seemed somewhat chaotic in their inattention to visual word units. In the manuscript tradition, copyists would create paragraphs of equal size, paying more attention to their equality in length than to the actual content. Thus, words with more than three or four letters were quite unproblematically chopped and transferred to the next line in order to maintain conformity with the length of the previous line. Early printers, too, quite commonly divided words between separate lines, playing havoc with modern notions of textuality. Krishnachandra Sharma Shiromoni's *Puran Bodhodwipani* (1827) had such a division of letters. The word *swetdwipé* on page 143, was divided up as *swetdwip*, in that page while the next page carried the single disjointed letter *pé*.[98] There was also the problem of title pages, which in the beginning tended to summarize the contents of the book itself, acting both as an index and advertisement for it. Bhabanicharan Bandyopadhyay's *Nababibibilas* (1822), had a thirteen line title (inclusive of the date of publication). It declared the subject, the contents of its four parts, and the implication of its name, all within the title page.[99] Later policies on printing and composing were, as a result, rigorously directed around the simplicity of title pages, for it was claimed that fancy and embellished ones diminished the 'gravity' of the work.[100]

[97] Sripantha, *Jokhon Chapakhana Elo*, pp. 121–2. Similarly Radhakanta Deb had established a press at his own house and had a set of types prepared under the designation of 'Raja's Types'. See *A Rapid Sketch of the Life of Raja Radhakanta Deva Bahadur, with some Notices of his Ancestors and Testimonials of his Character and Learning By the Editors of the Raja's Sabdakalpadruma* (Calcutta, 1859), p. 21.

[98] Jatindramohan Bhattacharya, 'Punthir Pare Bai' in Chittaranjan Bandyopadhyay, ed., *Dui Shataker Bangla Mudran O Prakashan* (Calcutta: Ananda, 1981), p. 24.

[99] Reprinted in Bhabanicharan Bandyopadhyay, *Rasarachanasangraha* (Calcutta: Nabapatra Prakashan, 1987), p. 8.

[100] Pannalal Sen, *The Master of Printing or the Manual of a Printing Office* (Calcutta: The Hindustan Publishing Company, 1921), p. 49.

Punctuation within the text was another area of confusion for early print, for it could take no leads from the manuscript, and it seemed an entirely novel method of organizing a text, both to the printers and the early writers. The *Samchar Darpan* in 1829 published an anonymous letter, in which the author asserted, that the only way new punctuation would find a place in Bengali was to create an entire grammar for its application, and taught in the indigenous pathshalas. The letter was without any punctuation except for the finishing sign of the *dari* (|).[101]

Rammohan's *Vedantagrantha* (1815) was an excellent example of the old punctuation style. It used most of the punctuation marks of the punthi tradition, including the dari, the double dari (||), *kashi* (—), the *kashi* after a single dari, (| —), and after a double dari (|| —), and the point between two double daris (||° ||). The *dari* not only acted as a full stop, but also substituted for the colon and the dash throughout the text.[102] The preface or *bhumika* ended with a || — sign, and the text itself began with the words *Om Tat Sat* within two double daris, traditionally regarded as sanctified signs in Bengal.[103] From this his later work *Subrahmanya Shastrir Sahit Bichar* (1820), was both an indication of Rammohan's individual comfort with new signs of punctuation, and the progress of print. This book incorporated the quotation mark, the full stop, the coma, and the semi-colon.[104]

The School Book Society embodied the first institutional effort in laying out the grids of European printing technology. One of its first books the *Nitikatha* (1817), a collection of Bengali lessons, compiled by the Rev. May, John Harley, and J.D. Pearson, and supervised by Eustace Carey and William Yates, was designed to be a 'novelty' in Bengali print. It was marked by the 'introduction of a regular punctuation, similar in principles, and for the most part in its marks, to that employed in books printed in the Roman

[101] Brajendranath Bandyopadhyay, *Sambad Patre*, Vol. 1, pp. 52–3.

[102] Brajendranath Bandyopadhyay and Sajanikanta Das, eds., *Rammohan Granthabali* (Calcutta: Bangiya Sahitya Parishad, n.d.), pp. 2–113.

[103] See Dilip Biswas, *Rammohan Samiksha* (Calcutta: Saraswat Library, 2nd. ed. 1994), pp. 177–90.

[104] Rammohan Roy, *Subrahmanya Shastrir Sahit Bichar* (Calcutta: Baptist Mission Press, 1820), p. 2. A copy of the first edition of this book has been preserved by the William Carey Library at Serampore.

character'.[105] The Society was using print in exactly the way that best suited it, that is, changing the content of a particular practice by altering its form. In a letter to Marshman, one Captain Irving explained how useful it would be to approximate the printed characters as much as possible to the writing of the manuscript. He argued that it would present the people with a consistency between what they were already familiar with and what was being introduced: 'the curvilinear *matro*' he said, was 'justly considered by the Natives far more beautiful than the rectilinear'. Their taste with regard to elegance in printing and manuscript should, he felt, be readily allowed for. He proposed that both the forms be introduced in the Society's printing. While the curvilinear form, like the manuscript could form the main body of the works, just as the upright Roman did with English texts, the rectilinear form could be used as italics. He capped his proposal with the following rationale that by 'exhibiting to the Natives the spectacle of advantageous innovation continually introduced', the Society could shake 'their inordinate attachment to ancient custom'.[106] This system of reworking traditional practices was evident in the fundamental principles of the Society. Appalled though they were at the nature and contents of the Bengali books produced, they nevertheless maintained that it was not desirable to '*supersede* ... the labours of independent authors, editors, and compilers, but rather to *direct* them'. They preferred to render their interposition as 'gratuitous *middlemen*' who would only provide 'salutary guidance' to the native publishers.[107]

The technology of print thus found the required compatibility with the idea of print as a *devise* for civilizing. More than just the ideology that print helped to generate, the means of its production via the technology was duly emphasized. Principally, the permanency of the printer's ink was taken for a primary wonder that had the power to immortalize all literature and knowledge. We find a corroboration of this position in the didactic and pedagogic texts of our period. Valmiki, claimed one, should express gratitude to print, since for the first time it had saved him from literary

---

[105] *The First Report of the Proceedings of the Calcutta School Book Society, Read at the Annual General Meeting of the Subscribers, held at the Town Hall of Calcutta, July 4, 1818* (Calcutta, 1818), pp. 2–3.

[106] *The Second Report of the Proceedings of the School Book Society, Second Year, 1818–1819* (Calcutta, 1819), pp. 52–3.

[107] Ibid., p. 41.

extinction.[108] Printing was the only technology of the time that was specifically connected with the abstraction of an idea. It dealt in them, altered them, and produced them. In that regard, its concreteness in the garb of its permanence and indelibility was like the material traces of its abstractive possibilities. Hence, not only were the ideas within the printed book regarded as important, the mechanics of the reinscription of those ideas were also considered equally significant.

The Location of Print

The two seminal works on early Bengali print by Graham Shaw and D.E. Rhodes do not mention any Bengali printer in their checklist of printers and publishers before 1800.[109] According to contemporary sources, Gangakishor Bhattacharya's *Annadamangal* (1816), printed at the European press of Ferris and Co., was the first Bengali book with a Bengali publisher.[110] The presses before 1800 were quite naturally located around the residential and commercial quarters of the European community which were concentrated in and around Tank Square (modern Dalhousie Square).[111] These presses according to the subject analysis of Shaw, printed almanacs and calendars, lists, registers, and directories of civil/military personnel, government publications in English, Persian, Bengali, and Hindustani, periodicals like the *Asiatick Miscellany*, the *Asiatick Researches*, and others.[112]

---

[108] Gopalchandra Bandyopadhyay, *Hitashiksha*, Part 4 (Calcutta: Hitaishi Press, 1869), pp. 65–7. Also see for a similar viewpoint, Maheshchandra Bandyopadhyay, *Anubadsar* (Calcutta: n.p., 1864), pp. 51–2.

[109] See Graham Shaw, *Printing in Calcutta to 1800-a description and Checklist of printing in late 18th. Century Calcutta* (London: Bibliographical Society, 1981), p. 10; and Dennis E. Rhodes, *The Spread of Printing, Eastern Hemisphere India, Pakistan, Ceylon, Burma and Thailand* (Amsterdam: A.L. van Gendt, 1969), p. 31.

[110] The *Friend of India* in 1820 wrote, 'The first Hindu who established a press in Calcutta was Babooram, a native of Hindoosthan .... He was followed by Gangakishor formerly employed at the Serampore Press', *Friend of India*, Quarterly Series, No. I, 1820. The *Samachar Darpan* (30 January, 1830) also confirms Gangakishor as the first Bengali publisher, and the *Annadamangal* as the first book to be printed for sale. Quoted in Bandyopadhyay, *Sambad Patre*, Vol. 1, p. 85.

[111] See P. Thankappan Nair, *A History of the Calcutta Press: The Beginnings* (Calcutta: Firma KLM, 1987), pp. 215–16.

[112] Shaw, *Printing in Calcutta to 1800*, p. 4.

Their location around the administrative and commercial centres of town, was thus in accord with their publications. After 1800 and the beginning of Bengali enterprise in this field, Bengali printing moved further northwards, around Bowbazar and Chitpore Road, the residential quarters of Babu Calcutta.

The three most detailed sources that serve as a point of departure for any discussion on print from our period are the catalogues compiled by James Long, apparently prompted by his own intellectual curiosity. The first, *Granthabali, An Alphabetical List of Works Published in Bengali*, was published in 1852; it contained a total of 1,084 titles, arranged alphabetically, but classified according to subjects. It was incomplete, in the sense, that it only had the titles of the books, and did not mention their authors or publishers.[113] In 1855, he produced *A Descriptive Catalogue of Bengali Works*, a more detailed version of his earlier effort. This contained 'a classified list of Fourteen Hundred Bengali Books and Pamphlets which have issued from the press during the last sixty years with occasional notices of the Subjects, the prices and where printed'.[114] In 1859, Long prepared his third and final catalogue as a set of *Returns Related to Publication in the Bengali Language, in 1857, To Which is Added, A List of the Native Presses with the Books printed at each, their Prices and Character, with a Notice of the Past Condition and Future prospects of the Vernacular Press of Bengal and the Statistics of the Bombay and Madras Vernacular Presses*.[115] Evidence from these three reports and other contemporary sources show the Bengali press to be a burgeoning enterprise from 1852, at least statistically speaking. According to the last estimation by Long, the number of printed books for sale was 3,03,275 in 1853, and 6,00,000 in 1857, despite the latter being the year of the Mutiny.[116] Taking into account the relevant sociological data, that these books were not always read, but also 'listened to', Long allowed each book an average of ten 'hearers' and/or readers, which would mean that there was an impressive two million book reading/listening public.[117]

[113] Reprinted in Jatindramohan Bhattacharya, ed., *Bangla Mudrita Granther Talika, Vol. 1, 1743–1852* (Calcutta: A. Mukherjee, 1990), pp. 1–14.

[114] See Preface to James Long, *A Descriptive Catalogue of Bengali Works* (Calcutta: Sanders, Cones, 1855).

[115] Ibid.

[116] Long, 'Returns', pp. 10–11.

[117] Long, 'Returns', p. 15.

In the excellent subject analysis done recently by Tapti Roy, she notes that in the period between 1844 and 1852, when Long was preparing his first catalogue, scriptures and mythologies (18.26 per cent) still formed the largest category, followed by Christian tracts (11.49 per cent), which had enjoyed in the earlier phase of 1818–43, the highest production. In the older subjects, which had had a formidable presence since the beginning of the century, (for example, scriptures and mythologies, moral tales, classic tales, histories, biographies, dictionaries, and grammars) reprints outnumbered first editions. In biographies, for instance, there were seven reprints but only two new books.[118] Allowing for incomplete data, it can still be assumed then, that till 1852, the tide was still strongly in favour of older subject categories, and that the presses were still producing the reading tastes of the earlier period. Long himself commented on this trend and said that it was only from 1850, that the tide turned in favour of 'useful works'.[119]

Scriptures and mythologies, through which print had originally found its foothold in the beginning of the century, lost its dominance from 1852. Within a period of five years, that is, in 1857, the category that Long broadly named as 'Educational' not only had the largest average copies per title (3,158.70, compared to only 1,1131.17 of 'Mythology and Hinduism'), but was also the second largest category in the list.[120] The quantitative study conducted by Jatindramohan Bhattacharya shows that between 1853 and 1867, books on social sciences, natural sciences, technology, history and geography, and language formed 35 per cent of all the books, excluding 'original compositions' which under the head of literature formed 30 per cent of the total.[121] We have noted earlier that Chitpur Road with its presses on either side, was the main artery of Bengali print. But Battala did not participate at all in the publication of the new genre of the so-called 'educational' books. In the 1857 Returns of Long, among the forty-six presses that he listed, twenty-five of them were established before 1852, and most of them were located in the complex of Battala. In 1857, the earlier category of 'Mythology and Hinduism', still formed nearly 100 per cent of their

---

[118] Tapti Roy, 'Disciplining the Printed Text', pp. 39–41.

[119] Long, 'Returns', p. VII.

[120] Roy, 'Disciplining the Printed Text', pp. 41–3.

[121] See the pie-graph in the appendix to Jatindramohan Bhattacharya, *Mudrita Bangla Granther Panji*.

publications. Where, then, were the new books on educational subjects being printed?

The Bangla Press, in 1857, was one that solely catered to the new genre. Though located in Battala, it was marked by its impressive publication list, which included, Dwarkanath Vidyabhushan's *Greece Itihas*, Kshetramohan Dutta's *Dharapat*, and Gopalchandra Bose's *Bhugol Sutra*. The other presses that were commissioning similar books, were the Baptist Mission Press, Bishop's College Press, Satyarnab Press, Sucharu Press, the Vidyaratna Press (1856), and of course Vidyasagar's Sanskrit Press, and the Bramho Samaj's Tattobodhini Press.[122] From Long's records it appears that that the presses almost had a streamlined division of printing material. Categories were almost never confused except in the case of well known publishers, who could afford to 'switch' genres without being typed. The Anglo Indian Union Press (1844) for instance, was one of the presses of Battala, whose publications in 1857 were, the Ramayan in its various parts, *Annadamangal*, Mahabharat, *Mahinma Stab*, or praises of Shiva, and various 'erotic' titles such as *Adiras*, *Rasamanjari*, *Prem Natak*, and others. Similarly the Kamalalaya Press (1848) at 265 Chitpur Road had printed the *Chandi* by Kabikankan, two parts of the Mahabharat, and the *Shishubodhak*, which according to a terse comment by Long, 'taught lies'.[123] In sharp contrast, the Satyarnab Press or the Vidyaratna Press was printing Long's own *Dhatumala*, the *Education Gazette*, the *Krishi Sangraha* or the organ of the Agri-Horticultural Society, the books of the Vernacular Literature Society, and books like Shyamacharan Sarkar's *Byakaran*, which had earned the approval of being 'the fullest grammar yet published in Bengali'.[124] Needless to say, that the Tattobodhini Press managed by the Brahmos, and the Sanskrit Press under Vidyasagar and Madanmohan Tarkalankar, had scrupulously 'tasteful' publications.

It is perhaps noteworthy that the Hindu College was originally located on Garanhata Street in Chitpur. In 1825, it was shifted to Pataldanga and the Sanskrit College was set up next to it in 1826. The area from then onwards was called College Square and College Street, the principal centre

---

[122] Long, 'Returns', pp. 1–62.

[123] Ibid., pp. 2–3, 28–9.

[124] Ibid., pp. 44–5, 55–8.

of education and scholarship from the middle of the century.[125] The School
Book Society in 1826 opened an outlet for books next to the Hindu College
and Vidyasagar's Sanskrit Press Depository was established there in 1847.[126]
Before this the only other private press in this area was Iswarchandra Bose's
Stanhope Press, established in 1840, which had a reputation for printing
books of a superior quality.[127] Most of Michael Madhusudan Dutta's works
were published here, along with journals such as the *Bamabodhini Patrika*.
The location as well as the type of books printed in these presses, marked
the emergence of specialized hierarchies among the printers of Bengali books.
It also marked the spatialization of print in a particular way, such that the
'better' presses were discerned by their proximity to educational institutions.

There were certain definitive indices that classified the presses of this
era. A press which dealt mainly in educational works would in no instance
print certain kinds of books, like the ones in Mochalmani Bengali. In 1857,
the presses that were printing such books fell squarely in the 'inferior'
category, their lists comprising the various parts of the two epics, Vaishnav
hagiography, or the 'erotic'. Neither the Rozario Press which had to its
credit Derozio's poems and the first edition of Pearychand Mitra's *Alaler
Gharer Dulal*, nor the afore-mentioned Stanhope Press ever included even
one copy of any work in Mochalmani Bengali. The constitutive split between
presses producing 'good' and 'bad' literature, and their physical positioning
in the respectable and non-respectable areas of town, was further deepened
by yet another criterion of selectivity, the quality of production. By 1865,
Bengali books were actually priced higher than English ones.[128] But Battala,
even in this phase, continued to uniformly produce books of an inferior
quality on inexpensive paper with not much attention to spelling or printing
errors. They were truly 'cheap books'.

[125] There were in the early part of the century a number of important schools in the
Chitpur area. From Garanhata the Hindu College was shifted to the nearby Jorasanko,
while its earlier building was used for the Oriental Seminary. The St. Paul's School,
established in 1821, was also in this area. For details on individual institutions see Kamal
Choudhury, *Kalkatar Tinsho Bacharer Itihas: Sanskriti Kendra* (Calcutta: Pratibhash,
1990), pp. 106–15, 174–5.

[126] See Gopalchandra Roy 'Bangla Baier Byabsa', pp. 351–63.

[127] Sukumar Sen, 'Battalar Bai', p. 272–3.

[128] Letter No. 3790, from S.C. Bayley, Junior Secretary to the Government of
Bengal, to The Secretary to the Government of India, *General Proceedings*, 1865, No. 4.

This ideology of printing in Battala was actively determined by two major considerations. First, the reading public of Battala had by this time been more or less determined. There is little actual historical evidence to prove this in exactitude, and we can only proceed from derivation. In Long's 'Returns' the presses that he listed to be in the Battala area, were not old presses, that is, they were not presses that had continuity with Battala in the earlier part of the century. The earliest among them—the Shastra Prakash Press—was established in 1835, and the latest date was that of the Bengal Superior Press in 1858. Thus it would seem that there was a spurt in the number of presses at Battala from the 1830s. We have shown earlier how from the 1840s onwards, after the Hindu College had been shifted to College Street, the concentration of printing and publishing come to be centred around it. But here was an anomalous trend of reoccupying the older network, and also of printing in the older manner. The reason for this lay in the official policy on education, which created in the wake of Bentinck's Resolution of 1835, a new social promise for English education. The new augmentation of Bengali presses at Battala was the apotheosis of the schism between the high learning of the new middle class and the more general popular reading by the kerani. These presses were set up expressly to meet the needs of that class which had not been 'chosen' by the Social Darwinism of the 'Downward Filitration' project. Hence Battala from this period was to become the bearer of the 'low' tradition, printing not only purely Bengali books but also purely 'non modern' versions of knowledge such as mythologies and the scriptures.

The other reason for Battala's inferior quality of book production was intimately connected to the first. The printers from 1835 onwards were confronted with an entirely new set of ideological imperatives of print. Not only had the constitutives of knowledge changed with the primacy of English education, but so had print's location in that epistemology. The contents of a book was now as important as its production, including the quality paper it was printed on, the clarity of the printed characters, the arrangement of words on a page, and so on. Efficient printing was not only synonymous with 'good literature', but actually *produced* it.[129] Thus, when it came to the

---

[129] Vidyasagar's *Rijupath* (1857), was a collection of tales from the *Panchatantra*, and the Mahabharat in Sanskrit. In the Bengali Preface he noted that the original two texts had been much maimed by the carelessness of the copyists, so he was attempting to correct the situation through decent and clear printing and the omission of obscene passages, Prafulla Kumar Patra, ed., *Vidyasagar Rachanabali*, p. 661.

ownership of presses, the middle decades saw publishers from a very different class background than the previous eras.

Prananath Dutta (1840–88), the owner of the Sucharu Press, which had earned a name for good printing, was a scion of the famous Duttas of Hatkhola. Prananath himself had at least three dramatic publications to his name *Praneswar Natak* (1863), *Premadhini Natak* (1866), *Sanjukta Swayambar Natak* (1867)), besides being the editor of *Basantak* (1874), one of the most popular satirical magazines of the time. He and his brother Girindrakumar Dutta also prepared the illustrations for the journal. *Basantak*, as could be expected, came down strongly on the errant printers of Battala. The poets Valmiki, Krittibas, and Kasiram confided to *Basantak* at a séance: 'It is not our fault ... what you see of us are just the disjointed limbs and headless torsos of the of the original. The publishers have done this to us, if some of our bones had been spared by the copyists, the imbeciles at Battala have pulverized even those'.[130] The Sanskrita Press and the Tattobodhini Press we know had thorough supervision from the leading intellectuals of that era. Bankim had his own press at Kathaltala, from where his *Krishnakanter Will*, was first published.[131] Upendrakishor Roychoudhury, scion of another talented family, introduced the half-tone picture. The U. Roy block was consequently used in all the major contemporary journals, like the *Mukul, Pradip*, the *Modern Review*, and the *Prabasi*.[132] Print's insistent association with education in a marginal sense, and knowledge in a broader perspective, had shifted the priorities of publishing. The educated reader would now read *Annadamangal* not for what it was worth, but because it had been reinscribed by Vidyasagar.

How far were the books produced in Battala or the educational books circulated? According to Long, the books printed in Calcutta had their chief circulation within Calcutta and in a radius of twenty miles around it, which would include the older centres of print along the river like, Serampore, Chinsurah, Halishahar, and Burdwan.[133] But what about the

[130] Quoted in Debipada Bhattacharya, 'Bangla Samayikpatra', in Chittaranjan Bandyopadhyay, ed., *Dui Shataker*, p. 292.

[131] See Haraprasad Shastri, 'Bankimchandra Kathalparaye', in *Rachanasangraha*, pp. 22–3.

[132] Kedarnath Chattopadhyay, 'Upendrakishor: Satabarshik Sraddhanjali', *Viswabharati Patrika* (Kartik–Poush, 1963), pp. 108–19.

[133] Letter to G.F. Cockburn, Chief Magistrate of Calcutta, dated 24 June 1844, in the General Proceedings, No. 26, February, 1855.

rest of Bengal? Almost twenty years earlier Adam had reported from the district of Rajshahi a dismal picture regarding the accessibility of print in that district. In his survey he had come across only two printed books—a missionary tract and an almanac, the latter having been procured from Calcutta by an 'official or wealthy native'.[134] In his 'Returns' Long did not mention the state of things in these parts of the country, so in 1864, Rev. John Robinson, the Bengali translator to the government, was given the undertaking of preparing another catalogue (from 1855–64) which would encompass, besides all the presses in Calcutta, those in the 'interior', including Dacca and Chittagong in the south-east, and Monghyr, Patna, Cuttack, and other districts of the north-west.

Robinson's report after touring the Presidency was remarkable in its disparity. He ascertained that the number of presses in the town of Calcutta was eighty-three, and in the rest province, only twenty-nine. Of these, most were clustered within the twenty miles circle mentioned by Long, in Serampore, Uttarpara, and Burdwan.[135] The presses at Cuttack, Muzzafarpore, Midnapore, and Shibsagar in Assam, were run by missionaries and so were not included within the list of Bengali printers. In Purneah, in Bihar, there was just one press, owned by the local zamindar, which only printed forms for use in the zamindar's estate. There were two at Patna, which printed Urdu, Persian, and Arabic tracts, and none at all in Bogurah, Dinajpur, Maldah, Pabna, or Rajshahi. There were four presses in Burdwan, all owned by the Rajah of Burdwan, Mahatab Chandra Bahadur. Only in Dacca, did Robinson find three private presses which were worth mentioning.[136]

---

[134] Long, ed., *Adam's Report*, p. 97.

[135] Letter from J. Wenger, officiating Bengali translator to the government, to S.C. Bayley, junior secretary to the Government of Bengal, General Proceedings, No. 46, April 1865. A not so publicized fact about the famous Serampore Press was that, it was established under the auspices of the Danish Government in 1800, Lord Wellesley having positively refused to allow the establishment of a press beyond the limits of Calcutta. See 'Letter No. 169, dated 14 July 1874, From C.T. Buckland, Commissioner of the Burdwan Division, to The Officiating Secretary to the Government of Bengal, General Department', in *Bengal, Miscellaneous Public Documents 1843–87* in the British Library Collection.

[136] See General Proceedings, January 1864, No. 66; March 1865, No. 72; and June 1865, No. 4.

The relationship of Calcutta to its neighbours was primarily determined by the fact that the city was the only centre for higher education for a considerable period of time. Its neighbourhood or mofussil did not possess the institutional apparatus to generate and back a local literati. The traditional élite in the mofussil towns, as we noted earlier, sent their children away to study in Calcutta. In 1873, the district reporter of Hooghly, Mr Pellow mentioned in connection with the dearth of local newspapers in the district that 'the natives who might be expected to support such a paper probably support some Calcutta paper subservient to their interests or giving prominence to their views', a fact that in the long run did away with the need to develop any initiative on the part of the district altogether.[137] The book readers and subscribers to newspapers in these regions consisted of the English-educated class who were generally employed in the courts or government offices of the district.[138] Their professional status bound them necessarily to large towns within the districts, and the Reports note them to be very 'occasional visitors to their homes'.[139] The distance from Calcutta significantly affected the educational system and consequently the production of the press in the district towns.[140] Even in the case of textbooks, the districts were dependent on the metropolis, in the form of either the depositories of the School Book Society or the Government Book Agency.[141]

[137] General Proceedings, File No. 1-85/89, September, 1873.

[138] Most district reports compiled by the colonial state attest this phenomenon, see the Annual General Report of Dacca Division in General Proceedings, November 1874, Nos 32–4; and General Report on the Rajshahye Division for 1873–4 in General Proceedings, September 1873, Nos 72–7; and Annual General Report of the Chittagong Division in General Proceedings, November 1874, Nos 23–8.

[139] General Proceedings, File No. 1-85/89, September, 1873.

[140] The report of the Chittagong Division makes this connection quite clearly: 'In the matter of secondary and higher education for which there is necessarily less demand or requirement in these districts, the returns are unfavourable when compared with those of other districts situated nearer Calcutta', General Proceedings, November 1874, Nos 23–8.

[141] The government book agents in the districts were responsible for the supply of textbooks to the government or aided schools. A certain monthly credit was allowed to each school (or college as the case may be) and each institution indented for its required number of books. These books were supplied either from agency stores, or more generally from the shops in Calcutta, and their prices were debited against the schools. See Letter No. 943, from Gordon Young, Director of Public Instruction, to W. Grey, Secretary to the Government of Bengal, General Proceedings, July 1855, No. 123.

The books that the mofussil did publish, were not the progenitors of any alternative disciplines, but as we saw earlier, fell well within the boundaries of the educational discourse. Abhaycharan Sen's *Abidyar Das Ain* (1853) published from Dacca was popular in the schools of the Dacca and Mymensingh region.[142] Others like Umesh Chandra Chattopadhyay's *Nitimala* (Serampore, 1856), or Kalimoy Ghatak's *Charitashtak* (Hooghly,1867) were sets of either educational or moral precepts.

The Avenues of Distribution and Sale

In the absence of book shops, till the last decade of the nineteenth century, hawkers, as we have mentioned before, were the most common agents for distribution or sale. In 1857, Long estimated there to be more than 200 hawkers in connection with the Calcutta presses. According to Long, they sold books eight months in a year and were employed in agriculture during the rainy season:

These men may be seen going through the native part of Calcutta and the adjacent towns with a pyramid of books on their head. They buy the books themselves at wholesale price, and often sell them at a distance at double the price which brings them in probably 6 or 8 Rupees monthly, though we know of a man who realizes by book hawking more than 100 Rupees monthly.... The natives find the best advertisement of a Bengali book is a *living agent* who shows *the book itself....*[143]

Long was probably right in his assessment of the hawker being a living symbol of his wares, for the eminent essayist Ramendrasundar Trivedi, when young, had so integrated the book with the bookseller, that for a considerable part of his childhood he was under the impression that the hawker who sold the *Bornoporichoy*, and other educational works in his village was Vidyasagar the author of those books himself.[144] The Vernacular Literature Committee had in their employment a female hawker who had full entry into the *andarmahals*, for the sale of their works.[145] The Battala publishers

---

[142] See Srinath Chanda, *Bramho Samaje Challish Bachar* (Dacca: Bharat Mahila Press, 1913), p. 14.

[143] Ibid., p. 14.

[144] Ramendrasundar Trivedi, 'Charit Katha' in Brajendranath Bandyopadhyay and Sajanikanta Das, eds., *Ramendra Rachanabali* (Calcutta: Bangiya Sahitya Parishad, 1949), p. 195.

[145] *Report of the Transactions of the Vernacular Literature Society From July 1st 1858 to December 31st. 1859* (Calcutta, 1860), p. 6.

went a step further in their hawking enterprises. They would employ very young boys to sell their sensational literature, because they had easy ingress to the female quarters on account of their tender age.[146] There were other more unorthodox channels of dissemination. Prasannamayi Devi, sister to Asutosh and Pramatha Chaudhuri, noted in her autobiography incidents of her having copied out entire issues of the *Bangadarshan* and posted it to relatives in villages who did not have access to the journal.[147] The Postal Department was, in fact, an important distributive channel for print. After the change in the nature and scope of print from 1850, the bhadralok, realizing its potential, demanded a lower and uniform postage rate to facilitate the distribution of their journals and newspapers to their subscribers. They were no doubt inspired by the Penny Postage legislation passed in England, at the initiative of Sir Rowland Hill in 1840. They submitted their demands in a memorial to the government in 1850, and accordingly influenced Lord Dalhousie's decision to pass a new law on postage in 1853, by which rates were standardized and regulated, and magazines and newspapers received the special privilege of lower charges.[148]

The general practice of the state in supplying books to the vernacular schools was to sell the books through the book agencies which had been established throughout the Presidency. A certain monthly credit account was allowed to every school and college, which then indented their requirements. The books were supplied by the book agent either from the agency stores or more generally from shops in Calcutta, their prices being debited in account against the respective institution. The price of each of the books as were sold by the school to its pupils or others was remitted from time to time by drafts, the amounts of which were then again credited in the account current of the school and could be thus drawn against by an indent.[149] Though the procedure was very complicated, and there were frequent irregularities in the indents that the schools made out, the book agencies when first established, had a busy trade in the mofussil. The School Book Society, previously the only source of books in the interior, admitted in 1848 that the sales at its depositories were suffering due to the

---

[146] *Report on the Native Papers for the Week Ending 17th. August 1889*, p. 743.

[147] Prasannamayi Devi, *Purba Katha*, p. 118.

[148] Kedarnath Majumdar, *Bangla Samayik Sahitya* (Mymensingh: Narendranath Majumdar, 1917), pp. 188–90.

[149] Letter No. 943, from Gordon Young to W. Grey, General Proceedings, July 1855, No. 123.

establishment of the government book agency.[150] However, this system did not ultimately prosper, partly due to the large number of books that the schools indented and could not ultimately pay for, and partly due to the supply exceeding the demand, particularly in the mofussil towns.[151] So in 1855, the government formally declared the abolition of the book agency and transferred its duties to the School Book Society.[152] To meet this new situation the Society opened six new depositories at Balasore, Bankura, Barasat, Burdwan, Howrah, and Uttarpara.[153]

The School Book Society, however, had its own problems. Initially, when the Bengali press was still in its infancy, the Society had attempted to engage native booksellers to dispose of its works on commission, for they felt it would 'introduce the Society's works into circles to which they would otherwise be debarred all access'.[154] They found some amount of success in the project, and some dealers applied to the depositories for a 2 anna discount on the cost price.[155] As the Bengali press gained in strength, and particularly after the advent of the printers at Battala in the arena of print, the most popular works of the Society, began to be pirated indiscriminately, complete with the Society's imprimatur C.S.B.S. on the title page. The printers at Battala, as we have noted were known for their inexpensive publications, and they simply reprinted on cheap paper the Society's books and maintained their market.[156] The Bengali printers, in fact, forced the Society to reduce

[150] *Fourteenth Report of the Proceedings of the School Book Society, 28th. to 30th. Year, 1845–1847* (Calcutta, 1848), p. 15.

[151] There were repeated complaints from the book agent against the collectorates for having asked for more books without having cleared the previous outstanding balances. The school and college libraries had to sell off books from their stocks to meet the amounts. See General Education Proceedings, July 1850, Nos 16–24. Also for the problem of unsaleable books, see General Education Proceedings, March 1850, No. 20, and October 1851, No. 15.

[152] Letter No. 278 from W. Grey to the Director of Public Instructions, General Proceedings, July 1855, No. 126.

[153] *The Eighteenth Report of the Proceedings of the School Book Society, 38th. Year, 1855* (Calcutta, 1856), pp. 9–13.

[154] *The Sixth Report of the Proceedings of the School Book Society, 6th. and 7th. Year, 1824–1825* (Calcutta, 1825), p. 16.

[155] *The Seventh Report of the Proceedings of the School Book Society, 8th. and 9th. Year, 1826–1827* (Calcutta, 1828), pp. 14–15.

[156] *The Seventeenth Report of the Proceedings of the School Book Society, 36th. and 37th. Years, 1853–1854* (Calcutta, 1855), p. 15.

its prices in order to make it less profitable for the printers at Battala to print pirated versions.[157] The Society also had to take into account the competition from the missionaries, who consistently sold their own publications at prices lower than both the government and the Society.[158] But if the Bengali printers were forcing a lowering of prices, a very different demand was being made upon the Society's policies by the European printers. In 1867, J.B. Knight, on behalf of the Calcutta Trades Association, submitted a memorial to the Governor-General demanding either the abolition of the government grant to the Society, or restrictions upon the Society's dealings in imports of books from England. The Association claimed that government patronage put the Society in an advantageous position in comparison with the general trader 'who relying upon the demand which he has hitherto been prepared and accustomed to meet, now finds himself forestalled and superseded by the operations of a society, carried on not only under no risk, but with positive aid from the public purse, an aid which is applied to a reduction of price below legitimate trading'.[159] In defence the Society resorted to the powerful motif of its civilizational functions. 'The correct view to be taken of the Society' was not it argued, as one of a rival establishment to any bookselling firm, but as 'a voluntary public organization of the educated members of the various classes of the community'. It was not motivated by 'even the smallest pecuniary profit'. Due to the fact that native authors could not 'afford to place his books within the reach of the people in remote districts', or to dispose of them 'at prices within the means of the middle and lower classes', free enterprise of publishers and booksellers of Calcutta, it argued, could not yet replace the Society in this respect.[160]

The state found the logic of this argument acceptable and the Society's rights were not interfered with. It was the first to open a formal book shop for Bengali books at College Square. Till that time Bengali books were sold within the premises of the presses where they had been printed, or at a venue, usually a private home, or the authors' work place, which was advertised at the back of the text, as a place where the book could be

---

[157] Ibid.

[158] General Education Proceedings, August 1850, Nos 21–2.

[159] Letter from J. Lindley, Secretary to the Calcutta Trader's Association, to the Secretary to the Government of Bengal, General Proceedings, November 1867, No. 16.

[160] Ibid.

obtained.[161] English books, as one contemporary source noted, were sold mostly at the China Bazar: 'If the visitor wishes to have a non-scientific work recently published in London and already popular, he is certain of obtaining it in the new or old China Bazar'.[162]

The exodus of book shops and presses to College Street, we have noted, began with the Sanskrit Press Depository and the Stanhope Press. The real concentration of booksellers in this area began in the last two decades of the nineteenth century. The proprietor of the famous Bengal Medical Library, Gurudas Chattopadhyay, started his career as a help in the Hindu Hostel. From there he began his business of selling books to students and then moved on to open a shop, first at Bow Bazar in 1867, and then in front of the Medical College in 1885. Gurudas was the publisher of the acclaimed *Sipahi Judhdher Itihas* by Rajanikanta Gupta, and several writers, including Bankim, depended on his funds for printing their works.

The book had created as its appurtenant an educational grid so firmly entrenched in the perceptual sphere of the late nineteenth century, that the educated middle class covered all aspects of printing, publishing, and selling of 'good' literature. Sarat Chandra Lahiri, son of the famous Ramtanu Lahiri, opened his shop on College Street in 1883. Rajkrishna Roy (1814–94), who had even before Michael Madhusudan Dutt, experimented with the blank verse in Bengali poetry, had his book shop at Thanthania in 1881.[163] By the end of our period of study, College Street and its adjacent areas formed the indisputable locus of the educational ideology of print. Print had united spatially and contextually the ideological determinations of the bhadralok.

---

[161] For instance, Chandramohan Chattopadhyay's *Shishuranjan* (1868), printed at the Stanhope Press, listed its places of availability as the Press itself, the Sanskrit Press Depository, China Bazar, and the Bali Anglo-Vernacular School. Similarly the back over of *Satyabati Natak* (1875) advertised the Pataldanga Canning Library as a place where it could be bought.

[162] Quoted in Shyamal Chakrabarti, *Chapa Harafer Hat* (Calcutta: Sahitya Sadan, 1970), p. 32.

[163] Brajendranath Bandyopadhyay and Sajanikanta Das, eds, *Sahitya Sadhak Charitmala: Rajkrishna Roy* (Calcutta: Bangiya Sahitya Parishad, 1948), p. 16.

4

Education and its Necessary Virtues

Nagare anek kele Hindur kalej
gelo tar Hindu nam ghuchiache tej
kaj nai niye ar English knowledge
Kalejer nam holo khichuri Kalej [1]

(Hindu's College: the city's familiar site
Loses its Hindu name loses its might
What need further of English knowledge
The college is renamed Gumbo College)

So far in our discussion the bhadralok has been mainly engaged in what
Therborn has called 'ideological mobilization'. He defines it as the setting
of a common agenda by summing up the 'dominant aspect or aspects of
the crisis' (in this particular case the reduced glory of India as compared to
Europe or Britain), identifying the 'crucial target' (British rule in varying
forms such as English education, Westernization, and loss of traditional
values) and 'defining what is possible and how it should be achieved'.[2] The
last criterion of the definition is beyond the scope of this work. The concept
of ideological mobilization, however, brings to the fore the question of how
any ideology or ideologies are sustained in a social formation. Any belief
has to have some material basis in order for it to survive. No amount of
ruling class coercion or general social persuasion could, for example, make
a twelfth-century peasant believe in the nuclear family. Similarly, the ideas
that constituted what a bhadralok must be, and what was to be his
appropriate mode of social conduct, had to have certain concrete material

---

[1] The poet Iswarchandra Gupta registering his poetic protest at the renaming of
Hindu College to Presidency College.

[2] Göran Therborn, *The Ideology of Power*, p. 116.

structures to both survive and also to rally others to such a body of ideas. The investigation of such structures is, in the main, the subject of this chapter.

We have already seen that the rhetoric of the new middle class about education and culture attempted to separate these issues from material wealth. This had an important implication. In a situation where social life was determined by market forces, no matter how weak (underdeveloped capitalism, whatever its features may be, is *not* feudalism), the negation of wealth makes authority appear divorced from wealth. Chances of success in these spheres then appear to be solely dependent on individual merit or failing. In other words, an individual's literary and/or educational achievements are assumed to be purely based on inner talents or steadfast perseverance, as the case maybe. This attitude is very much in keeping with modern bourgeois-democratic notions of equal 'citizenship' where it is widely believed that capitalism creates equal opportunities and makes social boundaries fluid. Disparities of social standing are only explicable in terms of individual 'lacks' in effort, intelligence, or hard work, as traditional inequalities of wealth, class, or property are irrelevant.[3]

There is, however, considerable room for doubt about such enthusiastic interpretations. In the course of this chapter we shall see how the changing nature of social mobility (there is no doubt that under colonialism there was greater social mobility than before) was in actuality very much dependent on the individual's class position, and how the education system itself was geared to it. Career opportunities became more predictable as they came to depend on formalized scholastic achievement. The chapter focuses on the following three problems: first, the generalization of educational opportunities by colonialism in comparison to the pre-colonial order; second, the effect this had on social classes, and third, the various class-specific cultural attributes which came to be connected with education and which concealed the actual relationship between classes and formal and informal educational networks.

Yielding Place to the New

In the pre-colonial social order, the investment in education was fairly class specific. The landed class of the zamindars or local princes allocated

---

[3] The notion of the 'American dream' is a classic example.

rent-free land grants to Brahmins who maintained tols or *chatuspathis* from the income of such land. According to the Brahmanical tradition, education was supposed to be imparted free of cost by the guru to his pupil. The student was to reside with the teacher in the *gurukul*, until his education was completed, during which time he served the guru in the performance of various household duties, including cattle herding. This was, of course, the classicized tradition of the scriptures, and there is evidence to suggest that it was not followed in the monetized economy of the seventeenth–eighteenth century by non-Brahmanical traditions of education. Poromesh Acharya's study shows pathshalas, the elementary schools for the masses, to have been almost entirely supported by fees and occasional gifts from villagers.[4] One of the reasons for this was probably because such institutions did not find much favour with the nobility, who were more partial in their grants to the institutions of Sanskrit learning which generally catered to Brahmin students only. Beside the land lease and frequent help from their noble patrons, these institutions also collected dues from the local people during such social ceremonies as weddings or funerals.[5]

One of the first detailed contemporary histories of education in the nineteenth century was complied by the Bramho reformer Upendranath Mukhopadhyay. In his account, he marked out the geographical limits of the centres of education before English rule to be between Barahanagar and Nabadwip on either sides of the Bhagirathi river. He claimed that the number of tols, chatushpathis, Brahmin teachers, learned Vaishnavs, and litterateurs within this radius of twenty-five *kroshas*, far exceeded the rest in the entire province of Bengal.[6] A list of Brahmin pundits of Bengal was compiled sometime in the nineteenth century. In this list Nabadwip, Kumarhatta, Tribeni, Bansberia, Shantipur, Shalika, Janai, Chatra, and Garalgacha featured as prominent centres of Sanskrit learning.[7] William Ward's history of the Hindus specifies some of the courses that were taught at these institutions. According to him, Nabadwip was famed for its *Nyaya*, *Smriti*, Sanskrit poetics, grammar, and astrology. Calcutta had a total of

---

[4] Poromesh Acharya, 'Indigenous Education', p. 99.

[5] For details, see Panchanan Mandal, ed., *Chithipatre Samajchitra*, Vol. 1 (Calcutta: Vishwabharati, 1968), pp. 225–8.

[6] Upendranath Mukhopadhyay, *Hindujati O Shiksha*, p. 111.

[7] Panchanan Mandal, *Chithipatre* Vol. 1, pp. 225–6.

twenty-eight centres of Sanskrit education, all of which taught the Nyayas and the Smiritis.[8] Besides these centres of formal Sanskrit training, there were pathshalas for the Hindus and *maqtabs* for the Muslims, in almost every village as institutions of primary education. Hindus were not barred from the maqtabs and muslims were not barred from the pathshalas. The munshi or *maulavi* taught at the maqtab, while the pathshala was managed by the guru.[9]

The entire system of education was highly localized and specific. There were five different types of institutions, each marked out for a definite social group: Sanskrit tols for the Hindu upper classes and Brahmins, Arabic madrassas for the upper echelons of Muslim society, pathshalas of secular learning for the poor, and maqtabs for the ordinary Muslims. In addition to these there were Persian schools, for both the Hindu and Muslim élite to learn the language of the court. Acharya has noted how all these 'were separate institutions without any link or relation of any kind between them, each catering to a distinct class or community'.[10]

One of the important things that a Hindu child learned even before he or she began school, were the names of his/her forefathers, including a detailed account of the subdivisions of his/her particular caste and clan. It was important for maintaining the intricacies of the kinship networks, in a familiar world which was at most times bound within the ancestral village.[11] In the first quarter of the century, Rajnarayan Basu began his education with the recitation of the Sanskrit shlokas of Valmiki, the Chanakya shlokas, and a mnemonic recitation of English words with Bengali meanings, like God—*Ishwar*, Lord—*Ishwar*, I—*Ami*, You—*Tumi*, and so on.[12] A child grew up in an atmosphere steeped in the kathkatha and story-telling traditions and picked up the stories of the epics from old punthis preserved in the

[8] William Ward, *A View of the History, Literature and Mythology of the Hindoos*, pp. 588–94.

[9] For details, see M.A. Rahim, *Social and Cultural History of Bengal* (Karachi: Pakistan Historical Society, 1963), pp. 193–203; Kalikinkar Datta, *Studies in the History of the Bengal Subah* (Calcutta, 1935), pp. 1–6; also Benoy Ghosh, *Badshahi Amal* (Calcutta: Aruna Prakashani, 1967), pp. 220–5.

[10] P. Acharya, 'Indigenous Education', p. 98.

[11] Kartikeyachandra Ray, *Jibancharit* (Calcutta: Indian Association Publishing Company, 1956) (Calcutta, reprint 1956), pp. 4–6.

[12] Rajnarayan Basu, *Atmacharit*, p. 11.

family, or from reading sessions held in the neighbourhood. The reading of Persian texts was also fairly common among the middle classes.[13]

The entire mechanism of the pre-colonial education order was challenged by colonialism. Some scholars have portrayed this conflict as the destruction of the rich and complex knowledge system of a 'culturally plural' society by the pragmatic state-oriented approach of colonialism.[14] Once again one has to avoid such romantic notions of pre-coloniality to reach any kind of critical historical judgement about colonialism. The pre-colonial system was a rigid hierarchical structure and thoroughly exclusive in its essential operations. C.A. Bayly has argued that it consisted of several forms of non-pragmatic knowledge.[15] The Brahminical order of education, on the contrary, was highly pragmatic in its social operation. By institutionally debarring lower castes and women from the system, it legitimized through caste the place of the producer and the ruler.

The encounter between the two knowledge systems is best judged by avoiding purely cultural registers. Colonialism introduced a generalized system of education in accordance with capitalist principles. The policy makers were very clear about this. In 1854, the Court of Directors sent a despatch to the Governor-General of India stating this in no uncertain terms:

This knowledge [Western education] will teach the natives of India the marvellous results of the employment of labour and capital, rouse them to emulate us in the development of the vast resource of their country ... confer upon them all the advantages which accompany the healthy increase of wealth and commerce; and at the same time, secure to us a larger and more certain supply of many articles necessary for our manufactures and extensively consumed by all classes of our population.[16]

What colonialism introduced was the *formal principle* that everybody, irrespective of caste or creed, had a right to education. This had two implications. One, it *legally* denied discriminatory practices and thus closed all avenues of social acknowledgement of such practices; second, as a result

[13] Srinath Chanda, *Brahmo Samaje Challish Batsar*, pp. 7–8; also see Girishchandra Sen, *Atma Jibanbrittanta* (Calcutta: Gupta, Mukherjee and Co., 1906), pp. 1–7.

[14] C.A. Bayly, 'Colonial Rule and the "Informational Order" in South Asia' Nigel Crook, ed., *Transmission of Knowledge in South Asia*, pp. 281–2.

[15] Ibid.

[16] Despatch from the Court of Directors of the East India Company to the Governor-General of India, No. 49, 19 July 1854, reprinted in J.A. Richey, *Selections from Education Records*, Part II (Calcutta: Superintendent, Government Printing, 1920), p. 365.

the individual was made solely responsible for his or her failures. Dadabhai
Naoroji fighting for the admission of Indians in the civil service thus argued
that the government should adopt rules as they thought fit to get Indian
candidates to come up to the same level as the English 'whether in
acquirements, *character, physical energy*, or any other particular'. Then if the
Indian failed 'it would be their own fault: *they only ask a fair trial*.[17] The
irony of this expectation points to a fundamental contradiction in
colonialism. While capitalist relations continuously strove to homogenize
the polity under the 'fairness' of a rule of law, the political domination of
colonialism denied this to classes who otherwise would have been its
beneficiaries. In 1858, for example, Pearychand Mitra's brother, Kissorychand
Mitra, was dismissed from his job as native magistrate. The reporting of
this incident in the native and European press points to the depth of feeling
among the new middle class about such issues. The *Friend of India* admitted
that Mitra was 'by no means a bad specimen of an educated native', coming
as he did from an 'enlightened' family. What he lacked, however, was 'a
moral sense', something which 'neither knowledge, nor Milton, nor high
position' had managed to give him.[18] The *Hindoo Patriot* responded sharply
to this condescending attitude. It pointed out that it was a 'notorious fact'
how the 'ministerial classes of native officials are dismissed, fined and
suspended from office at the whim and pleasure of their immediate superior'.
However, it concurred that there was no complaint regarding 'the conduct
of native officials being tested by a stricter standard of official morality
than is applied to the conduct of European officials'.[19]

Let us go back to our original point about homogenization. The vast
network of educational institutions set up by the colonial state, following a
regularized and fixed syllabus, was of course the most palpable instance of
this process. The effects, however, were not merely limited to the starting of
formal institutions. The Sanskrit College, whose system of knowledge was
slightly incongruous to this process, had to effect some significant changes

[17] Lecture read before the East India Association on 17 April 1868; Dadabhai
Naoroji, *Admission of Educated Natives into the Indian Civil Service* (London: Macmillan
and Co., 1868), p. 4.

[18] *Friend of India*, 4 November 1858, reprinted in Benoy Ghosh, ed., *Selections
from English Periodicals of Nineteenth Century Bengal*, Vol. 5, pp. 309–10.

[19] *Hindoo Patriot*, 11 November 1858, reprinted in Ghosh, *Selections*, Volume 5,
pp. 91–5.

in its running to fit the current atmosphere. Following the indigenous scale of time, the College enjoyed a holiday twice every fortnight on the lunar days of Ashtami and Pratipad and not on Sundays as in other Government institutions.[20] Vidyasagar as Assistant Secretary to the College proposed in 1851 that 'every Sunday be substituted' in place of the lunar calendar. The proposal was accepted.[21] Vidyasagar also regularized the manuscript collection of the College by printing them, and, from the request lists for books that he made out for the government to supply, it is clear that the students read Locke, Newton, Dryden, Chaucer, and even Robert Burns, as supplements to their Sanskrit training.[22]

The contestation between the old and new methods of learning was quite stark. As early as in 1835, the year that marked the victory for the Anglicists in policy making, a letter in *Friend of India* remarked on the extent to which the spread of British rule had succeeded in 'closing the native seminaries [...] either by the political extinction of their patrons, or by the absorption of their resources'.[23] With the shift of the middle class to English education and the actual disintegration of the landed class as patrons, the traditional institutions of learning were facing the threat of extinction. We have already seen the state of decline faced by the traditional rural literati. According to a petition filed by pundits from Nadia in 1863, they had been reduced to begging for alms to support themselves and their pupils.[24]

An interesting contrast between the old and new orders was recounted in a poem about the education of a young zamindar in the 1870s. In 1855 the government had established a Court of Wards for the education of young zamindars who were still minors. Instituted on Maniktala Road in Calcutta, this establishment housed young boys from various parts of Bengal, and the government was responsible for supervising their education. The renowned scholar, Rajendralal Mitra, was made the director to this

[20] *Samachar Darpan*, 22 January 1825, reprinted in Brajendranath Bandyopadhyay, ed., *Sambad Patre Sekaler Katha*, Vol. 1, p. 25.

[21] See Arabinda Guha, ed., *Unpublished Letters*, p. 11.

[22] Ibid., pp. 59, 77.

[23] Junius, *Two Letters on the Education of the People of India* (Serampore: Serampore Press, 1835), p. 3.

[24] General Proceedings, Education Department, October 1863, Nos 24–7.

institution, and he remained so till its abolition in 1881.[25] The poem narrates the fate of one such ward, Krishnachandra, the minor ruler of Hetampur in Birbhum. The Court of Wards ordered the boy to be brought to Calcutta for a modern English education, for it stated that an education in the village tol would render him unfit to rule his people; he would be cheated by pundits into believing a lot of superstitious nonsense, and would as a result bring misery to his subjects.[26] Opposition to this order came from the boy's grandmother, who wanted him to go to Varanasi for a Sanskrit education if at all he was to be sent away from his native village. Finally, he was taken away by force to Calcutta, where he spent his days in misery, and longed for the Sanskrit education of Varanasi. At this point Rajendralal Mitra, greatly enraged by this apparently unsound desire, decided to intervene. What the poet records to be Mitra's opinion on the matter, stands as vivid testimony to what the new education involved, not only in its cognitive utility, but also in terms of a range of other priorities which were seen as being constitutive of it.

Mitra said, the poem goes on, that if the boy, were to go to Varanasi, he would be turned into a fool. Here in Calcutta, he would be bound by such excellent regulations that his education would be half accomplished just by being in the system. In the morning, upon awakening he would be taken for a brisk morning walk, whereupon on his return he would be served a hot cup of tea. After that he would have study for four hours, and later have a full breakfast of select milk products. At eleven a carriage would take him to college, and bring him back again at four. After an hour's rest, the carriage would take him for an evening drive, and he would be served tea once more when he returned at six. Every Wednesday, arrangements were made for him to attend tasteful cultural performances, and at the end of each year he would be given new clothes. Fish and meat would be a part of the regular diet, and a qualified doctor would conduct medical examinations every week. Clearly the new education was not the mere reading or learning of things, it also specified a certain way of life. It was the complete overhauling of notions of health, body, and even time: a new ordering of the social rules and perceptions.

[25] 'Raja Rajendralal Mitrer Jibani', *Janmabhumi*, Part 1, No. 8 (Shravan issue, 1891), pp. 547–8.

[26] Nilkantha Mukhopadhyay, *Balya Kahini* (Hetampur: Harinath Bhattacharya, 1904), pp. 83–4.

As Mitra characterizes the situation in Varanasi itself, in the poem, this new ordering becomes even clearer. In Varanasi, he says, the first thing the boy would be required to do in the morning was a ritual dip in the Ganges followed by various religious ceremonies to be observed as a part of the system. All through the year a vegetarian diet of little amounts would be offered, and one would have to walk to college. Five hours of rigorous study were to be capped by working in the garden as a leisure activity. Very little clothes were provided to students and any disobedience was promptly punished by imprisonment in dark, stuffy rooms.[27] The new education did not only involve the social impairment of the older channels of knowledge, it was an altogether new social code which moved the signs of education beyond institutionalized learning.

The Attributes of Education

The new educational system, or *shiksha*, incorporated within itself several elements which were not directly correlative of reading and writing. One of the issues that united the various classes of the bhadralok as a social group was, as we mentioned before, the threat that mass education would enable the lower orders to rise above their station. This fear of mass dissemination of formal learning moved education, in the bhadralok rhetoric, to a culture which a degree could not buy.[28] As a part of the campaign for the Hindu Mela, Manomohan Basu outlined in his speeches some of the necessary requirements of a modern education. The basic contention was to make education a comprehensive totality that regulated every aspect of life of the social being. Basu emphasized that just as it was necessary to work hard at reading prescribed textbooks, it was equally important to play games, have leisure activities, and undertake regular physical exercise. There were ten vices specifically marked out as being dangerous for a diligent student. These were laziness, indifference, sleep, bad company, an overt fondness for sports,

[27] Ibid., pp. 89, 135–6, 475–86.

[28] The endowment of education with various social attributes was also a recurrent theme in contemporary British thought. In 1859 the *Friend of India* outlined this in their description of men who had been loyal to the British in the 1857 mutiny. 'There is an education', it said, 'other than of books, an education in active life, in politics, in national resources'. The men who possessed such education was said to have 'stood by us almost to a man'. *Friend of India*, 13 January 1859, reprinted in Ghosh, *Selections*, Volume 5, p. 315.

too much socializing, that is, the custom of sending young boys especially in Brahmin households to every social occasion in the community, wasting time in the numerous religious festivals, the reading of unnecessary books, long windedness, and narcissism.[29]

The ordering frame within which all these prescriptions were enumerated was that of a complete social vision which was to be outfitted by a band of newly-educated agents. Education was to extend beyond the printed pages of the book, and embrace the playground, the body, family life, and even the affective senses of the converts.[30] The need to extend it beyond the book, was particularly strong. One of the major drawbacks of the new liberal education, according to the new middle class, was its *punthigata* (bookish) nature. Akshaykumar Maitra, an eminent historian, wrote at the end of the century about the ills of a modern education:

Modern education is only the education of the book [....] In the olden days education was the pure fruit of *brahmacharya*, it was not possible to buy it for a price.

In the *gurukul* characters were built. Education did not end with the reading of prescribed texts. One had to lead ones life in accordance with those texts .... Modern schools emphasize only the importance of the texts in themselves. Reading them puts an end to their educational function. And reproducing them at the right time earns one the appellation of a pundit. School education draws attention to the mind, but never reaches the heart.[31]

By the middle of the century, printed books had become easily and cheaply reproducible tools of knowledge, and it was difficult to build any hierarchy of learning on denying accessibility to books. Thus, other factors were inserted as accompaniments to education. The educated were to be distinguished from the uneducated through a series of social marks, which could not depend only on their formal institutional training, or ability to read and write. The notion of physical exercise grew to be one such mark of the middle class.

[29] Manomohan Basu, *Baktritamala* (Calcutta: Madhyastha Press, 1873), pp. 61–8.

[30] Bhudev Mukhopadyay's seminal work on education determined three spheres in which education was to extend its hold. These were the *sharir* (body), *dharma* (moral and religion), and *garhya* (the domestic). Mukhopadhyay, *Shikshabidhayak Prastab*, pp. 59–70.

[31] Akshavkumar Maitreya, 'Shiksha Samasya', *Utsaha* (Magh issue, 1900), pp. 348–55.

All contemporary treatises which catered to the educational ideology devoted a chapter on health and the care of the body in the form of physical exercise. Recent scholarship has drawn our attention to the ideological contest around notions of masculinity in the colonial context.[32] However useful this scholarship may be, it fails to explain the material logic of the stereotypes imposed by colonialism. Why, for example, were 'ethnic' differences (manly Pathan, effeminate Bengali) imposed within overall racial (Indian) categories? The answer should perhaps be sought in the needs of capitalism, which, as a social order, requires the subordination of labour to capital in a general sense, but in the colonies it also required that the labour force was internally divided. Eric Wolf has noted how this allocation of workers to invented ethnic categories was doubly effective in this respect, first, 'by ordering the groups and categories of labourers hierarchically with respect to one another', and second 'by continuously producing and recreating symbolically marked 'cultural' distinctions among them'.[33] On the one hand, groups were allocated specific roles both within the production process and within social life more generally. On the other hand, they were encouraged to identify with these roles and defend them against other groups. Sometimes these built on existing divisions of labour within pre-colonial society; sometimes they were wholly new and based on the division of labour within the new industries that the Europeans established.[34] The rhetoric against the 'effeminate' Bengali babu, developed by the new Bengali middle class, from the middle of the century was thus not merely a response to cultural and personal humiliation. It was tied to the genuine material dissatisfaction of chakri and the decreased opportunities in the political economy. The discourse on the development of the body that filled the pages of contemporary tracts on education has to be seen as this need for a class to go beyond the social role that colonialism forced upon it.

Contemporary Bengali school textbooks vividly documented this anxiety. One of the prominent writers of these textbooks, Gopalchandra

[32] See for example Mrinalini Sinha, *Colonial Masculinity* (Manchester and New York: Manchester University Press, 1995); David Omissi, '"Martial race": Ethnicity and Security in Colonial India, 1858–1939', *War and Society*, Vol. 9, No. 1 (1991), pp. 1–27; and Paul Hoch, *White Hero, Black Beast: Racism, Sexism and the Mask of Masculinity* (London: Pluto Press, 1979).

[33] Eric Wolf, *Europe and the People Without History* (Berkeley and Los Angeles: University of California Press, 1982), p. 380.

[34] Ibid., p. 381.

Banerjee wrote: 'Without having a clear policy on ways to make the body sturdy, virile and healthy, it was pointless to dictate ways of improving the mind'.[35] This particular text added a chapter on gymnastic exercises in its second edition. Directives on a proper and regular diet, formed an important element of concerns on health and the body. Too much oily food, the standard fare for most Bengali meals, was considered eminently disagreeable.[36] Physical fitness and a healthy body was necessary for the building of a healthy *jati*. One text used the example of the 'uncultured' and less civilized Yavanas in India, and the Gauls in Europe, who managed to overthrow superior cultures by sheer physical prowess.[37] But this linkage of a hardy masculine body with the future nation had its pitfalls. Ordinarily it would imply that those in the possession of such a physique would become fit leaders of the nation. Such a criterion would inevitably include the lower classes or the *chotolok*, known for their physical strength, and bodily dexterity.

Rajnarayan Basu expressed such fears indirectly when he observed that in the past the bhadralok, due to their participation in some sort of regular physical exercise, had greater longevity. 'Now', he observed ruefully, 'one does not see too many old men who are bhadraloks. We see more of chotolok older people'. This, according to him, proved 'that the bhadraloks were becoming short-lived'.[38] The discourse on physicality had to thus strike a balance in order to bypass this contradiction. This was done effectively by emphasizing the need for mental strength *simultaneously* with physical strength.

The famous poet Rangalal Bandyopadhyay won the Hare Anniversary prize, as a student, for his essay on 'The Importance of Physical Education'. In this essay he made clear that humanity's happiness was dependent on a symmetry of both mental and physical strength. He stressed that 'whenever a jati had excelled in physical prowess, and disregarded the mind, it had spelt evil for the world'. In such a ideological stratagem, the discourse of the *asabhya jatis* conquering the civilized fit in perfectly; for Bandyopadhyay the neglect of physical strength by the civilized meant their defeat at the

---

[35] Gopalchandra Bandhopadhyay, *Shikshapranali: An Elementary Treatise on Education* (Calcutta: Hitaishi Press, 1868), p. 297.

[36] Manoranjan Guhathakurata, *Chatrera Khabe Ki* (Calcutta, 1917), p. 6. The writer had also published an article in a similar vein in the journal *Pratibasi* in 1897.

[37] Somnath Mukhopadhyay, *Shikshapadhdhati* (Calcutta: New Sanskrit Press, 1866), pp. 2–3.

[38] Rajnarayan Basu, *Sekal ar Ekal*, pp. 52–3.

hands of the uncivilized.[39] A distinction was also made between exercise and labour. Resorting to the Ayurvedic notion of *shaktardhya byam*, by which a person needed exercise in proportion to the individual's own physical abilities, the texts cautioned against too much exercise.[40] It was made very clear that what was being recommended was physical exercise and not the physical labour that came with some professions. One text spelt out that exercise was meant only for the moneyed people: for the common man his labour was enough.[41] This was why cautionary boundaries were set up against too much exercise, which might border on physical labour. The forms of exercises recommended also made very clear which class of people they were intended for. Riding, morning walks, rowing, swimming, wrestling, all the forms of activities that would ensure them as leisurely pastimes of particular classes, were listed as being forms of good exercise.[42] It was thus quite clear, that it was the body of the bhadralok that had to be groomed, in order to constitute a healthy body for the future jati.[43] This carefully nurtured body, of course, could not be exposed to the vagaries of the older system of education, with its approbation of physical punishment. We find that the other aspect of the new education was its violent prohibition of physical punishment.

In the indigenous pathshalas of the past, the gurus were objects of terror due to the harsh punishments meted out to students.[44] Rajnarayan Basu commented that the guru's punishment techniques far excelled his

[39] Runga Lal Banerjea, *On the Importance of Physical Education* (Calcutta, 1860), pp. 3–11.

[40] Banerjea, *On the Importance of Physical Education*, p. 54; also see Radhanath Basak, *Sharirtatvasar* (Calcutta: Vidyaratna Press, 1863), p. 84; and Gaurinath Sen, *Sharirik Shasthya Vidhan* (Calcutta: Sambad Sajjan Ranjan Press, 1862) pp. 64–5.

[41] Jadunath Mukhopadhyay, *Sharirpalan* (Hooghly: Budhoday Press, 1868), pp. 62–3.

[42] Mukhopadhyay, *Sharirpalan*, pp. 63–4; also see Harimohan Moitra, *Shasthyarakshar Prosnottar* (Calcutta: H.C. Gangooly and Co., 1872), p. 22.

[43] *Chikitsa Sammilani*, a popular journal on health published from 1884 carried various essays on the subject. Including Vidyasagar's friend Annadacharan Khastagir, all the editors of this journal were renowned doctors. See for instance, "Jatiya Dainik Punarajjiban", *Chikitsa Sammilani*, Baishakh, 1885.

[44] James Long in his Introduction to Adam's Reports mentions fifteen different kinds of punishments that the gurus inflicted on their students. Long, ed., *Adam's Report*, pp. 10–11.

teaching skills. These included the *narugopal* posture, by which the erring student had to kneel down, while heavy bricks were placed on his outstretched palms; students were often whipped with the *bichuti*, a kind of poison-ivy which caused severe skin irritation.[45] The Bramho reformer Girishchandra Sen never completed his education in the pundit's school for the fear of excessive physical torture.[46] Dineshchandra Sen recollected in his memoirs how he and his fellow-students learned difficult Bengali words by rote, without comprehending their meanings, for any lapse in the obedience of the guru's orders was instantly met with heavy caning. The entire neighbourhood, wrote Sen, would ring with the cries of the hapless students.[47] The new manuals on education wholly rejected such direct and physical disciplinary methods. In fact, there were instances of teachers being dismissed from service when they had adopted such methods.[48] Correction, claimed the texts, was to be effected gently through affection, display of understanding and the adoption of a loving relationship with the students.[49] 'A sign with a glance', said one, 'was the best form of discipline'. To look once at the student with displeasure was enough of a reprimand to make him do what the teacher wanted. But to achieve this, the text continued, the teacher should be in possession of sufficient uprightness, and a strong moral fibre, which was only possible through vidya and a pure character.[50]

Discipline, was to thus move inward to the self such that physical punishment, a violent rejection of bourgeois notions of human dignity, was rendered unnecessary. *Shikhshapranali: An Elementary Treatise On Education* (1864) was a popular text written by Gopalchandra Bandhopadhyay, which

[45] Basu, *Sekal ar Ekal*, p. 7.

[46] Girishchandra Sen, *Atma Jibanbrittanta*, pp. 8–9.

[47] Dineshchandra Sen, *Gharer Katha O Jugsahitya* (Calcutta: Shishir Publishing House, 1922), p. 41.

[48] See Prasannamayi Devi, *Purbakatha*, p. 77.

[49] Dwijendranath Neogi, *Uchcha Shikshak Sahachar* (Calcutta, 1902), pp. 286–304. From the preface we learn that this author had wide experiences in teaching, having served as the principal at the government high schools in Shillong, Darbhanga, Jalpaiguri, Dibrugarh, and several other cities of the Presidency. His books *The Senior Teacher's Manual* and *The Junior Teacher's Manual* had been approved and recommended by the government to be translated into Bengali, Hindi, Urdu, and Oriya.

[50] Aghornath Adhikary, *Vidyalaya Vidhayak Vivida Vidhan* (Calcutta: Sanyal and Co., 1909), p. 55.

incorporated the dominant strands of this principle. The teacher was the 'undisputed and only sovereign', according to Bandhopadhyay, in the kingdom of the school. Irrational behaviour on his part, in the form of harsh punishments, would only result in the students growing rebellious and defiant. His omnipotence lay precisely in his ability to rationally explain the rules of administration within the school, such that the students would see a father-figure in him, and learn to love and respect him. He was to be omnipresent. Mingling with his students, Bandhopadhyay's ideal teacher was supposed to keep a vigilant watch upon all their actions without revealing his presence. Later they were to be rewarded or reprimanded, according to their individual behaviour: 'just as God stays out of earthly vision and judges human beings for their actions'.[51] Our reading of Foucault fits such an approach to discipline within his framework of the enactment of power.[52] There is, however, another relevant connection to be made between this conceptualization of the teacher as the virtual God of the education system and the changes in the class structure of the men who were being recruited as teachers in this period.

Gurumashai to *Mastermashai*

The Bengali pathshalas and their gurus came under sharp criticism from the bhadralok with the introduction of English education and particularly with the introduction of new model textbooks and primers by the School Book Society and other such agents. The middle class took up the English critique of immoral and even licentious teachings by the gurus and the older methods of teaching suddenly appeared insufficient and corrupt in the light of the new educational discourse. Kartikeyachandra Ray remembered with relief that he never had to study under a guru for:

The youth of today will be unable to imagine the heinous conduct of the gurus of those times and their terrible methods of teaching. They did not have a single book that was fit for children in their pathshalas, and no sweet moral lessons entered the ears of the students. They merely had their palmyra or plaintain leaves clutched tightly on their laps, the marks of ink all over their bodies and the angry vision of the guru before them with his fearful and ubiquitous cane.[53]

---

[51] Gopalchandra Bandopadhyay, *Shikshapranali*, pp. 88–9, 97–111, 117–27.

[52] Michel Foucault, *Discipline and Punish*.

[53] Kartikeyachandra Ray, *Atma Jibancharit*, pp. 6–7.

Hutom noted the pathshala to be more terrifying than hell itself, and the guru to be as dangerous as the tiger.[54] In a paper read at the Bethune Society, Hurchandra Dutt said that the guru encouraged the same practical modes of instruction 'so keenly satirized by the gifted Dickens in his description of Dotheboy's Hall'.[55]

It is worth mentioning that this severe criticism of the indigenous pathshalas was not universal until the middle of the century. In 1815, Lord Moira had called the gurus a 'humble but valuable class of schoolmasters'. He said that the first rudiments of reading, writing, and arithmetic taught by these men, were sufficient for the purposes of the village zamindar, the village accountant, and the village shop-keeper.[56] In 1814, the Court of Directors referred to the system 'with particular satisfaction'. In their despatch they referred to it as one of the most distinguishing features of internal polity, and urged the government to extend its protection to the village teachers in all their just rights and immunities, for they believed that 'humble as their situation may appear if judged by a comparison with any corresponding character in this country, we understand that those village teachers are held in great veneration throughout India'.[57]

By the middle of the nineteenth century, however, the guru had lost all his credibility as a fit dispenser of knowledge and was thought instead to 'teach bad morals, and inculcate deception, theft' and the like.[58] Who were these gurus, who had served their purpose so well until this time and were then suddenly considered totally unfit for teaching? From contemporary evidence provided by the bhadralok it appears that the gurus were usually Kayasthas in the villages, who had at some point served as the personnel to the zamindari and learned his accounts and writing skills at the zamindar's kachari, or office.[59] These gurus did not hold education as a traditional or

[54] Arun Nag, ed., *Satik Hutom*, p. 125.

[55] Hurchandra Dutt, *Bengali Life and Society* (Calcutta: Sanders, Cones and Co., 1853), p. 3.

[56] Quoted in Jogeshchandra Bagal, *Banglar Janashiksha* (Calcutta: Viswabharati, 1949), p. 3.

[57] See H. Sharp and J.A. Richey, *Selections from Educational Records*, Part I (Calcutta: Superintendent, Government Printing, 1920), pp. 19–21.

[58] William Gordon Young, *Training Schools for Teachers of the Ryots* (Calcutta: Sanders, Cones and Co., 1858), p. 1.

[59] Bhudev refers to this practice with derision and attributes this to the declining state of education in the land. Bhudev Mukhopadhyay, *Shikshabidhayak Prastab*, p. 6.

hereditary profession, like the Brahmin pundits of the Sanskrit tols, and were generally simply dressed, simply spoken and without much proficiency beyond the preliminary stages of reading, writing, and arithmetic.[60] The education they afforded equipped student to do book-keeping and maintain accounts in the offices of the zamindar.

In 1853, the Council of Education proposed to follow Adam's recommendations by establishing experimentally in four districts or zillahs, model vernacular schools and to organize the necessary staff to visit and inspect the existing vernacular schools of those districts. The plan was to provide instruction to the teachers, rewards to the best pupils, supply books to the schools, and to connect the whole with the workings of Hardinge's resolution of 1844.[61] This experiment was carried further in 1855, with the plan of sanctioning government grants for the village schools and completely overhauling their syllabus in favour of more 'moral' and educational training. The schools were arranged into circles according to their districts and money rewards were offered by the state to the gurus for improving the education of their pupils.[62]

The cash reward programme was firmly institutionalized by the Lieutenant-Governor, J.P. Grant, in 1860. In this scheme, the gurus of selected pathshalas in a district would be awarded cash grants dependent on their pupil's performance. New subjects like geography and Indian history were introduced in the schools.[63] The guru became eligible for the grant if

---

Kartikeyachandra Ray mentions such kayastha teachers near his village, and also refers to the fact that due to a dearth of schools in his own village, most children would learn elementary reading and writing from the staff of the zamindar's office. Karikeyachandra Ray, *Jibancharit*, pp. 4–7. For a similar example, see Krishnakumar Mitra, *Atmacharit* (Calcutta: Prabasi Press, 1937), p. 17.

[60] For an eloquent description of the guru's attire and behaviour, see Mahendranath Datta, *Jibankahini* (Calcutta: Shishia Kumar Mitra, 1924), pp. 16–17.

[61] Lord Hardinge's resolution of 1844 was an effort to reverse Bentick's resolution of 1835 which had started the era of English education in Bengal. Hardinge put forward a plan to establish a limited number of vernacular schools in several districts of Bengal and Bihar in order to give vernacular education its due importance. See General Proceedings, Education Department, October 1860, No. 62.

[62] A.M. Monteath and A.P. Howell, eds., *Selections*, p. 67.

[63] General Proceedings, Education Department, October 1860, No. 64. In a recent study, Manu Goswami has incisively documented the historical significance of these disciplines in the colonial pedagogical order. See her *Producing India: From Colonial*

his students were able to take dictation and spell three-letter words, and also recite the multiplication tables up to ten. The grant would increase exponentially, one paisa to one anna to two annas, etc., depending on the proficiency of the students. The highest grant, four annas per month, was accorded for the satisfactory completion of the highest course by the pupils, that is, geography, history, Bengali grammar, zamindari and mahajani accounts, and different forms of letter writing.[64]

In the budget of 1862–3 Rs 30,000 was set aside for the extension of this vernacular education. Henry Woodrow, the Inspector of Schools for East Bengal, who had initially started the 'circle' method, realized that in order for Grant's project to succeed, the gurus themselves would have to have special training. He thus initiated another project of transferring a certain numbers of gurus from their native village schools to a Normal School, where they were to remain for a year and 'receive instructions in their proper duties as teachers'. In the meanwhile, the Normal School pupils were to act as their replacements in the village schools.[65] The guru's monthly stipend for a one year period of study in the Normal School was Rs 5, while the Normal School pupil officiating on his behalf received Rs 12.[66]

The fallout of such plans of disciplining the pathshalas and their gurus along modern lines was that the traditional gurus were increasingly replaced by the urban middle class. Kazi Shahidullah has shown this change in its precise details from an analysis of eleven gurus chosen by Bhudev Mukhopadhaya for training in the Normal Schools in 1863 (Table 4.1).

Only three out of ten gurus in this year came from the former class of men. The changes made in the curriculum, and more importantly the change in the discipline of schools, made the traditional gurus redundant. The pathshala regime, previously allowing for a long break in the middle of the day, was changed to a continuous session from ten to four. The palm and plantain leaves for writing were replaced by slates and chalk. Payment to gurus by pupils were strictly regularized and the previous system of part payment in 'cash' and part in 'kind' was replaced with a pre-determined

Economy to National Space (Chicago: University of Chicago Press, 2004), see especially pp. 143–53.

[64] General Proceedings, Education Department, July 1862, No. 64.

[65] General Proceedings, Education Department, July 1862, No. 63.

[66] Ibid.

TABLE 4.1   Social background of gurus in Normal Schools[67]

Name of guru	Village he came from	Whether traditional
W.C. Chakraborty	Baloor	No
Brojoraj Roy	Jamna	Yes
J.C. Bannerjee	Bagnaparah	No
J. Chakraborty	Beejor	No
J. Roy	Pallah	Yes
Ramkisto Dutt	Garaghatta	No
Issan Chunder Sircar	Doomoordah	Yes
B.M. Ghosh	Nobogram	No
P.C. Ghosh	Astai	No
Kedarnath Ghosh	–	–
Dwarkinath Mullick	Chachai	No

Source: Kazi Shahidullah, 'The Purpose and Impact of Government Policy on Pathshala Gurumohashoys in Nineteenth-Century Bengal', in Nigel Crook, ed., *The Transmission of Knowledge in South Asia*, p. 126.

school fee.[67] Attendance registers were introduced and the spatial imagination of students scrupulously territorialized by teaching them to draw maps which plotted natural river courses along with the essential colonial institution, the railways.[68]

Unsurprisingly from this period the new middle class assumed the guru's place in the village schools under government supervision. In the autobiographies of this period, we thus find mention only of this class of men as teachers, even in villages. Recalling his school days in the Dhamrai Village of the Dhaka District, Dineshchandra Sen listed several such 'respectable' men, including Dinanath Sen the father of the famous high court lawyer Priyonath Sen, who took up the selfless job of teaching students in remote areas. It is worth mentioning that Sen specifically mentions in his account, that they called their teachers 'mastermashai' instead of

[67] General Proceedings, Education Department, January 1863, No. 51.
[68] *Report of Public Instruction* (Calcutta, 1863–4), pp. 342–3.

'gurumahashay', perhaps to mark the difference.[69] With the bhadralok manning the village schools with their new printed books and scientific teaching methods, they never tired of pointing out how the guru was a 'perfect ignoramus in geography, history, and all the rudimentary branches of study' required in a 'good secular education'.[70]

This denigration of the guru, was in tandem with the notion of an ideal teacher, whose specificities were worked out in this period, and to whose standard the guru could never quite measure up.[71] Gourmohan Addhya who founded the Oriental Seminary at Calcutta was one of the earlier representations of this ideal teacherhood. The texts on his life portrayed him as gentle and God fearing, and one who loved his students like his own children. He would not accept fees from needy but meritorious students, and took personal care of such boys by visiting their homes if they were ill.[72] Similar images were drawn for the more prominent teachers of the period like David Hare and Ramtanu Lahiri.[73] Several short stories around this period promoted the romantic figure of the poor but extremely scholarly teacher, who often sacrificed his life for his students.[74] In a long article entitled 'Shikshaker Upajogita', or the utility of a teacher, Saratchandra Chaudhuri insisted upon the personal purity necessary for the profession, alongside its needs of scholarship. The two, he stated, however, went hand in hand, and all true scholars were essentially pure hearted. One important criterion was mentioned by him, which spoke of the sentiments of the period surrounding the teaching profession. He explained to the uninformed that the teacher did not accept such a profession in order to make a living,

[69] Dineshchandra Sen, *Gharer Katha O Jugasahitya*, pp. 3031. In this context also see Srinath Chanda, *Bramhosamaje Challish Bachar*, pp. 9–10; Debaprasad Sarbadhikari, *Smritirekha*, pp. 22–4; and Girishchandra Sen, *Atmajiban*, p. 16. Sen was one of the teachers in this scheme himself.

[70] Quoted by Dr Lees in his letter of 10 October 1859, in A.M. Monteath and A.P. Howell, eds., *Selections*, p. 74.

[71] Baradababu in Pearychand Mitra's *Alaler Gharer Dulal* is a classic example of this stereotype.

[72] See Subalchandra Mitra, *Kalikatar Itihas* an adaptation from Raja Binaya Krishna Deb's *The Early History and Growth of Calcutta* (Calcutta, 1917), pp. 130–1.

[73] See Pearychand Mitra, *A Biographical Sketch of David Hare* (Calcutta: Jijnasa, 1979); Shibnath Shastri, *Ramtanu Lahiri*.

[74] See for example, Hemendraprasad Ghosh, 'Mastermahashay', *Sahitya* (Jaishtha, 1898), pp. 101–11.

he came willingly to fulfil a greater responsibility to the community.[75] Another similar text echoed his sentiments:

If one wishes for wealth and money, then he is advised not to enter the profession. If it is glamour and social standing they want, they are advised to stay away. If they are looking for fame then this is not their calling. Only those who strive to be like the selfless, guileless Brahmin scholar of the past, satisfied only by a meal of tamarind leaves, should accept the mantle of a teacher.[76]

The virtues of the new model teacher that these texts ceaselessly emphasized, and which brought into prominent relief the inadequacies of the older class of gurus, were in effect the virtues of the bhadralok. As a result the *Calcutta Review* in 1876 analysed the situation in retrospect:

At the very outset ... the indigenous *Guru* found himself superseded and degraded in the eyes of his pupils from the rank of a teacher and director into that of a subordinate usher.

... he and all his pupils at once assumed that the *pathshala* had changed its character and become a unit in the Government scheme of *Kerani* manufacturing education. Those of the pupils ... who already intended to use their education as a ladder to employment, were delighted at the change ... while the masses ... who knew that appointments were beyond their ambition, would desert the *pathshala*, as no longer a place they had any right to frequent.[77]

The pathshala, the sole place of rudimentary knowledge for the lower classes, had been 'reformed' to such an extent by the fair and equal educational policies of colonialism that the peasant no longer had any right to it.

The Discriminating Metropolis

When Lalbehari Dey came for higher education to Calcutta from his native village of Talpur in Burdwan, he had the choice of four main English schools.

[75] Saratchandra Chaudhuri, 'Shikshaker Upajogita', pp. 10–11.

[76] Aghornath Adhikary, *Vidyalaya Vidhayak Vivida Vidhan*, p. 3. The reference is to the popular myth of the nineteenth century of Buno Ramnath, a scholar in the times of Raja Krishnachandra of Nadia, who was allegedly offered immense wealth and riches by the king for his scholarly achievements, but who said that the simple fare of a curry of tamarind leaves cooked by his wife, was enough reward for his work.

[77] 'The Midnapore System of Primary Education', *Calcutta Review*, 63, 125 (January–June, 1876), p. 133.

The Hindu College and the Oriental Seminary were immediately ruled out by his father, due to their high fees.[78] The Hare School was an option which could not be taken up as admission there depended entirely on the individual decision of Hare himself and hence was too unpredictable for their liking. The only choice for him, therefore, was the General Assembly's Institution, run by the missionary, Alexander Duff.[79] Dey's case stands as a marked refutation of the myths of equal opportunities and the separation of money from knowledge that were the hallmarks of the educational ideology. While the discourse actively promoted the ideals of poverty, the invincibility of individual merit, and the superiority of knowledge over wealth, in the material sphere of social reality, the educational networks underscored social position and wealth.

The financial layout of education in Bengal had evolved from the policies of the colonial state at different points of the nineteenth century. As mentioned earlier, in the first half of the century official opinion was not averse to the system of indigenous education, primarily due to the fact that it placed the pecuniary responsibility on the concerned native community. In their Despatch of 1814, the directors were all praise over the system, 'by which the instruction of the people is provided for by a certain charge upon the produce of the soil and by other endowments in favour of the village teachers who are thereby rendered public servants of the community'.[80] It is important to note that this praise was accorded only to the monetary organization of the system, for even Lord Moira, one of the greatest advocates of the existent educational structure, noted its 'sad defect', namely the fact that 'the inculcation of moral principles' formed 'no part of it'.[81] The principle of sharing the cost of education and absolving the state of the full responsibility was an appealing prospect, and it formed the basis of the establishment of three premier institutions of education under Moira's rule—the Hindoo Vidyalaya (1817), the Calcutta School Book Society (1817), and the Calcutta School Society (1818). These institutions were formed on the basis of donations and grants of private individuals, both Bengali and European. While the state was thus saved

[78] Hindu College charged Rs 5 per month, and the Oriental Seminary Rs 3.

[79] See Manmathanath Ghosh, *Sekaler Lok* (Calcutta: Gurudas Chattopadhyay and Sons, 1923), pp. 158–9.

[80] H. Sharp and J.A. Richey, *Selections from Educational Records*, p. 23.

[81] Ibid., p. 25.

from direct financial investment, prominent state functionaries including the Lieutenant-Governor himself, extended their support on an individual basis.[82] The system invited the support of the native elite who were to provide the financial backbone to the institutions. While this arrangement displayed its relative autonomy from direct state supervision, and emphasized initiative on the part of the organizers, the constitution of the managing committees with important functionaries of the state, maintained sufficient ground for observation; from the very start thus, the 'private' initiative in education was not totally free from monitoring by the state. Moreover, this important initiative was monetarily dependent, to a large extent, on native subscriptions. A practice which constituted from the beginning the elite nature of the institutions and tied up educational opportunities firmly with wealth and social position.

The Hindu College was an extreme example of the workings of the educational ideology. Though there were no official policies barring admission in a democratic manner, the high fees that it charged determined the class composition of the students in general, and an instituted practice of the sons of most prominent families taking admission there, constituted it as 'an institution that acted as a key socialization agency for ... [an] earlier generation of bhadralok'.[83] We shall take up here only one aspect of the long history of this institution—its transition from the Hindu College to the Presidency College—in order to demonstrate how statements of exclusion and class barriers, officially uncharted could nevertheless dominate very material policy decisions.

The Hindu College was formally declared to be open to non-Hindu students, when it was re-established as the Presidency College in 1855. The fee was raised from Rs 5 to Rs 10 as the price of this open policy.[84] One very dramatic incident that preceded the government's decision to alter the nature of the college, and which might have had some bearing on the matter, was the radical protests from the bhadralok community in 1853–4 over the

[82] Lord Moira and his wife paid liberal donations to both the School Society and the School Book Society; Sir Hyde East, the Chief Justice of Calcutta, and other prominent Europeans like Bishop Middleton and Joseph Baretto were among the early subscribers to the Hindu College funds. For a detailed study see N.L. Basak, *History of Vernacular Education in India* (Calcutta: Educational Publishers, 1974), pp. 235–7.

[83] John McGuire, *The Making of the Colonial Mind*, p. 47.

[84] A.M. Monteath and A.P. Howell, eds., *Selections*, p. 17.

issue of admission of the son of a prostitute into Hindu College. This incident caused several students to break away from the college and start a rival institution, the Hindu Metropolitan College, where they felt their social purity would not be compromised.[85] The sequence of events was so rapid and dramatic that even the Lieutenant-Governor could not be informed of them through the official channels, and in fact learned of the incident through the newspapers. Subsequently, he sought a full report from F.J. Mouat, the Secretary of the Council of Education, on the matter. Mouat denied any responsibility for the course of events, as he claimed that the admissions were regulated by the Hindu College managers and were 'not even reported for the information of the Council'.[86] In this correspondence, however, Mouat admitted that it was true that the question of whether it might be proper to open the Hindu College, like other government institutions to all classes of the community, had recently occupied the attention of the Council. The question, he stated, first arose in connection with the education of Muslims and with the question of what opportunities the government was providing to encourage the study of English for that community.[87]

Though the College had started out originally with private donations, the collapse of the Barretto Bank and other financial crises had prompted the managers to ask for government support which was sanctioned in 1824. The mode in which it was proposed to aid the institution was in the first place to endow at public cost, a Professorship of Experimental Philosophy, the lectures of which was to be open to the senior students both of the Hindu and the Sanskrit College. It was further resolved to supply from public funds the cost of school accommodation to be provided in the vicinity of Sanskrit College, and to grant an allowance of Rs 280 per month for house rent. Finally, the General Committee was given 'a certain amount of authoritative control over the concerns of that Institution in return for the pecuniary aid'.[88] It was decided, however, that in case of differences of opinions the managers would have the final say in their right of veto.[89]

---

[85] Brajendranath Bandyopadhyay, *Sambad Patre Sekaler Katha*, Vol. 2, pp. 702–3.

[86] Letter No. 245, from Cecil Beadon, Secretary to the Government of Bengal, to the Secretary to the Council of Education, General Proceedings, June 1853, No. 103.

[87] Ibid.

[88] Quoted in Mukhopadhyay, *Hindujati O Shiksha*, p. 278.

[89] Mukhopadhyay, *Hindujati O Shiksha*, pp. 279–80.

By the mid-century, with the spread of educational facilities and the access to books by a large number of people, the state was forced to consider the establishment of a college where there were no *official* bars to the entry of all classes. It was, however, unwilling to spend any money for this purpose, and rather sought to provide the necessary funds by stopping its aid to the Hindu College on the grounds of fair and democratic admission policies. In its correspondence with the managers the government agreed that it would not 'insist' upon opening up the College to all classes, as it was contrary to the wishes of the native managers:

But, as the Government feels it to be its duty to provide a College in Calcutta, where all may meet for instruction without distinction of classes or creeds, and as the Government will not consent, when it incurs this expense, to burden the public revenue at the same time with a continuance of the whole of its present payments to the Hindoo College, for the benefit of the sect of Hindoos *alone*, the Government must now give notice that the united management and maintenance of the Hindoo College by the government and the Native Managers must cease.[90]

This not too subtle threat on the part of the government brought matters to the fore for the managers. While it was necessary that the government grant be continued in order for the college to function, years of traditional hold over the institution by the upper classes of the bhadralok was not something that could be easily erased. In the series of negotiations that followed, the actual workings of the admission policy and the social attitudes that had determined it since its inception were voiced for the first time.

The Maharaja of Burdwan, otherwise widely known for his patronage of the arts and education, declared that as far his interests in the College were concerned, he had not the slightest hesitation in at once resigning from the management of the College as it stood on its new footing. Prasanna Kumar Tagore, after stating that he was individually opposed to any exclusive system in education or in other matters, also resigned, for as a trustee and the representative of the surviving co-heir of his late father, one of the principal founders of the Hindu College, he could not be a 'consenting party to revolutionize the College', and transferred the rights and privileges he possessed in the institution and its funds to the government. Asutosh Dey, an elected member of the Committee, deeply regretted the organic

---

[90] Letter No. 527, from the Secretary to the Government of Bengal, to the Secretary to the Council of Education, in *Selections from Records of the Bengal Government Papers on the Establishment of the Presidency College of Bengal*, Vol. 14 (Calcutta, 1854), pp. 34–5.

changes proposed and retired from the management. The remaining native members, among them Debendranath Tagore and Srikrishna Sinha, expressed no opinion on the matter.[91] It is worth noting in this context that the severance of ties between the managers and the College was not as complete as it appeared to be. Since 1834 there had been no elections for the Managing Committee of the College, and the management appeared 'by tacit consent to have become a permanent body'.[92] Further, members of this Committee were appointed to the General Committee of Public Instructions, on the government's recommendation in 1841, and two members were granted a vote in the workings of the Committee. Thus, as members of the government's committee on education in general, the managers were not totally without a say in the affairs of the College.

It would seem, however, from this turn of events that the new Presidency College as supervised by the state, would be run along different lines from the old Hindu College. In reality, however, matters were altered insofar as exclusivity was only officially removed from the annals of the college's history. The fees were fixed at Rs 10 per month which even the Council admitted to be 'more than the fees as yet paid at any Mofussil College', and lectures were 'opened' out to all upon paying Rs 15 for each course of lectures. It was strongly recommended by the Council that 'all free studentship should at once be abolished'.[93] There were, however, scholarships for students who could not afford to pay the high fees so instituted. After the resignation of his position from the Managing Committee, Prasanna Kumar Tagore had expressed his wish that with all powers being wrested from the managers, the Council should see to it that the scholarships should be distributed in a manner that was consistent with the known wishes and intentions of the subscribers. It was thus decided that the scholarships in question were to be assigned to students in the junior department of the Hindu College or the Hindu School exclusively, thus ensuring that they went only to the Hindu students. The strongest voices of opposition to the new Presidency College, Prasanna Kumar Tagore and the Raja of Burdwan remained Hereditary Governors of the College and even their families were given the privilege of choosing a member of the governing committee. The Hindu College thus

[91] Letter No. 598, from F.J. Mouat, Secretary to the Council of Education, to Cecil Beadon, Secretary to the government of Bengal, in *Selections from Records*, pp. 40–1.

[92] *Selections from Records*, Appendix VI.

[93] Letter No. 598 in *Selections from Records*, p. 67.

attained its democratic credentials as the Presidency College without any actual changes in its policies.

The Hindu College with its bias for Hindu students from the upper class was, however, not the only institution that was anxious to maintain its exclusivity. In admitting boys to the Calcutta Madrassa, the only institution of higher education for the Muslims, the applicant was required to produce a certificate of 'respectable parentage' from some well known person. The certificate also required the counter-signature of some member of the Madrassa Committee. In 1871, the Principal of the Madrassa, J. Sutcliffe, sought to end this 'unnecessary' practice. As a reformed policy it was agreed that the boys 'should not be the sons of menial servants'. This was sanctioned by the government in 1872.[94] The Sanskrit College, with its faculty of Brahmin pundits, adopted a more rigid stand. In 1851, F.J. Mouat, Secretary to the Council of Education, requested Vidyasagar, as Principal of the College, to report on the question of admission of students belonging to castes other than Brahmins and Vaidyas, and to submit to the Council the opinions of the principal professors of the institute. The professors, Joynarayan Tarkapanchanan, Bharatchandra Shiromoni, and Premchandra Tarkabagish, stated in no uncertain terms their objection to allowing Kayasthas and other mixed castes 'who rank with Shudras' to study grammar and other shastras which according to them were allied to the Vedas. They opined that the 'study of the ... Shastras by Shudras' was 'forbidden by Manu and other Law-givers' and was 'contrary to custom'.[95] In spite of this opposition, Vidyasagar in his letter to the Council saw 'no objection to the admission of other castes than Brahmanas and Vaidyas or, in other words, different orders of Shudras' to the Sanskrit College. But as a matter of expediency he suggested that 'at present only Kayasthas be admitted'. As an explanation Vidyasagar said:

The reason, why I recommend the exclusion of the other orders of Shudras at present, is that they, as a body, are wanting in respectability and stand lower in the scale of social consideration. Their admission, therefore, would, I fear, prejudice the interests of the Institution.[96]

[94] Letter No. 982, from J. Sutcliffe to the Director of Public Instruction, General Proceedings, Education Department, February 1872, No. 15.

[95] Quoted in Arabinda Guha, ed., *Unpublished Letters*, p. 20.

[96] Letter No. 702, from Vidyasagar, to F.J. Mouat, Files for Letters Sent 1849–51, Vol. 6, Sanskrit College File for Letters Collection, Volume 6.

Three years later when the caste barriers were finally removed from the policies of the College, it was in favour of 'admission of boys of all respectable classes of Hindoos' which was sanctioned by the Council in 1854.[97] The 'respectable' class, that is, the upper layers of the bhadralok, thus retained unqualified hold over all premier institutions.

The grids of educational institutions were laid out in such manner as to encourage only the 'respectable' class to attain higher education. In 1864 the *Dacca Darpan* published an editorial on this phenomenon:

Though in each village there may be one or two Aided or Circle Schools, yet only children of the higher or middle classes receive instruction, while the poor, who though not anxious to acquire knowledge, if they do sometimes wish to learn, are excluded on account of their lowness [...] but for this class prejudice we might see one or two of the poor waiting at the door of learning, and might hope that their condition would yet be changed. But as things now stand we dare not even dream of such prospects.[98]

What the editorial pointed out was merely the effects of the half-century-old colonial educational policies, which had scrupulously on grounds of finances excluded the access of the lower classes to education. From mid-nineteenth century onwards this overall principle found ardent support from the Bengali middle class, whereupon the official discourse began to lay the blame for exclusivity at its door.

The General Committee of Public Instruction, constituted in 1823, in its report of 1831 clearly outlined the priorities of the official policy on education. It said that the village schools had been continued or aided by the Committee either from an unwillingness to undo what had required much trouble to effect, or with the hope that the seminaries might eventually become more advanced. With the limited means available to the Committee they considered that the education of a whole people rendered a selection necessary. 'The Committee', they claimed 'have always sought to teach the respectable in preference to the indigent classes'. The education of the latter, they further declared, 'in fact scarcely merits to be called education'.[99] An editorial in the *Friend of India* pointed out in 1836, that the Committee

[97] Education Department Proceedings, April 1863, No. 83.

[98] General Proceedings, March 1864, No. 4.

[99] Minutes and Proceedings of the General Committee of Public Instructions, Vol. V (Calcutta, October 1831).

was yet to take its first step towards the education of the masses.[100] From the letter written by Sutherland, the Committee's secretary to the government, it was clear that 'two great principles' had been laid down earlier by the Committee as 'fundamentally essential'. One of these was that 'the Committee should in all things endeavour so to shape its conduct and proceeding as to win the confidence of the educated and influential classes of the people, and if possible, to carry these classes with them in all the measures they might adopt for the revival and improvement of the literature of the country'. The other principle was that, 'whereas the funds at their disposal were quite inadequate to any purpose of general and universal instruction, the best application that could be made of them consistently with the ends in view was to assist the seminaries of more advanced education through which only the Committee could hope to revive and improve the literature of the country, and to encourage the learned men'.[101] This attitude was tied up with the necessity to push the claims of English as the medium of instruction. Macaulay went on to say that 'the intellectual improvement of those classes of the people who have the means of pursuing higher studies, can at present be effected only by means of some language, not the Vernacular among them'.[102] A connection had been thus carefully laid out in the official policy with English education as the representative of a particular class and the access of that class alone to higher education.

The attendance report of schools for 1859–60 bears testimony to this policy of exclusionary practices. The number of primary schools was in this year reported to be 220, with an average attendance of 10,336 students. Compared to this impressive number, the number of higher class schools were only 45, with an attendance of 5,309 for the whole of the Presidency.[103] Nearly half the students who began their education were thus weeded out from the system during the course of their study.

Since the publication of William Adam's reports on primary education, the government was anxious to appear as being concerned about the education of the masses. The government was also eager to test in Bengal the system of *Hulkabundee* schooling as it existed in the North-Western

[100] *Friend of India*, 24 September 1836.

[101] H. Sharp and J.A. Richey, *Selections from Educational Records*, pp. 107–17.

[102] Quoted in N.L. Basak, *History of Vernacular Education*, p. 253.

[103] A.M. Monteath and A.P Howell, eds., *Selections*, p. 40.

Provinces.[104] In 1860, a circular was issued from the government to some select members of the bhadralok community, seeking their opinion on the practicability of promoting these cheap schools for the masses in Bengal. Of the fifteen men who received the circular, including Radhakanta Deb, Vidyasagar, Pearychand Mitra, the Rev. K.M. Banerjea, Debendranath Tagore, and Shibchandra Deb, men of various political and religious persuasions, all agreed that it was impracticable to introduce any such system.

Prasanna Narain Deb, the Dewan to the Nizamat at Murshidabad, ruled out the proposition on the grounds that (according to him) there existed in Bengal no sharp line of demarcation between class and class as viewed in the English sense 'where all distinctions are purely secular and rest ultimately in the possession of property, or its equivalent, a sound education'. Thus, he claimed 'any improvement of the lowest and very indigent must be attended by a corresponding movement amongst the middle classes'. Vidyasagar felt that the condition of the labouring classes was so low that they could not afford to incur any charge on account of the education of their children; under such circumstances he emphasized that it was 'needless to attempt the education of the labouring classes'. The government should, he felt, confine itself to the education of the higher classes on a comprehensive scale, for 'by educating one boy in a proper style the government does more towards the real education of the people, than by teaching a hundred children mere reading, writing and a little of arithmetic'. Prasanna Kumar Ghosh favoured the adoption of Adam's plan whereby the existing mass schools could be improved *without entirely changing their character*. He, like the other members of his class, regarded the education of the masses as solely consisting of the rudiments of reading, writing, and arithmetic, which could be improved by superior textbooks, but was not be compromised by any efforts to raise the level of education imparted. Echoing a similar position, Pearychand Mitra suggested the extension of the knowledge of practical agriculture and horticultural skills for the masses, for he felt that 'they can apply that knowledge to the

---

[104] The *hulkabundee* system of vernacular education was introduced in the North Western Province in 1850. According to this, a model school known as the *Tehseel School* was established by the state in the center of each *tehseel* or revenue district. Teachers and textbooks were provided to each school at government expense and the schools functioned as models for the neighbouring indigenous schools included within the 'halka' or circle.

promotion of their interest more than their knowledge of English or Bengali literature, or proficiency in calligraphy'.[105]

While some members of the bhadralok community were totally opposed to granting education to the lower orders due to the fact that higher education would render them too proud to follow their traditional professions, the majority were in favour of a limited and controlled access to learning. What resulted was a controlled participation of the lower classes in terms of how far and what they could study. The district reports were an indication of the situation. In 1860 the magistrate of the twenty-four Parganas reported that the great majority who frequented the government Anglo-Vernacular schools, were 'of that class who, from their caste and position in society, would have been literate and gained their livelihood by sedentary occupation'. It appeared to him that the school committees and masters took 'pride in keeping their schools select and excluding the classes who live by manual labour'. It was not so much a question of access to primary education, which the system allowed to some degree to the lower orders, but of entry into schools of higher education. The magistrate of Jessore reported in 1872 that the percentage of sons of cultivators attending schools as compared to the number of boys of the higher classes was very small. He noted that even boys who were entered as sons of cultivators were not really the sons of men who supported themselves by manual labour, but of small *gautidars* and others who lived on the produce of their holding without personally engaging in agriculture. According to him, it was the very smallness of the percentage of sons of agriculturists attending school which had given rise to the impression that the education of the *chasas* or peasants was a mistake. In a detailed account of his district he remarked:

An educated *chasha* who feels that from his education he has acquired something which in the opinion of himself and his fellows has always been the distinguishing mark of the *bhadra loke*, naturally feels inclined to separate himself from his uneducated companions ....

There is at present the impression prevailing that the education of a *chasha* unfits him for practical work, which means manual labour. The parents of the *chasha* thinks so; the chasha himself thinks so; the bhadraloke, both educated and uneducated (and the educated are quite as jealous of the progress of the chotolok as the uneducated) think so too. There is not quite so much feeling on this point as regards

[105] General Proceedings, Education Department, October 1860, Nos 52–63.

the very elementary education that the ryots' sons receive in a pathshala; but as regards any higher education, the *chasha* is not considered as deserving of any encouragement, but rather of repression.[106]

In 1866 even a largely racist article in the *Calcutta Review* noted that education was essentially of two kinds, that of the farm labourer or mechanic, and that of the lawyer or clergyman.[107] It was thus clear from the outset that this concern from all quarters on the issue of mass education was determined specifically by the kind of education that the masses were allowed to receive.

Mythologies of Democracy

So far we have seen that the education afforded by the colonial state was to a large extent responsible for not only the creation of a specific attitude towards learning, but also served an important ideological function for the new middle class. While the discourse on education or shiksha persistently separated it from wealth and material concerns, and emphasized democracy in opportunity, in actuality it was very much dependent on the individual's class background or gender as the case maybe.

The majority of the bhadralok being salaried, jobs were important in determining one's location within the group. The connection between an English education and employment was first established by Lord Hardinge in his Resolution of 1844 in which the Education Council was instructed to prepare returns for meritorious students to be printed and circulated to the heads of all government offices. The offices were instructed to 'omit no opportunity of providing for and advancing the candidates' and 'in filling up every situation of whatever grade'. This would, Hardinge felt, show people the 'invariable preference over others not possessed of superior qualifications'. It was clearly stated in the resolution that 'in every instance a man who can read and write be preferred to one who cannot'.[108]

[106] Letter No. 356E, from J. Monro, Officiating Magistrate of Jessore, to The Commissioner of the Presidency Division, General Proceedings, Education Department, April 1872, No. 46.

[107] 'The Native Press of Bengal', *Calcutta Review*, 43, 86 (July–December,1866), pp. 377.

[108] Hardinge's Resolution of 10 October 1844, reproduced in General Education Proceedings, May 1850, No. 1.

Accordingly, the Council furnished the government with returns of candidates it considered suitable. Such returns usually favoured the pupils of leading institutions like the Hindu College, and also was a living reference to their character and abilities.[109] Within eight years of its institution it was found that the greater number of these candidates had entered the Education Department, as teachers in schools and colleges and even as librarians.[110] Of the 1,589 students who obtained arts degrees from the University of Calcutta between 1857 and 1882, 526 had in 1882 entered the public service, 581 the legal profession, and twelve had become doctors. The state officials speculated that of the 470 who remained many were 'no doubt, largely employed as teachers in the colleges and the high schools'.[111] We have already commented on the disproportionately large numbers that flocked to the public services from the middle of the nineteenth century. In 1901, 11 per cent of the total population of Bengal was recorded as being in the service sector. According to the census, this included 18,950 people in government services and 22,530 people working in what it called the 'professions'.[112] It is important to bear in mind, however, that the number of literate persons in 1901 was 210,253.41.[113] This meant that even by that date only a small number of people, about 20 per cent, were within the ambit of white-collar jobs. The ratio must have been considerably less in the nineteenth century.

If the distance between the majority of the population and the service sector was quite large, the correlation between the kerani and the upper layers of the middle class was not too distant. As we mentioned before, Bankimchandra Chattopadhyay's brother had started out as a kerani. Rajnarayan Basu's father also started his career as a kerani in the *Hurkaru* office from where he subsequently went to other similar posts.[114] Sumit

[109] In one of the earliest of such returns, F.J. Mouat, the Secretary to the Council, listed four candidates, all of whom were from the Hindu College. See General Education Proceedings, January 1850, No. 8.

[110] General Education Proceedings, January 1852, No. 1.

[111] *Selected Chapters of the Report of the Calcutta University Commission* (Calcutta, 1919), p. 101.

[112] *Imperial Gazetteer of India: Provincial Series, Bengal*, Vol. 1 (Calcutta, 1909), p. 400.

[113] Ibid., p. 418.

[114] Rajnarayan Basu, *Atmacharit*, p. 8.

Sarkar draws attention to the social closeness between the two groups whereby the 'most eminent of the bhadralok', he argues, 'could have kinsmen eking out a living from clerical *chakri*, or among the ranks of the educated unemployed'.[115] It was fairly common that newcomers to the city, whether Calcutta, or any large sudder town would usually stay either with a distant relative or a village-cum jati affine, till he found a job or completed his education, as the case may be. Akshaychandra Sarkar, a fairly well known author of the nineteenth century confirms in his autobiography that in the mid-nineteenth century, it was the custom of high earning bhadralok to shelter insolvent relatives and others in his house.[116] A well-paid job in the city usually signified taking responsibility for a number of indigent dependents. Sarkar says that 'looking for a chakri' was the main pre-occupation of these men.[117] The wealthier rentier class, who could afford it, institutionalized this practice to a large extent. Kailashchandra Basu, the grandson of the Company's dewan, Bhabanicharan Basu, utilized a part of his family wealth in this way. It is said that once a student approached him saying that he had earned his graduation degree through his financial help, and in gratitude, would like to offer him some sort of service. Kailashchandra is said to have asked the student to help four more poor students in a like manner.[118] Similarly Narendranath Mitra, the youngest son of Raja Digambar Mitra, ran a charitable boarding house for students at Jhamapukur.[119] Debendranath Tagore and Ramaprasad Roy, the son of Rammohan Roy, had established a school at Bansberia, and was advertised as being based on ancient Hindu principles of non-montesied education.[120]

Social permeability between the two groups did not necessarily erase all difference. Difference lay in the choices that were available to each group and the informal networks of patronage and favours. Here financial considerations played a crucial role. First, the institutional complex of education was structured in such a way as to allow only a few to attain a B.A. degree. Primary education was entirely in the vernacular and in principle

[115] Sumit Sarkar, *Writing Social History*, p. 228.

[116] Harimohan Mukhopadhyay, ed., *Bangabhashar Lekhak*, Part I (Calcutta, 1904), p. 505.

[117] Sarkar, *Writing Social History*, p. 228.

[118] See Manmathanath Ghosh, *Sekaler Lok*, p. 73.

[119] Shibendranarayan Shastri, *Kalikatar Paribarik Itihas*, Vol. 1, pp. 99–101.

[120] Manmattanath Ghosh, *Sekaler Lok*, p. 100.

accessible to all. The pathshalas had 'their system perfectly adapted to the state of things existing before the art of printing was known', and were attended in large numbers by the 'children of those poorer orders of the people who send them to School merely because it [was] the custom to do so'.[121] However, in order to get state funding or a state scholarship which would allow these students to go on to higher education, the following criteria had to be strictly adhered to: writing the vernacular of the district and reading it in printed books as well as manuscripts, command over arithmetic up to the first four rules both simple and compound, knowledge of bazaar and zamindari accounts and simple mensuration.[122] These rules eliminated the lower classes to a great extent, as printed books, though available, were not in plenty. The scholarships thus mainly went to children of the bhadralok, both from the high income and low income range. The colonial authorities admitted in 1876 that despite the catholicity of scholarships it was 'doubtful whether the lower stratum of native society ... [would] force its way through the upper by force of intellect'. The reason for this was not, it was pointed out, the 'apathy and idleness' of the poor, but due to material exigencies which compelled 'the young to begin earning a livelihood before their education is properly completed'.[123] The first level of education thus managed to weed out the very bottom rung of society. The remarks of the Commissioner of Jessore is a fitting tribute to the situation. In 1872, he observed:

There is at present the impression prevailing that the education of a chasa unfits him for practical work, which means manual labour. The parents of the chasa think so; the bhdraloke, both educated and uneducated (and the educated are quite as jealous of the progress of the chota lok as the uneducated) think so too. There is not quite so much feeling on this point as regards the very elementary education which ryots' sons receive in a pathshala; but as regards any higher education, the chasa is not considered as deserving of any encouragement, but rather of repression that this must be the result of a free education policy at the stage which it has ... reached in Bengal.[124]

Education at the middle, or secondary level, was imparted partly in vernacular and partly in English. This level saw the 'infusion of the scientific

---

[121] General Proceedings, Education Department, February 1864, No. 6.

[122] *Report on the Administration of Bengal*, p. 81.

[123] Ibid., pp. 78–9.

[124] General Proceedings, Education Department, April 1872, No. 46.

element in instruction'. The bhadralok from all class backgrounds generally studied up to this level, the chasas having gotten rid of at an earlier stage. The Commissioner for the Presidency division, G. Graham, conducted a survey in 1872 to see how many students from the labouring classes attended these schools. He reported that 'school committees and masters feel some pride in keeping their schools select and excluding the classes who live by manual labour'. When asked whether any such pupils attended these classes 'the answer in the negative was given with an appearance of pride rather than of regret'.[125] But despite the solidarity within the bhadralok vis-à-vis the lower orders, this camaraderie did not extend too far.

Notwithstanding the demand for English education, according to official estimates, the majority of secondary students in the 1870s still learnt their lessons in Bengali. The total number of students in the secondary schools in 1872–3 was 517,239, of whom 453,578 studied in the vernacular and had no access to English books. Thus, eight out of nine students were educated in the vernacular.[126] In institutions of higher education, that is, in colleges, the medium of instruction was almost exclusively English. The gap between the middle and the top level was hence sufficient to complete the final elimination process, this time from within the bhadralok rank. Also the fees for colleges were high enough to keep unwanted elements out. The monthly fees for all government colleges, except Presidency College, in 1872–3 was Rs 5. For Presidency College it was Rs 12. In view of the fact that the average income of the majority of the service sector was roughly around Rs 12 per month, it was impossible for the sons of members of this layer to continue their college education. The discrepancy was evident in the attendance record of the colleges, keeping in mind that nearly 600,000 students reached the secondary level (see Table 4.2).

One student in 600 thus reached college from the secondary level. Also, as Table 4.2 shows, Presidency College records the highest numbers compared to the provincial Colleges through the years. It is hence safe to assume that most of the students who went into higher education could afford to pay the required high fees thus pointing to the class character of higher education in general.

[125] Ibid., No. 47.
[126] *Report on the Administration of Bengal*, p. 82.

TABLE 4.2   Student attendance in colleges

Government college	Monthly fee	1871	1872	1873	1874	1875
Presidency College	Rs 12	405	442	385	353	350
Sanskrit College	Rs 5	26	23	26	26	25
Hooghly College	Rs 5	152	142	120	93	113
Dacca College	Rs 5	112	102	124	116	130
Krishnangar College	Rs 5	116	96	52	46	61
Berhampore College	Rs 5	41	21	24	20	25
Patna College	Rs 5	84	79	97	92	90
Total		958	924	854	803	851

Source: Report on the Administration of Bengal, p. 450.

In 1872, H.A. Cockerell, the Commissioner for the Presidency division, correctly surmised that under the present system every boy at a higher class English school commenced to read the University Entrance Course, irrespective of his class background. However, he remarked, that for the son of a poor clerk with a monthly salary of Rs 20, the passing of the examination 'reaps nothing beyond the barren honour of a certificate, as he is too poor to attend the University'. Thus, according to Cockerell, it would be much wiser to give this class of students 'a sound professional education, comprising a good acquaintance with their own vernacular, a knowledge of English book keeping and vernacular zemindaree accounts', for they would have to 'look forward to earning their livelihood as clerks'.[127]

The trajectory of life for the upper layers of the bhadralok was, in contrast, significantly different. As a student at Sanskrit College in 1876, Haraprasad Shastri won a prize for his essay titled 'On the highest ideal of woman's character as set forth in [sic] ancient Sanskrit writers'. When he finally got his B.A. degree the following choices were open to him: his education at the M.A. level was assured by his scholarship (he knew that a job would not be immediately available) and he could get his essay published as an article in one of the literary journals. His first target was *Aryadarshan* edited by Yogendranath Bandyopadhyay. In Shastri Shastr's own words Bandyopadhyay 'was a fellow alumni from the Sanskrit College so he might

[127] General Proceedings, Education Department, April 1872, No. 45.

consider my request'. Bandyopadhyay, however, turned him down. Some days later he bumped into an old acquaintance, Rajkrishna Mukhopadhyay, who was then a Professor at Presidency College and already had a long list of scholarly publications to his credit. Mukhopadhyay hearing of his plight with *Aryadarshan* said that he could get the essay published in Bankimchandra's *Bangadarshan*. The young Haraprasad was sceptical, as *Bangadarshan* by then was an extremely prestigious journal. Mukhopadhyay assured him: 'that is not your concern, meet me at Naihati Station on Sunday [Bankim was then living and editing the journal from Naihati]'. When Haraprasad was finally introduced to Bankim, the latter commented 'You are from Naihati? You are a Brahmin's son, a B.A. from Sanskrit College, why have you not come to us previously?' Bankim's incredulity was obvious. Haraprasad, with the correct attributes of such social circles had been so far missing out on vital networks of power. His essay was consequently published in the *Bangadarshan* and earned him much acclaim.[128]

This outlines the structure of what we have called the informal networks of education. Most of the new middle class, as we have shown before, were related to each other, either by blood, marriage, or as fellow scholars from premier educational institutions. It was a fairly tight circle of intellectual interaction beyond the ken of the ordinary kerani, let alone the peasant. The subscription rates for a popular newspaper like the *Hindoo Patriot* was Rs 8, Rs 4 and Rs 1 on an yearly, half-yearly and monthly basis. No subscriptions were received for less than a month. Also for the unfortunates in the mofussil towns, the newspaper had a strong policy of not registering any requests for subscription 'unless a year's or six month's subscription ... [was] remitted'.[129] It is doubtful how many of the peasants that the paper defended during the Indigo uprising, or the kerani whose plight worried the editor, actually got to read the paper.

Bankim's comment about Shastri's caste and educational background sums up the reigning social attitude. Beginning with that encounter, Haraprasad had unlimited access to the privileged circle that gathered at Bankim's house. He also became a regular contributor to the *Bangadrashan*. In 1880, he published a long article in the journal on education in colleges.

---

[128] Satyajit Chaudhuri et al., eds, *Haraprasad Shastri Rachana-Sangraha*, pp. 15–17.

[129] *Hindoo Patriot*, 6 April 1854, reprinted in Benoy Ghosh, *Selections from Records*, pp. 142–3.

The main thrust of his argument was in favour of making Bengali the medium of instruction. The English language he felt unnecessarily made education a chore and also limited its accessibility.[130] Nurtured in the select literary circles of Jorasanko (the Tagores) and Kanthalpara (Bankim) the new middle class from this period had started to blame the English language for fractures in social relationships. The next chapter studies the politics of this cultural upsurge in the language.

<hr/>

[130] Brajendranath Bandyopadhyay and Sajanikanta Das, eds., *Sahitya-Sadhak Charitmala: Haraprasad Shastri* (Calcutta: Bangiya Sahitya Parishad, 1949), pp. 35–7.

5

Bewarish Bangla Bhasha
Language and its Guardians

> *When conversing in our native tongue [Bengali] we tend to use very many English words. Eleven years ago, in a short English treatise, I proposed that we establish purity of speech when conversing in Bengali. A few days after the publication of the tract, on a visit to an affluent Calcutta household, I found therein a civilian youth of that same household engaged in a new sport. The game was as follows: any individual who used an English word during conversation would have to pay a fine of one paisa. Later all the money collected would be spent in buying treats for all. I also took part in this novel game. Of the players some were fined 7 annas, some six annas ... even I was fined 2 paisa.*[1]

The first formal history of the Bengali language was written in the late nineteenth century by the famous pandit, Ramgati Nayaratna, in an attempt to trace back its sources as a comparatively new language and document its formative literature.[2] The major achievement of this work, which remains a seminal text of its kind, was to establish language as an object of history. For the first time language, hitherto the operative ground for grammarians and the nebulous creative material for literature, was peopled with human achievements, with names, figures, dates, and events. Bengali as a language was given an individual particularity distinct from its past 'sources' of Sanskrit, Maithili, or Magadhi, and narrativized as a generative sum total of individual artistic creativity. The genesis of the language was shifted from the previous assumptions of the grammarians as a system of forms, to a high drama of human agency and intentions. Hence the famous grammar

---

[1] Rajnarayan Basu, *Bangla Bhasha*, pp. 66–7.

[2] Ramgati Nayaratna, *Banglabhasha O Banglasahitya Bishayak Prastab.*

of Rammohan Roy was mentioned only in passing by Nayaratna in his history. While fully acknowledging Rammohan as one of the pioneers in consolidating the language, his grammar was summed up in two lines—as 'using the laws of English grammar' and containing 'some useful facts for students learning the language'.[3]

In this chapter we will trace the significance of this shift in linguistic perception. We will argue that this shift was not an arbitrary romanticization of the language, or the linguistic community, but a necessary historical change. However, it cannot be seen in abstraction as a *development*, or *maturation*, of the language as such but must be contextualized within contemporary historical developments. Broadly speaking, we will argue against the structuralist position that the system of language and its history are alien to each other, and try to show that the historicization of language, as distinct from its actual history, was significantly related to broader changes within the social formation in terms of the emergence of new classes and their ideologies. Recent works on print have investigated its role in standardizing the language and have tried to show how the emergence of print pushes the multiplicity of utterances (different dialects, norms of spelling) to the borders of social acceptance.[4] Benedict Anderson, thus, argues that printing in Europe strove to create stable uniform languages, which in turn were established as the languages of particular nation states.[5] While agreeing with the conclusions of this literature, we would like to emphasize that print was not serving any essential technological function in any absolute sense. In fact, print was used within the linguistic paradigm and its location and form changed according to the historical needs of the social agents.

The Word as Utterance

Any discussion on the Bengali language in the nineteenth century should be contextualized within two general points that formed essential axes of the linguistic discourse. First, to restate the obvious, the emergence of formal linguistics (in the modern sense of the term) was initiated in India through the efforts of the intrepid Orientalists of the late eighteenth and the early nineteenth century, in the works of men like William Jones, Nathaniel

---

[3] Ibid., p. 163.

[4] See for example, Walter J. Ong, *Orality and Literacy*, pp. 130–5.

[5] Benedict Anderson, *Imagined Communities*, pp. 44–5.

Brassey Halhed, Charles Wilkins, and H.T. Colebrook. Second, due to such beginnings, linguistics, had from its very inception a very specific historical task. As Jones eloquently put it, the acquisition of languages was necessary because they held the key to the 'history of the human mind'.[6] Thus the history of language and linguistic investigation always shared an anxious intimacy with the imperatives of rule.

Michel Pecheux identifies Leibniz as one of the first major figures from the late Enlightenment period, who according to Pecheux, 'decentred the seventeenth century's world of eternal truths', by prioritizing the empirical principle as the premise of all philosophical understandings of the world. What this meant in terms of conceptions about language was that for the first time language was abstracted as a stable, irreversible *system*, which could be studied under specific *laws* very much like the natural sciences. This stable abstract structure of language, which was assumed to be applicable to any linguistic community, irrespective of its individual and specific variations formed the theoretical basis of Leibniz's notion of universal grammar. It also formed the organizing principle of William Jones's position on comparative linguistics.[7]

There have been two major trends in recent scholarship in the analysis of the emergence of language as an abstract category in the late eighteenth and early nineteenth century. Michel Foucault has argued that previous to the nineteenth century, words were investigated on the basis of their representative values, as virtual elements of discourse that prescribed one and the same mode of being for them all.[8] This epistemology of language, according to Foucault, underwent a change in the last phase of the eighteenth century and the early decades of the nineteenth century. From a

---

[6] Quoted in O.P. Kejariwal, *The Asiatic Society of Bengal and the Discovery of India's Past: 1784–1838* (New Delhi: Oxford University Press, 1988), p. 31.

[7] For a detailed analysis of Jones's method see Prabal Dasgupta, 'On Sanskrit and Indian English: Some Linguistic Considerations', *New Quest*, 67(1988), pp. 15–25.

[8] Foucault uses the idea of general grammar, one of the fundamental principles of which implied that all languages had an absolute origin, whether mythical or not, and all the words of any language were bearers of a 'more or less hidden, more or less derived signification whose original *raison d'être* lay in an initial designation'. As a result, lateral resemblance with other languages were noted and listed only in order to confirm 'the vertical relation of each to these deeply buried, silted over, almost mute values'. Michel Foucault, *The Order of Things: An Archaeology of the Human Sciences* (London, New York: Routledge, 1994), pp. 232–8.

categorization based essentially on the representation of similitudes, differentiation between languages moved to address 'a form intermediary between the articulation of contents and the value of roots: namely inflection', such that grammar through inflection became the point of analogy between languages.[9]

Let us state Foucault's case more clearly. The basic point about the epistemic shift, Foucault argues, is in the functioning of grammar. Whereas previously languages were presumed to be similar to each other on the basis of their common primary origin, mythical or otherwise, from this period the constitutive link between languages was sought through the grammatical *form*. The grammatical inflection, says Foucault, constituted the 'solid, constant, almost unalterable totality whose sovereign law' was 'so far imposed upon the representative roots as to modify even those roots themselves'.[10] Thus, we find from this time onwards, the appearance of what Foucault has rightly called, the 'dimension of the purely grammatical'.

There has been another line of argument about the implications of language as an immutable system, first propounded by V.N. Volosinov, and later developed in the works of Mikhail Bakhtin. This argument is based on the proposition that the emergence of language as a system of stable laws was an abstraction of language from its social context. The principle of language being constituted as a system of normatively identical linguistic forms, argues Volosinov, denies totally that linguistic connections have anything in common with ideological values. It tries to prove that language phenomena are not 'grounded in ideological motives' and that no 'connection of a kind natural and comprehensible to the consciousness or of an artistic kind obtains between the word and its meaning'.[11] The most significant aspect of this thesis is the formulation of language as a dialogic utterance, and for our purposes this needs elaboration.

Language, according to Volosinov, is a purely historical phenomenon, and hence signs can arise only on inter-individual territory, where it is essential that the individuals be *organized socially*. Consciousness takes shape and being in the material of signs created by an organized group in the process of its social intercourse. To generalize then, language is something

[9] Foucault, *The Order of Things*, p. 234.

[10] Foucault, *The Order of Things*, p. 235.

[11] V.N Volosinov, *Marxism and the Philosophy of Language*, tr. L. Matejka and I.R. Titunik (Cambridge, MA: Harvard University Press, 1996), p. 57.

that should be viewed primarily as *communication*, as a dialogic utterance between people, situated in their specific socio-historical context. The word, says Volosinov, 'is a two-sided act'. It is 'precisely the product of the reciprocal relationship between speaker and listener, addresser and addressee. Each and every word expresses the "one" in relation to the "other"'.[12] The abstraction of language as a system of stable signs precisely denies this and treats languages as dead monologic utterances, fixed in a trans-historical sense, where individual speech acts become arbitrary in relation to an immutable law.[13]

Both Foucault and Volosinov, then, seem to be in agreement in their recognition of language as an abstraction having a fundamental social significance, though they arrive at different conclusions as to its implications. For us to place the history of the Bengali language in the perspective of these two positions two issues are of relevance. First, it is important to note that the cognitive ability to situate language in objective abstraction through its laws, is an entirely modern phenomenon, and must be seen in distinction from pre-modern grammatical perceptions. Second, this entailed a new approach to the issues of form and content. Volosinov makes a relevant argument on this issue when he attributes the concept of formalism to a thinking focused on a 'ready-made and, so to speak, arrested object', or dead languages. The only way that the form and content can be separated, and made objectively available to a linguist, is through the study of a language that had lost all social contextuality, and was hence dead, or 'alien'.[14] In this respect Sanskrit proved to be the ideal ground for the linguistic speculations of Jones and his colleagues. As a dead language, it could be used to shed light on the life of living languages. Deliberations on the linguistic question in Bengal was thus overdetermined from the very start by the Orientalist perceptions of language in general, and Sanskrit in particular. What is perhaps most remarkable about this epistemology is its veneration of the linguistic *form*, as distinct from its *content*. Taking their lead from the

---

[12] Ibid., p. 86.

[13] Volosinov's major critique is against the structuralist dualism of *langue* and *parole* which divide up the whole linguistic phenomenon into its synchronicity, which is assumed to be fixed across time, and the historical diachronicity, which is considered to be arbitrary, and unconnected to the former. In other words, he argues against the position that the history of languages can be seen in separation from its so-called laws. See particularly Part II of his *Marxism and the Philosophy of Language*.

[14] Volosinov, *Marxism and the Philosophy of Language*, p. 78.

developments in the European scientific and linguistic paradigm noted earlier, the structure of Sanskrit through its grammatical laws, became the point of departure for Jones and his contemporaries. Given this objectification of language, it is no surprise that Jones actually maintained that Sanskrit was a language that was to be respected rather than studied.[15]

The celebrated grammar of Halhed (1778) was intended as a grammar of the 'pure Bengali dialect', in distinction from the 'modern jargon' that actually prevailed in the province.[16] Grammar, Halhed had hoped, would provide the much needed structure to the language, which was missing in the spoken tongue of the people and was absent even their written correspondence.[17] Languages earned their linguistic credibility through their grammars in this formulation, and, more importantly, languages were perceived primarily from the point of view of their forms. It was of secondary consideration for this conceptualization what the content of the language was, that is, what the language in its texts spoke about. In fact, the content of the language was considered to be determined by its form. This relationship between the form and content of languages is of fundamental importance to our understanding of the subsequent historical developments of the nineteenth century, and it is this conceptual distinction that informed a range of linguistic changes.

The Search for Sources

'The grand source of Indian Literature', stated Halhed in his preface, 'the parent of almost every dialect from the Persian Gulph to the China Seas, is the Sanscrit'.[18] This position in keeping with William Jones's famous speculations of 1776, established the dead past of Sanskrit onto the present. We have already mentioned Volosinov's argument about dead languages. Here we would like to make a related but different point. While it was true that the deadness of Sanskrit was of significance, its pastness was also of no less importance. One of the major agendas of the comparative linguistics of the Oriental school was the construction of a remote past, to which

[15] S.N. Mukherjee, *Sir William Jones: A Study in Eighteenth Century British Attitudes to India* (London: Cambridge University Press, 1968), p. 46.

[16] Nathaniel Brassey Halhed, *A Grammar*, p. xx.

[17] Lamenting on the lack of any proper prose form in Bengali, Halhed mentioned that the letters of business, petitions, and public notifications that were written in prose lacked any grammatical form. Halhed, *A Grammar*, p. 36.

[18] Halhed, *A Grammar*, p. iii.

contemporary speakers had no access. Historical linguistics as a whole postulated processes of linguistic change without the consciousness of the speakers perceiving or affecting them in anyway. Etymology became the prime determinant in the story of the past, and the greatest achievement of Orientalism, the construction of a classical Indian Hindu past was firmly established.[19]

Due to this curious linguistic approach to the past, it is not surprising that Sanskrit would be fetishized in this discourse not only as the sole link with the ancient civilization, as the word of the gods as it were, but as the only language worth claiming inheritance from. Sanskrit also proved to be one of the links that tied together the classical antiquity of Europe with that of India. Jones, for example, precipitously sought similarities between Hindu and European gods. In an enthusiastic letter to Earl Spencer in 1787, Jones thus wrote:

To what shall I compare my literary pursuits in India? suppose Greek literature to be known in modern Greece only, and there to be in the hands of priests and philosophers; and suppose them to be still worshippers of Jupiter and Apollo: suppose Greece to have been conquered successively by Goths, Huns, Vandals, Tartars, and lastly by the English; then suppose a court of judicature to be established by the British parliament, at Athens, and an inquisitive Englishman to be one of the judges; suppose him to learn Greek there, which none of his countrymen knew, and to read Homer, Pindar, Plato, which no other Europeans had even heard of. Such am I in this country; substituting Sanscrit for Greek, the *Brahmans*, for the priests of *Jupiter*, and *Valmic, Vyasa, Calidasa*, for Homer, Plato, Pindar.[20]

Sanskrit, according to Jones, was a language possessing a 'wonderful structure, more perfect than the Greek, more copious than the Latin, and more exquisitely refined than either'.[21]

[19] Historical investigations through word similarities reached such a height that one Edward Pococke attempted to prove, on the basis of the similarity of words in Greek and Sanskrit, that a group of Brahmins and Rajputs colonized Greece. *Friend of India* (Vol. IX, 1853) wrote a scathing article on this proposition declaring its absurdity. Jones himself had to issue a warning to the dangers of making such deductions based solely on the similarities of sounds in different languages. See William Jones, 'On the Gods of Greece, Italy and India', *Asiatic Researches*, Vol. 1 (Varanasi: Bharat-Bharati, 1972, first edn 1784), pp. 188–91.

[20] Garland Cannon, ed., *The Letters of Sir William Jones*, Vol. II (Oxford: Clarendon Press, 1970), pp. 755–6.

[21] Quoted in Thomas R. Metcalf, *Ideologies of the Raj* (Cambridge, reprint 1998), p. 14.

As noted earlier, it was the *form* of Sanskrit that came under European scrutiny, and carrying this formalism further, it was the form of Sanskrit that was also assumed to determine its content. William Carey, one of the firm believers in the use of Sanskrit in building up the Bengali language wrote:

The people do not venerate the language for the idolatrous ideas it contains, but the ideas for the dress they wear. What can be a more effectual mode of counteracting this influence, than that of depositing ideas of genuine science in this very language, and by dividing the attachment of the people, finally transferring all their regard to those just ideas which it is proposed to inculcate.[22]

This very separation was to be used later by James Mill to prove the depravity and decadence of the Indian civilization. Taking his lead from Jones, Mill argued that *Shakuntala* as a text embodied the true spirit of India, that of superstition and irrationality. The flamboyant volubility of Sanskrit lyricism was, according to him, irreducible proof of a self-indulgent and ultimately despotic society.[23]

Approach to languages through their forms, as in the European paradigm, had some important consequences in Bengal in the beginning of the nineteenth century. First, due to the determination of languages through their grammars, Bengali as a language was rendered linguistically unviable until it had a stable grammatical structure. It is hence not entirely coincidental that the first Bengali book to be printed was one of Bengali grammar. Second, a strong distinction was made between the spoken language of the people, what Halhed called the 'modern jargon', and the prose that was born within the confines of the Fort William College. Carey, not noted for his love of the spoken language, made this hierarchy clear in one of his letters:

The language spoken by the natives of this part, though Bengali, is yet so different from the language itself, that, though I can preach an hour with tolerable freedom, so as that all who speak the language well or can write or read, perfectly understand me, yet the poor labouring people can understand but little.[24]

---

[22] William Carey, 'On the Importance of Sungskrita to the Future Improvement of India', *Friend of India*, Vol. 2, No. xvi (1819), p. 374.

[23] James Mill, *History of British India*, Vol. 2, pp. 37–9, 111.

[24] From a letter written to S. Pearce, 2 October 1795 in Eustace Carey, ed., *Memoir of William Carey* (Hartford: Canfield and Robins, 1837), p. 242.

It is important to note that before the attention given to it, Bengali as a language, occupied a very specific social space in the early nineteenth century. We have already commented on the overall dynamic of the pre-colonial order of knowledge which was localized and fractured in both its transmission. The medium of transmission also varied according to specific tasks. Bengali was, as Sudipta Kaviraj has argued, the language of the quotidian, of everyday life. Sanskrit, by contrast, was the language of religious ceremonies and of formal institutional education in the *chatushpathis*. The language of state was predominantly Persian, till it was replaced by English. Thus, 'functions like dealing with God, or the King, or property' were done in different languages.[25]

In the linguistic hierarchy then, as Kaviraj has argued, Bengali performed the low functions. But while the perception of this hierarchy is certainly true for the nineteenth century, it is unlikely to have existed in such a form before the specific canonization of Sanskrit in this period. That is not to say that Sanskrit did not represent a 'high' language before the Orientalist project. Medieval poets like Jayadeva and Vidyapati used it in their poetic compositions. However, one of the major achievements of Vaishnavism in Bengal, after Chaitanya, was carrying its strong anti-Brahamanical drive into the linguistic domain, and according to the reformer's implicit theory, touching the everyday with the divine. Kaviraj makes an interesting proposition about this tradition of vernacular writing in the pre-colonial era. According to him, the greatest achievement of Vaishnav poetry was its use of a 'dual language', a language which not only utilized and altered the canonical traditions of Sanskrit literature, but also brought the vernacular closer to Sanskrit, as an *inclusionary* literary strategy, to appeal to a larger audience.[26] Bharatchandra, as the prestigious court poet of Krishnachandra,

---

[25] Sudipta Kaviraj, 'Literary Culture in History: Bengali', unpublished paper.

[26] Since the vocabulary of the vernaculars was based on Sanskrit, either in the form of identical words (tatsama), or derived ones (tatbhava), this tradition used tatsama words primarily, but minimized the use of the verb, drawing the poetic play as much as possible from the use of nouns and adjectives, thus making the vernaculars closer to Sanskrit. In this stratagem it was not to make literature more exclusive that Sanskrit was adopted, but to widen its scope. Jayadeva thus writing in Sanskrit could still be understood by the Bengali speaking audience, and Vidyapati though writing in Maithili was still very popular in Bengal. The high tradition of Sanskrit, thus instead of acting exclusively, was used by this tradition as a wide communicative devise. Kaviraj, 'Literary Culture'.

thus could use the grammatical structures of Sanskrit, and yet write in the Bengali language.

It is this idea of sectoralization of content in accordance to its form, that lay at the heart of the debates over *sadhu* and *chalit bhasha* in the nineteenth century and was to be refuted by the new middle class. In order to trace the origins of this debate, we have to go back to the days of the Fort William College, when the pandits writing the commissioned prose of the Empire, were for the first time challenged by a new social imperative in the scholarly objections of Rammohan.

Laying the Foundations

Rammohan's Bengali translation of the Vedantas (1815) surfaced as a challenge to social codes in two fundamental ways. First, it was an obvious attack on the existing religious sensibilities, advocating the invisible single God to be the organizing principle of Hinduism, and simultaneously displacing the long tradition of *Nyaya* and *Navya-Nyaya* that Bengal had been noted for. Second, this very important dissertation was written entirely in a language that had so far been considered unfit for any serious discourse, namely Bengali. In his preface to the text, Rammohan took up the issue of this use of Bengali and made it clear that it was a premeditated and purposive decision on his part. He said that the Bengali language, as of the present, only had words 'fit for household activities' and was dependent on Sanskrit. It was a language, he stated, in which prose had never been written, either to write out the Shastras or the Kavyas, and hence the people were ill-equipped to make sense of a full prose sentence in the language. It was this unavailability of an *easy* linguistic medium that, Rammohan maintained, prevented the people from grasping the true meaning and content of the Vedantas, and hence his effort to do so in Bengali.[27]

The text, published in 1815, found its best response in the *Vedanta Chandrika* (1817), by Mrityunjay Vidyalankar, the chief pundit at the Fort William College. Vidyalankar was supposed to have 'made a difference to Carey's Bengali',[28] and Carey acknowledged his 'great assistance' in the

---

[27] Rammohan Roy, 'Vedanta Grantha' in Brajendranath Bandyopadhyay and Sajanikanta Das, eds., *Rammohan Granthabali* (Calcutta, n.d.), pp. 9–10.

[28] S.P. Carey, *William Carey* (London: The Carey Press, 1934), p. 219.

compilation of his Sanskrit grammar.[29] In other words, Vidyalankar belonged to the class of traditional intellectuals in Hindu society whose assistance the British project at Fort William College secured in order to create a prose for Bengali. Much has been written in the recent times on the prose form of Fort William College, and how it was designed to be a prose for the Empire.[30] For our purposes what is perhaps of equal significance is the fact that the project of prose creation by the College gave such a shape to the Bengali language and built for it such a syntactic structure that Bengali came to be directly understandable to an European readership by applying the rules of English and Sanskrit grammar in a project of literal translation. It welded Sanskrit clauses to a structure of English verb patterns. The spoken form of Bengali did not figure in any way in this linguistic enterprise.

There was, in fact, as mentioned earlier, a conscious effort to move away from the spoken language, a phenomenon that was in part something that Rammohan was reacting to. Mrityunjay Vidyalankar was thus particularly scathing about Rammohan's use of the low spoken language:

The doctrine of the Shastras does not lie in extremely worldly language, but in sentences that resemble a ripe badari fruit [...] And as clever men, who understand the heart of a beautiful, ornamented and chaste woman, shun the sight of a naked, unchaste woman, so good men who understand the heart of ornate chaste language(*sadhu bhasha*) which contain the meaning of the Shastras, shun the very sound of the naked, unchained common language.[31]

We encounter two important theoretical formulations on language from this passage. First, it is another exemplification of the form and content debate, where the form of the language is taken to be determinate of its content. For Vidyalankar, the vulgar form of the spoken language made it an unfit bearer for the knowledge of the Shastras. Second, the very division between the spoken and written dominate both the social and the linguistic context of each of these. It was because a language was a spoken language that it lost its place to the written in the linguistic hierarchy, and sadhu

[29] William Carey, *A Grammar of the Sungskrit Language Composed from the works of the most Esteemed Grammarians* (Serampore: Mission Press, 1806), p. iv.

[30] See for example Anisuzzaman, *Puratan Bangla Gadya* (Dhaka: Bangla Academy, 1984); and Debesh Roy, *Pre-British Bengali Prose: Search for Sources*, Occasional Paper No. 48 (Calcutta: Centre for Studies in Social Sciences, 1982).

[31] Mrityunjay Vidyalankar, *Vedantachandrika*, pp. 67–8.

bhasha (literally meaning the language of the sadhu or good people), becomes co-terminus with the written, which in Bengal would have to be either Sanskrit itself, or its closest approximation, the highly Sanskritized Bengali of the Fort William College pundits. It is ironic that this emphasis on the written prose form for discourse, came from a Sanskrit pundit, whose entire scholarly tradition had revered the spoken word over the written and verse over prose. European linguistics, it is thus clear, had through the Orientalist enterprise, managed to set the terms for the debate, that was between the new social sentiments represented by Rammohan and the traditional intellectual in Vidyalankar.

What was particularly distinctive about Rammohan's linguistic project? We have noted in the context of his conscious use of Bengali that he was in search of a language that was widely understood, accepted and hence spoken. It was a project of particular significance because, on the one hand, Rammohan was trying to transform the social space of Bengali from its quotidian use to a language of scholarly discourse. On the other hand, he had chosen Bengali as the medium for the propagation of his own religious ideas of Brahmoism. Partha Chatterjee, in his analysis of separate sphere of the 'private' that the colonial elite devised in opposition to the colonial state's 'public', has seen language as one of the 'areas within the so-called spiritual domain that nationalism transforms in the course of its journey'. He has argued that the 'crucial moment' for the Bengali language came in the mid-nineteenth century, when the bhadralok made it a 'cultural project to provide its mother tongue with the necessary linguistic equipment to enable it to become an adequate language for "modern" culture'.[32] Chatterjee incisively argues that this 'modernizing' of the language was effected in this period through the agency of the numerous printing presses, newspapers, publishing houses, and literary societies that were set up outside the purview of the state. Modernization, however, was one of the effects of a larger project of *socializing* the language, and this process began with Rammohan. A process directly connected with the concept of an incipient but rising community of Bengalis who needed to be communicated with and spoken to. Rammohan's grammar, published posthumously in 1833, is an interesting text in this regard, as it tries to combine the contemporary presumptions of grammar with its own reversals.

[32] Partha Chatterjee, *The Nation*, pp. 6–7.

In keeping with the colonial linguistic anxiety that languages should be judged on the basis of their grammars, the first thirty years of the nineteenth century, following Halhed, saw a tremendous effort on the part of the Bengalis to fashion their own grammar. In 1789, right after the publication of Halhed's book, the *Calcutta Gazette* carried a letter requesting a 'bhadralok' to write a grammar of Bengali for the general well-being of the people.[33] The *Bangadoot*, in 1830, repeated the same appeal to its 'learned readers', for the uplift of the 'general masses'.[34] Rammohan's *Sambad Kaumudi* emphasized in its seventh issue that it was important for a Hindu to know the grammar of his mother tongue before learning a foreign language.[35]

The two significant grammars of Bengali published before Rammohan were those by Halhed and William Carey. Both these texts attempted to distinguish between the language as it existed on the ground, that is, as it was spoken, and that which it ought to have been, given a strong grammatical basis. We have mentioned earlier what Halhed had denoted as the 'modern jargon' of Bengal, and a very similar echo of the same position can be traced in Carey:

The language [Bengali] is very copious and I think beautiful.... Indeed there are two distinct languages spoken all over the country; viz., the Bengalee, spoken by the Brahmans, and higher Hindoos; and the *Hindoostanic*, spoken by the *Mussulmans*, and lower Hindoos; and is a mixture of Bengalee and Persian.[36]

From the start, therefore, there was an implicit recognition as to whose voice the new language was to represent. Within this paradigm, however, Rammohan's grammar can be regarded as a significant departure.

The very basis of his grammar was an exercise in social linguistics, as opposed to the formal structuralism of the Europeans. Explaining the origin and genesis of languages, the text proclaimed:

Of all living creatures human beings have the very specific nature of living close to each other in large numbers. Proximity of individuals to each other within a house or a town creates the necessity of mutually conveying each other's intentions and

---

[33] Quoted in Sushil Kumar De, *Bengali Literature*, p. 72.

[34] Brajendranath Bandyopadhyay, ed., *Sambad Patre Sekaler Katha*, Vol. 1, p. 56.

[35] From the subject index of *Sambad Kaumudi* published in the *Calcutta Journal* (31 January 1822), quoted in J.K. Majumdar, *Raja Rammohan Roy*, p. 288.

[36] BMS Mss, Carey to Sutcliff, dated 9 August 1794.

needs. Humans have multifarious needs and intentions, and different words-sounds are born of the contact and workings of the voice, the upper palate and the lips; in order to determine referentiality to different particular objects, words-sounds have been divided up country specifically.

Word-sounds cannot reach people who are located far away, hence letters are created inscriptionally, the reading of whose signs, can make people see words irrespective of whether they are near or far from each other, and the knowledge of those particular word sounds make apparent the meaning of the words.[37]

Clearly, Rammohan was trying to introduce a new ground for the theoretical underpinning of language. Moving away from the abstract validation of languages through their forms and structures, his text was trying to argue for human interaction as the only legitimate foundation for language. This particular move away from the structures of grammar must be seen in the context of the simultaneous opposition that Rammohan consistently maintained, both on a philosophical and a programmatic plane, to the Nyaya school in regard to its insistence on grammatical laws, regulations, and rules.[38] The function of grammar, thus, acquired an important qualification with Rammohan. It was no longer an autonomous rule to any language, but relevant only in respect to the social validity of the language and its speakers. In other words, the only reason that Rammohan thought it was necessary to write a grammar of Bengali was in order to dispel the dominant notion that Bengali, due to its quotidian use, could not become a language fit for serious writing or discourse.

We cannot overemphasize the importance of this position, nor ignore its inherent contradiction. While, on the one hand, it broke away from the previous assumption that a spoken language was an unworthy register of discourse, it also re-established, on the other hand, the necessity of a grammatical structure, albeit with its focus on social and inter-personal communication. The text seems to constantly attack the dominant linguistic presuppositions, but always within their own terrain. Rammohan's covert

[37] Rammohan Roy, 'Goudya Byakaran', in Brajendranath Bandhopadhyay and Sajanikanta Das, eds., *Rammohan Granthabali*, p. 5.

[38] In his famous letter to Lord Amerherst against the establishment of a new Sanskrit school, Rammohan said that such a seminary could only be 'expected to load the minds of youth with grammatical niceties and metaphysical distinctions of little or no practical use to the possessors or to society'. Jogesh Chunder Ghosh, ed., *The English Works of Raja Rammohan Roy*, Vol. II (Calcutta: Oriental Press, 1901), pp. 324–7.

critique of grammatical abstraction thus never established a parallel concept situated in a different problematic but merely introduced into the older paradigm a new aspect of the 'social'.

The text itself when published in 1833, was titled bilingually as *Grammar of the Bengali Language* and *Goudiya Byakaran*. More than half a century later Haraprasad Shastri was to point out the contextuality of *byakaran* and grammar as it applied to a bilingual intelligentsia. The word *byakaran*, Shastri rightly claimed, referred to the etymology of words in Sanskrit. The nineteenth-century grammars of Bengali, and this was also true of Rammohan's text, defined *byakaran* as the science which facilitated the correct reading and writing of a language. This definition was essentially an explication of the functions of an English grammar, which was divided into orthography, etymology, syntax, punctuation, and prosody. In Sanskrit, however, there existed separate shastras for each of these categories, in the form of *alankara* shastra, *badartha*, *chanda* shastra, and so on. The word byakaran, Shastri rightly claimed, referred to the etymology of words in Sanskrit or *vyakaran*. Thus, the grammars that went by the name of a *vyakaran* followed English linguistic rules, and hence, Shastri said, should be seen as such.[39] Rammohan was, in fact, quite clear in his objective when he wrote his text, and stated that his grammar was aimed at the European 'philanthropist gentleman' who had laboured much to communicate with the natives of India. The text was for such 'worthy persons' in order to facilitate the 'intercourse' between Bengalis and Europeans.[40]

The grammars and all linguistic suppositions that followed Rammohan had thus two theoretical agendas. First, they were aimed at socializing the spoken language in order to make it available to a larger audience; and second, this broadening of the scope of Bengali as a language was done strictly within the parameters of European linguistics. It is worth noting in this context that Halhed also advocated the adoption of Bengali in the administration of Bengal. The principles of English government demanded the general adoption of the mother tongue as much in the distribution of justice as in the transactions of business; the distance between the corrupt despotism of the Mughals and the 'vigour, impartiality and dispatch' of

[39] Haraprasad Shastri, 'Bangla Byakaran' in Satyajit Choudhury et al., eds., *Haraprasad Shastri Rachana Sangraha*, pp. 593–602.

[40] Quoted in Nirmal Das, *Bangla Bhashar Byakaran O Tar Kramabikash* (Calcutta, 1987), pp. 151–2.

English rule could be best measured by 'a proper attention to that dialect used by the body of the people'. The true beauty of Bengali for Halhed thus resided in its representative character.[41] We thus need to review the introduction of social linguistics by Rammohan, and the idea of a popular communicative medium of language in this light. The historical process realized by the imposition through print and the educational system of Bengali as the common language was aimed to impose an antagonistic differentiation in class linguistic practices. Within the use of a 'national' language, the free linguistic communication required by the new middle class was achieved, along with linguistic class barriers that were equally necessary for the reproduction of its own class hegemony. When the mid-nineteenth century raised the issue once more of sadhu versus the *chalit bhasha*, it was correlated once more within these considerations.

Sadhu Versus Chalit: The Debate Over Form

The less respectable words of the Bengali language once took their grievances to Saraswati, the mother of knowledge and language. The words claimed that, like the respectable words, they too were her children, and on such grounds deserved entry into polite society. Saraswati, caught out by the logic of equality, granted them their wish. Thus, armed with the goddess's blessings, the lower order of words turned up at Vidyasagar's library and said that they were Saraswati's children, and, though they were parts of the *itar bhasha* or low language, they had as much right to unrestricted entry into the language as their more respectable counterparts of the sadhu bhasha. Vidyasagar, not as amenable as the goddess, refused them access to his books. He said that they might have been in Saraswati's family, but they were not the children of Saraswati's son Sanskrit. Only the children of Sanskrit could

[41] The notion of the vox populi had been the cornerstone of English political thought since the late seventeenth century, when the populist upheaval of the Glorious Revolution of 1688 was philosophically justified by the works of Locke. The individual freedom championed by Locke had indeed been reaffirmed for the new international order by Adam Smith just two years before the publication of Halhed's *Grammar* in the *Wealth of Nations* (1776) in the figure of the freely exchanging individual of laissez-faire economics. True to Smith, Halhed envisioned a government 'for the people' in which industrious individuals are released from tyranny through the agency of an impartial and decisive system of law and allowed to pursue their individual proclivities in order to benefit the whole structure of society.

find entry in his books, and these were the sadhu words. Further, Vidyasagar explained to the hapless words, that they were, in fact, the illegitimate children of Sanskrit, born due to his past lecheries, and a few of them who had managed to gain entry into polite society, were condemned to carry the sadhu words on their backs. And with that he turned them out. The poor words next went to the Tattobodhini Sabha and tried to enter the *Tattobodhini Patrika*. There they were unceremoniously turned out by the Patrika's editors, Ayodhyanath Pakrashi. Similar treatment awaited them at all the other stops that they made around the town of Calcutta, and every man of letters from Rajendralal Mitra to Kaliprasanna Singha harassed and humiliated the unfortunate words. Thus treated by the Bengalis, the words, browbeaten and exhausted, gave up their quest. Some went back to Saraswati, while the majority returned to their old haunts of Narkeldanga, Beleghata, and Permit Ghat.

When the goddess learned of the tribulations that the words had faced from the mortals she was furious and set out to redress such discrimination against her children. She ordered the editors of the *Bangadarshan* and *Dharmatattava*, dramatists, and the authors of university entrance books, that if proper honour was not shown to the low words, she would send them all to hell. No one would escape her wrath from the government translators to the lawyers of the district courts. Hence Bengal saw the creation of *Hutom*, Vidyasagar and Rajendralal Mitra, staunch old timers acquired sickly constitutions, Ayodhyanath Pakrashi died, and Akshay Kumar Datta, raging a life-long war against the low words, developed a disease of the brain and retired to Bali.[42]

Such was the explanation given for the trend of writing in the itar bhasha by the Bengalis in an anonymous text published from Battala in 1882. From this period onwards there was a particular recognition, in practically every kind of literature, that the Bengali language was being given a definitive form. What was also clear was that there were two distinct possible futures that the language could apprehend. One was the *Alali* or *Hutomi* trend, set of by the two texts *Alaler Gharer Dulal* (1858) and *Hutom Penchar Naksha* (1861), and the other was the more chaste and Sanskritized prose of Vidyasagar and Akshay Kumar Datta. The former direction of Bengali writing was used in black satirical social sketches, or *naksha*, caricaturing contemporary life and society. The language was

[42] Anonymous, *Suraloke Banger Parichay* (Calcutta, 1882), pp. 29–33.

demonstratively colloquial and sentences abounded with idioms, proverbs, and words derived from non-Sanskrit sources. It was very much an exercise to reproduce common speech through written prose. Rajnarayan Basu commented in 1878 that the *Alali* language was, in fact, a conscious reaction to the *Vidyasagari* prose.[43]

Hutom actually popularized the concept of a *bewarish* Bengali, literally meaning heirless, but implying that the language lacked custodians. The term was quoted several times in later texts to substantiate the claim that the language needed guardians. Soon after *Hutom* was published, a popular weekly, *Bangabidya Prakashika*, carried a short entry of two columns under the heading 'Useless Writers should be Punished':

It is true that the Bengali language has no guardian. The Bengali language is like a dough for making *luchi*. People give it whatever shape they wish. In the absence of a guardian there is no one to prevent this.

With the coming of print, there have been unexpected improvements in the Bengali language. That we are now able to read books and newspapers that satisfy our minds is entirely due to the printing machines; it deserves our thanks. Especially the presses in Battala have made things really easy. Finding the rates cheap, people are writing and publishing whatever they please. We do not say that only useless and trivial books are published at Battala. A number of Puranas have also been printed there, but they smack of their Battala connections.

The more books are published in Bengali, the more propitious it would be for the language. However, some foolish men, lacking foresight, but with a great desire to become famous, have taken to writing books. They do not have enough sense to discern the good from the bad. In fact, these books have become like weeds in the language.[44]

It could be perhaps be argued that the uncontrolled proliferation of print, particularly within Battala, gave credence to the Hutomi language as it came about, and the guardian-less state of the language, though short-lived, explored the possibility of a form much closer to the spoken language. This is not to suggest that either Kaliprasanna Singha or Pearychand Mitra were forced to take into account the veritable surge of the 'popular' language as it emerged from Battala; for as our account of the itar words point out, they both used a different language and linguistic structure when it came to

---

[43] Rajnarayan Basu, *Bangla Bhasha*, pp. 26–7.

[44] *Bagabidya Prakashika*, 23 October 1865, cited in Tapti Roy, 'Disciplining the Printed Text', p. 53.

more serious forms of writing. It is perhaps unlikely that they would consider this language as a viable option for discursive prose. The case of the *Masik Patrika* clearly demonstrates this.

In 1854 Pearychand Mitra and Radhanath Sikdar started a literary magazine called *Masik Patrika*. In a short preface to its first issue, the editors made it clear that the magazine was being 'published for ordinary people, especially women'; articles would be 'written in the language in which we ordinarily converse'. The editorial also distinctly warned 'scholars' that they could read the journal if they so wished, but it was 'really not intended for them'.[45] This division between 'popular' language and language for serious issues was recognized and maintained almost till the very end of the nineteenth century. Writing in the 1880s about the *Masik Patrika*, Haraprasad Shastri observed:

Previously books written in Bengali prose drew their contents either from Sanskrit texts or were plays and novels. They were of such ugly taste that they could not be given to women. This journal was published such that women could read; it was for their amusement. It was full of good advice, conducive to happiness of both body and mind.[46]

In an earlier review of the journal, Long had inadvertently pointed to this separation between the two literary forms:

The Editor of the Masik Patrika has adopted the colloquial style—very good for females and others who have never learnt thoroughly their mother-tongue—but this is not the style of books generally acceptable. Natives consider language ought to have some elegance and not the baldness of the bazar. This latter style has not answered though the Editor Radhanath Sikdar devoted much time and zeal to popularize it.[47]

Ramgati Nayaratna substantiated Long's criticism in his history when he said that such simplified language was not conducive to writing books for a general readership.[48] What then were the imperatives of this particular trend in language?

The emergence of Bengali as a distinct language capable of being a language of discourse had its grounding in the effort to create a common

[45] Quoted in Haraprasad Shastri, 'Pearychand Mitra' in *Rachana Sangraha*, p. 143.
[46] Ibid., p. 144.
[47] Long, 'Returns', p. xviii.
[48] Ramgati Nayaratna, Preface to *Banglabhasha O Banglasahitya Bishayak Prastab*.

language of correspondence that would link a general audience to the issues raised by a particular class. While the socialization of Bengali as the language of the majority ensured this, its structuration into categories of sadhu and chalit emphasized the mechanisms by which linguistic stratification worked to uphold and reinforce class barriers.

The intervention by literary journals from the 1860s to determine the form and content of Bengali has been seen by historians as an effort by the new 'elite' to 'discipline the world of the printed text from within, by trying to enforce a set of normative literary practices'.[49] There is one significant development overlooked by this scholarship and that is that this 'disciplining', as it were, was done in comparatively accessible Bengali. A readable Bengali form was evolved in order to propagate a refined and cultured content. As early as in 1855, the *Hindoo Patriot* provided the real logic behind the need to simplify the language. The English newspapers, it said, were 'almost totally devoid of influence over any section of the community'. Language was thus clearly linked to the nation and to national mobilization. The *Hindoo Patriot* significantly added:

The vernacular press no doubt labours under one great disadvantage from the effects of which it will always suffer, namely its inapplicability to the purposes of polemical politics. The questions of Indian politics which must be debated in the English language, demand immediate adjustment at the hands of our rulers and the vernacular press must content itself with conveying but a faint reflexion of the lights shed by its more fortunate brother.[50]

This is not to deny that there was no conscious effort to create a standard prose form. What we are suggesting is that this argument about standardization has to be made within a more rigorous framework of class practice, which is absent from the general claims made about standardization in print. It is not enough to say that the new middle class effected standardization through print in the language, for the process of standardization was essentially twofold. The first stage involved the enterprise of socializing the language by distancing it from its Sanskritic bias with the corollary insistence upon simplifying the language in order to make it intelligible to a wider readership. This process was so successful that in

---

[49] Roy, 'Disciplining the Printed Text', p. 54.

[50] *Hindoo Patriot*, 3 May 1855, reprinted in Benoy Ghosh, ed., *Selections*, Vol. 3, pp. 168–9.

1855 the *Friend of India* grudgingly admitted that even though 'the works contained in Mr Long's catalogue' did not stand 'comparison with the great classics in our own language [English]', it was nevertheless undeniable that 'the Bengalee language ... [was] capable of conveying ideas which shall influence the mass of society'.[51] In the second stage, the language was colonized from within, with the imposition of the registers of sadhu and chalit, and concerns of literary taste and merit. Both these points can be best elucidated by the historical incorporation of the 'popular' or 'common tongue' within the language.

The literary journal *Nabya Bharat* published a series of articles in the 1870s about the future fate of Bengali. One of them, echoing this mood, urged the restoration of *khanti* or authentic Bengali, which could not be found in the heavy prose of Vidyasagar or Akshay Datta, but lay in the proverbs, songs, and poems of the spoken tongue.[52] All at once the spoken language, rejected and neglected so far, began to signify the authenticity of Bengal. Bankimchandra *Bangadarshan* carried a similar article by Haraprasad Shastri in 1881, where, lamenting the gulf between the spoken and the written language, he remarked that this distance was responsible for the appallingly low number of readers among the masses.[53] It was this traversal of the popular as a lost and yet fundamental space that the literature of this period traced.

This linguistic stratagem on the part of the new middle class, again, cannot be read as pure instrumentality. The dream of social reform through British rule had turned considerably sour by the 1870s. A very potent and visible proof of the ills of British rule was rural Bengal. We have to remind ourselves that most members of the bhadralok group had direct or indirect links to the countryside. There were very few factories and the workers were mainly drawn from non-Bengali immigrant labour. The overwhelming realities of the Bengalis were thus land and employment in the public and private offices. The Indigo Rebellion in the mid-nineteenth century had brought into sharp focus the exploitative and arbitrary nature of British dominance. As city life was mainly seen as an extension of the drudgery of chakri and ritual humiliation at the hands of British superiors, from this

[51] *Friend of India*, 7 June 1855, reprinted in Ghosh, *Selections* Vol. 3, p. 76.
[52] Bishnuchandra Maitra, 'Bangabhasha O Sahitya', *Nabya Bharat* (Shravan, 1897), p. 188.
[53] Haraprasad Shastri, 'Bangla Bhasha' in *Rachana Sangraha*, pp. 565–6.

period onwards the primary focus of educated writing was on the countryside. Rural Bengal appeared from this time on as the green and bountiful antonym for the harsh realities of city life. In the political polemics of the educated Bengalis a major concern was the destruction of handicrafts, a visible sign of the material transformation of the villages. Debaprasad Sarbadhikari, nephew of the famous mathematician Prasannakumar Sarbadhikari, recounts this change in an eloquent passage in his autobiography. He described the weavers of his native village at work while the soft humming of devotional songs mingled with the steady and happy rhythm of their looms. This, he said, was unique to the rural industry and could never to be found in the 'Manchester industry'.[54] The period, as a result, also saw the systematic investigation by the new middle class into the realm of the 'popular'.[55]

About our second claim about the stages of standardization, let us clarify at the outset that our difference with Tapti Roy was not about the ultimate outcome of the process, but about the implications of it. When she talks of the 'elite' effecting a normative prose for Bengali, a part of the story remains untold. Language can not only act as communication, which it is conceptualized as in the first stage, but also as definite non-communication, whereby in the second stage even Bankim was accused of crudity and vulgarity by the journal *Rahasya Sandarbha* in 1854.[56]

Language, in the first stage was hence conceptually designed to be one of the prefigurements of the future nation, where the notion of 'communication'

[54] There were, it seems, in his village 700 houses of weavers. Sarbadhikari lamented that later when he had wanted a 'desi' cover on his visit to the village, the weavers had brought him some machine made covers bought at Howrah *hat*. Debaprasad Sarbadhikari, *Smritirekha* (Calcutta, 1933), p. 11.

[55] Besides the pioneering works of people like Dineshchandra Sen, Dakshinsranjan Mitra Majumdar and Lalbehari Dey in the systematic collection of folk tales, songs, and other similar artifacts of the 'popular' tradition there were other minor efforts in this field. See for example, Prabodhprakasa Sengupta, *Dictionary of Proverbs* (Calcutta: A. Mukherjee, 1899); Upendrakrishna Bandyopadhyay, *Handbook of Proverbs: English and Bengali* (Calcutta: Bengal Medical and School Book Library, 1891); and Lalitmohan Raya, *Meyeli, A Collection of Sayings and Proverbs in Use by Bengali Women* (Mymensingh: Ananda, 1877).

[56] 'Bankim has certainly taken care' the reviewer of his first novel wrote, 'but it is to be regretted that he has not always kept in mind that Bengali books are now being read by cultured women'. *Rahasya Sandarbha*, second series, Vol. 21 (1854), p. 142.

emerged in its widest possible connotation. 'It is the mutual communicability among people achieved by a common language' stated one author in one of the leading journals, 'that makes it possible for a collectivity to work together. Unless we can work collectively we can never improve our present state'.[57] Let us retrace, once more, for the sake of contextualization, the linguistic trajectory from Rammohan. The status of language as a *social* tool, as opposed to a concern for the grammarian or linguist, was established in his translation of the Vedantas, and further developed in his grammar. The socialization of language in general, and Bengali in particular, was not sufficient to make the associative conjunction with either the nation or the idea of the collective. Therefore, in what we have called the second stage, from the 1850s, simplicity of the linguistic medium became one of the important registers of change within the language.

Simplification as a strategy was organized around the principle of autonomy from Sanskrit. Sanskrit derivations, it was argued, made Bengali unnecessarily dense and difficult to understand. Nayaratna's history anecdotally recounted an incident where one school teacher was asked to translate a Sanskrit Shastric injunction into Bengali. The Sanskrit pundits upon reading the text remarked 'What is this? It seems to be *Vidyasagari* Bengali, one can easily make sense of it'.[58] The *Bangabasi*, in 1889, printed a strongly-worded editorial, protesting against the refusal of Calcutta University to include Bengali as a subject in its higher examinations. It said that the University should not 'nurse or cherish the error' that the study of Sanskrit formed 'an indirect encouragement to the cultivation of the Bengali language', but that learning Sanskrit was, in fact, 'a disqualification for good Bengali composition'.[59] In tandem with a critique of Sanskrit there was the rehabilitation of the spoken language. The simplicity of the spoken word was actually an assertion of the primacy of the social location of language. Syamacharan Ganguli made an important contribution to this debate in a long article in the *Calcutta Review*, where, denoting language as 'faithfully mirroring every stage of human progress', he argued that the changes that languages underwent over time were reflective of social evolutionism. The flexibility of language was, in fact, a register of a given society's progress, or at least mobility, and new words first made their

[57] Bishnuchandra Maitra, 'Bangabhasha O Sahitya', pp. 182–90.

[58] Nayaratna, *Banglabhasha O Banglasahitya Bishayak Prastab*, p. 158.

[59] *Report on Native Papers 1889*, pp. 183–4.

appearance in colloquial speech and then made their way into books. In this respect he argued that the 'bias of learning [...] helped to keep the written language of every country [...] a little behind the spoken, a little archaic in comparison with the latter [...] and the *best* model for writers to follow would, therefore, be the spoken tongue'.[60] The spoken word was thus recuperated as the primary sign of social communicability. It should be remembered that the entire linguistic enterprise of this period was to fixate a stable language for written prose, or as Ganguli put it, to find the best 'model' for writers to follow. The project of making the spoken word speak to the written, was co-terminus with the recognition of one particular dialect as the 'spoken' tongue of Bengal, that is, that which could be best assimilated to the written form. The rules of literary usage of language were set such that Dwijendralal Roy had to justify his use of the dialect of Nadia in one of his plays.[61] Ganguli pointed out that 'the people of Bengal generally look upon the metropolis and the districts along the Bhagirathi as the parts where Bengali is spoken in its greatest purity'.[62]

It is interesting to note the opinions of the colonial authorities in this debate over sadhu and chalit were consistently resisted by the bhadralok. Adhering to the notion of the superiority of Sanskrit, the state, even as late as in 1872, tried to determine the sadhu form as one dominated by Sanskrit. In his correspondence with the government on the issue of the vernacular language of Bengal, the Bengali translator John Robinson insisted:

Among a people who have for ages past enjoyed but little or no instruction, and have had neither books nor literature, we are prepared to find the vocabulary of their vernacular very limited, and confined almost exclusively to words which their daily social duties bring into use [....] Contact with Mahomedans and foreigners would also introduce a few new words. But making allowance for these, the vernacular is found not only to be based upon Sanskrit, but to consist entirely of Sanskrit words [...] Bengali is simply a modification or we may say, a corruption of the ancient Sanskrit [... and the] introduction of Sanskrit words, judiciously chosen, does not corrupt but actually enriches the vernacular.[63]

[60] Syamacharan Ganguli, 'Bengali, Spoken and Written', *Calcutta Review*, 65, 130 (July–December, 1877), pp. 395–417.

[61] See Chintaharan Chakrabarty, 'Nadiar Bhasha', *Sahitya Parishad Patrika*, 51, 1–2 (1964), p. 185.

[62] Ganguli, 'Bengali, Spoken and Written', p. 400.

[63] General Proceedings, Education Department, June 1872, No. 111.

In sharp contrast, a satirical magazine published in 1873 voiced the dominant feeling about Bengali:

The Sanskrit language is too old, over the years it has dried up and is now as hard as a bone. One cannot understand it. If a new language is to be created then it must not carry any traces of Sanskrit. Persian, Arabic and Urdu are also not new languages and will have to be purged. There are certain primitive words native to Bengal [...] and all correspondence, spoken and written, should be carried through with these. Beware of using any other words lest you disturb the important process of creation.[64]

The space of the language as distinct from the discourse of the state was stated explicitly by all. Ganguli completed his piece with the following emphasis:

Whatever be the character of written Bengali at present, the State should not by any means interfere with its development. Languages grow spontaneously, and it does not rest with Caesar, however absolute the power with which he is armed, to mould or modify it.[65]

As the dead space of language-as-grammar was reconstituted as a chronicle of opposition, a larger imperative loomed in the horizon, and the nation acquired its primal nomination through it. Writing about the English influence on Bengali literature in 1885, Barada Charan Mitra drew out the deep living connection between the material and the epistemic in colonialism as a system of violence. He said that the English had 'de-nationalized' Bengal's literature, and just as he had to depend on Manchester for his clothing and Sheffield for his cutlery, the hybrid generation of Bengali writers depended upon Byron and Shelley for their poetical inspiration and upon Macaulay for the rounding off of their prose periods. His generation, he commented, had lost the heaven and hell of Vedavyas and could only glimpse the fires of the *Divine Comedy*.[66]

Language and Class

Let us remind ourselves once more about Partha Chatterjee's argument about the nature of colonial modernity. In his critique of Benedict Anderson,

[64] Anonymous, *Hak Katha* (Calcutta: Local Press, 1873), pp. 94–5.

[65] Ganguli, 'Bengali, Spoken and Written', p. 414.

[66] Barada Charan Mitra, 'English Influence on Bengali Literature', *Calcutta Review*, 80, 162 (January–June, 1885), pp. 330–45.

Chatterjee claims that the most powerful results of the 'nationalist imagination in Asia and Africa are posited not on an identity but on a *difference* with the "modular" forms of the national society propagated by the modern West'.[67] In our present aim to understand the emergence of Bengali as a language, we, however, noted certain trends which share the same epistemic and praxological ground with the development of vernacular languages elsewhere in the Western world. Renee Balibar and her colleagues have shown in the case of France, a similar development in the French language vis-à-vis the transformations in class relationships in France, first as the anti-feudal struggle of the bourgeoisie to conquer and secure political domination, and in the later stage, its anti-proletarian struggle to maintain it.[68]

We have argued in this chapter that the new middle class, by the mid-nineteenth century, arrived at two divergent trends in the language in the form of the Alali language and the Vidyasagari language. Though the apparent opinion seemed to be that the language would through its own social evolutionism choose one of the two trends as its constant, it was made explicit from the very start, as Rajnarayan Basu correctly pointed out, that there were certain subjects that would always use either of the two for its exposition. The language of history, biography or science, for example, would always remain Vidyasagari, while the Alali would always find its place in the comic, the ridiculous and the satirical.[69]

The incorporation of the 'popular' within the language was done with specific aims. An important author in his own right, Pramatha Chaudhuri (1868–1946), wrote a series of articles on the Bengali language at the beginning of this century. Though beyond the formal scope of the time-scale of the present work, these articles are an important pointer to the consequences of the process that we have discussed in this chapter. Pramatha Chaudhuri's family were big landowners and connected to the powerful Tagores by marriage. Chaudhuri himself was educated in Britain to become a barrister but never actually practised law, as there was no apparent financial need to do so. He was married to Rabindranath's favourite niece Indira

---

[67] Partha Chatterjee, *The Nation*, p. 5.

[68] Renee Balibar, *Le Francais National: Politique et Pratiques de la Langue Nationale sous la Revolution Francaise* (Paris, 1974).

[69] Basu, *Bangla Bhasha*, p. 27.

Debi. His opinions can hence be said to reflect a dominant sentiment amongst the prominent authors of the time. In his essay on sadhu bhasha, Chaudhuri argued strongly against the use of sadhu bhasha as he believed that the Bengali language was neither a product of '*bratya* [lower or bastardized] Sanskrit, nor was it English under-a-curse'.[70] According to him, two historical trends had robbed the Bengali language of its natural progress. The first was the language's preliminary dependence on Sanskrit. Rammohan's prose, Chaudhuri maintained, was not widely accepted as standard Bengali prose because of the former's use of Sanskrit structures. Similarly, the second trend, whereby the language became a derivation from English as seen in the works of Michael Madhusudan Dutt, Bankim, was also not acceptable. What should really form the basis of Bengali literature, Chaudhuri felt, was *moukhik bhasha*, or the spoken language.[71] Up to this point Chaudhuri's thesis is perfectly in accordance with the need for a language that would be understood by many, a language that was not merely the preserve of a few but could be used by all in communicating the exigencies of the 'imagined community'. Chaudhuri, however, clarifies further as to the exact nature of the spoken tongue. 'The wealth inherent in the spoken tongue of the educated in every country', he upheld, 'was sadly lacking in the language of the uneducated'. The poor, according to the distinguished author, were poor in 'both wealth and spirit'.[72] It was thus clear as to whose spoken tongue would form the basis of the language. It would not be the unrefined parole of the peasant but the cultured and educated voice of the Chaudhuris and the Tagores.

Challenging Marxist assumptions about language, Gareth Stedman Jones has recently made a case for Saussure and his adherents. In his history of the British working class, Stedman Jones has claimed that the structuralists and post-structualists have established 'the materiality of language itself, the impossibility of simply referring back to some primal anterior reality, "social being", the impossibility of abstracting experience from the language which structures its articulating'.[73] This conception of human action and

---

[70] Pramatha Chaudhuri, 'Atibhashan' in *Prabandha Sangraha* (Calcutta: Vishwabharati Press, 1974), p. 80.

[71] Ibid., pp. 78–9.

[72] Ibid., p. 79.

[73] Gareth Stedman Jones, *Languages of Class: Studies in English Working Class History 1832–1982* (Cambridge, 1983), p. 20.

interest is based upon the notion that the language that expresses them is our sole medium for understanding such interests and actions. In other words, we only have access to social reality through the agents' experience of it. According to this approach then, it is possible to recount historical reality exclusively on the basis of its textual representation. It is of course true that we talk about our reality using language, but does it then follow that realities themselves are constituted by the language that expresses them? Human beings rarely accept linguistic representations of the world or themselves without criticality. The word 'babu' used with such derision by the British ultimately became a mark of distinction for the Bengali middle class (a peasant or a worker is never referred to as one).

Marx's observations about language are inextricable from his conceptions about the larger social reality, where language is 'practical, real consciousness that exists for other men as well, and therefore exists for me'.[74] The relationship between discourse and the world cannot be one where the former determines the latter in a mechanistic inversion of actuality. Language, though constituting discourses, is finally related to social and class practices which they consecutively reflect.

By 1901, even before the tremendous efflorescence of patriotic Bengali songs, poetry, and prose of the Swadeshi era, the proportion of Calcutta's population speaking Bengali had fallen to 51 per cent, while that speaking Hindustani had risen to 36 per cent.[75] This was due to the concentration of migrant labour from the neighbouring regions of Bihar, Orissa, and the eastern districts of the United Provinces. These people, then, were truly 'outside the text' of the Bengali language.[76] It is worth remembering, however, that they, and others like them, were not outside the colonial reality of Bengal and it is their support that was urgently enlisted in the political struggles of the next century.

[74] K. Marx and F. Engels, *Collected Works*, Vol. V (London: Lawrence and Wishart, 1975), p. 44.

[75] Cited in B.R. Tomlinson, *The Economy of Modern India: 1860–1970* (Cambridge: Cambridge University Press, 1996), p. 124.

[76] This is a reference to Jacques Derrida's famous pronouncement 'There is no outside-text' (Il n'y a pas de hors-text), or, as it is more usually translated, 'There is nothing outside the text'. See J. Derrida, *Of Grammatology* tr. Gayatri Chakravoty Spivak (Baltimore: Johns Hopkins Press, 1976), p. 18.

Conclusion

This knowledge [Western Education] will teach the natives of India the marvellous results of the employment of labour and capital, rouse them to emulate us in the development of the vast resource of their country ... confer upon them all the advantages which accompany the healthy increase of wealth and commerce; and at the same time, secure to us a larger and more certain supply of many articles necessary for our manufactures and extensively consumed by all classes of our population.[1]

The period covered in this book, from the fall of the Union Bank (1848) to the formation of the Congress (1885), was undoubtedly for Bengal a period of intense social ferment, if not actual social change in certain areas. In just fifty years, for example, the debates around the position and status of women in society had changed from whether they should be burnt as widows to how far their education was being achieved. Even bearing in mind that such 'emancipation' was limited according to class positions, it was nevertheless a great leap forward. The total number of pupils in government schools, both English and vernacular, in the 24 Parganas in 1856–7 was 4,041. In less than twenty years, this number had increased more than four times to an impressive 17,558.[2] In 1873–4 the total number of people travelling by the newly constructed railways was 1,633,560. Of this number 94 per cent were third and fourth class passengers, that is, Indians in general, if not common people.[3] A post office was not an uncommon sight in most

---

[1] 'Despatch from the Court of Directors of the East India Company to the Governor General of India dated 19 July 1854', quoted in J.A. Richey, *Selections from Education Records*, Part II, p. 365.

[2] W.W. Hunter, *A Statistical Account*, p. 202.

[3] Ibid., p. 169.

villages and several parts of the countryside around Calcutta were dotted with schools for women and night schools for adults.

Yet the bulk of bhadralok projects ended in failure, personal bitterness, or plain cynicism. Shibnath Shastri's enthusiastic undertaking of a school for mature women, started in 1872, ended in him resigning from Kesab Sen's organization altogether and moving back to his native village of Changripota. Jyotirindranath Tagore, as we noted before, died an unhappy and broken man following the failure of his steamship venture. Vidyasagar, a classic case in this regard, moved to Karmatar and spent his last days amongst the Santhals, shunning so-called bhadra company.[4] Clearly, none of these figures, despite their personal commitment and promise, can be equated with a Marat or a Robespierre. A substantial volume of the historiography of Bengal, as a result, has been devoted to discovering the roots of this 'lack' and investigating the reasons for what has been called the unfulfilled bourgeois revolution.[5]

We have tried, in this work, to approach the question of class under colonialism from a different perspective. We began by questioning the cultural rhetoric of a section of the Hindu bhadralok and tried to ascertain the various social and economic elements that went into the making of such a discourse. Our first problem was to determine the class position of the bhadralok. The fact that they wielded such a powerful ideological discourse about culture, artistic production, language, and matters of political economy, has lead scholars down the following two paths. First, post-colonial theorists like Partha Chatterjee argue that 'culture' in itself was a private language of protest by the bhadralok against the public domain of the colonial state. Second, Marxist historians such as Sumit Sarkar have argued that the bhadralok was a bourgeoisie that lacked the economic power of its Western counterpart and was hence forever limited by the restrictive political economy of colonialism. The bourgeoisie, according to a Marxist understanding, is the class that owns and controls the means of production. One can allow a certain degree of theoretical manoeuvre, depending on

---

[4] He is reputed to have said that he preferred the company of the 'asabhya Santhals' to the 'bhadra Aryans'; See, Sankhya Ghosh, 'Iswarchandra Vidyasagar', in Sudhirkumar Gangopadhyay et al., eds., *Banglar Manisha*, Vol. 2 (Calcutta: Sarat Publishing House, 1987), pp. 411–16, 415.

[5] See for example, Ranajit Guha, 'On Some Aspects of the Historiography of Colonial India', Asok Sen, *Iswarchandra Vidyasagar*, and Sumit Sarkar, *Writing Social History*.

particular historical circumstances, to this definition, but the basic premise remains the same. Individual members of the bhadralok may have had a proportion of control over land, labour or even capital, but it would be erroneous to argue that they were in control of the means of production in the nineteenth century.

Two things are clear about the nature of national liberation struggles of the former colonial countries. First, that the bourgeoisie that arrives late on the international stage in comparison to its Western counterparts is fundamentally different from the latter, in that it fails to provide a consistent democratic opposition to the pre-capitalist forces and the imperialist onslaught. The new-born working class does not, for various reasons, provide any other alternative to the bourgeois national movement. Second, the role of the intellectuals or the intelligentsia in this context assumes great importance. In the absence of classes that in western Europe carried the historic task of nation-building, intellectuals and middle class professionals take on this substitutive role in the colonial countries. This work has tried to show the social roots of one such group in Bengal and the various ways in which it prepared itself for its future role.

The notion of colonial specificity has acquired, in recent years, considerable theoretical importance for scholars of post-colonialism. The claim by post-colonial theorists is that the manacles of colonial exploitation were forged in the West, while resistance was devised uniquely and specifically by the colonized. This curious understanding of colonialism brings to the fore several issues, some of which we tried to resolve within our limited scope. In conclusion, we can merely touch on some of the more general problems with such formulations.

The need to assert an independent agenda against 'Europe' or the 'West' by the post-colonial theorists is understandable, given that most of Asia and Africa is today reeling under the 'humanitarian' help of Western and European institutions like the International Monetary Fund and the World Bank. Formulating theoretical understanding under the aegis of moral outrage is, however, problematic. The notion that the colonial struggles of the Third World were somehow unique and specific compels one to theoretically disassociate from wider historical developments on a global scale. It also implies that the entire advanced capitalist world be treated as a unified ruling class and oppressor, endlessly producing its discourses of coercive enlightenment rationality. Actual history, however, was much more complex.

Let us consider one of the most contentious and productive industries of the high period of colonialism, namely cotton textiles. By all accounts there was an unprecedented rise in the export of cotton piece-goods to India from 1818 till about 1870. Manchester cotton found frequent mention in bhadralok writings, in itself symbolizing the shackles imposed on the Indian economy. But this period was not solely the history of colonial exploitation. Propelled by the pressures needed to maintain this trade, this period saw some of the most vicious attacks by the British ruling class on its own working population. In Manchester itself in the year 1837, some 50,000 workers were unemployed. The wages of the employed were cut as high as 27 per cent for the mill owners to maintain their profits in the face of recession.[6] It is worth bearing in mind that the various strikes and mass workers' movements that took place in this period (including Chartism), were directed against the very perpetrators of the colonial nexus. This world of struggle was very much a part of the history of the so-called 'West'.

The postcolonial critic conscientiously asserts that colonial discourse was all through interrupted by resistance of the colonized. If such is the case, then why is this analysis not extended to the West itself? Surely within western Europe there were several historical instances of resistance (Chartism, the Paris Commune to name only two notable examples), which questioned the fundamental basis of the system of which colonialism was a logical consequence. The fundamental problem of this kind of analysis is that political states tend to replace classes. Categories such as the colonizer and the colonized are ultimately unhelpful and largely nationalist categories, whatever may be their professed radical standpoint. The 'colonizer' had more in common with someone like Dwarkanath Tagore than with, for example, the black Chartist leader William Cuffay.

The history of the anti-colonial struggle only acquires its *specificity* against the *general* backdrop of world historical trends. The social relations that developed in Bengal in the nineteenth century cannot be analysed either in their isolated specificity or in comparison with western Europe. While the former method rules out the pressures on Bengal from the outside world of economic realities, the latter can only point to the difference and hence the 'lack' of some class force or the other. Colonialism ensured that capitalist relations be forcefully imposed onto a backward country and that

---

[6] For details see, Mark O'Brien, *Perish the Privileged Orders* (London: Redwords, 1995), pp. 42–43.

all resistance, whether economic or social, be met with direct political force, either in the form of laws or simple armed coercion. However, once the regime of market forces was introduced, it was bound to move the productive forces forward. If certain social classes, in this case the bourgeoisie and the working class, were not fully matured to carry forward this development in political terms that did not arrest this movement. New classes and new ideologies then arose to fill the space.

The bhadralok, as we have argued in the previous chapters, was not an incipient bourgeoisie. This point needs to be reiterated, for only in its substitute role can we begin to understand the reasons for the various uncompleted projects that they undertook and their unfulfilled dreams. The majority of them, whether an educated professional like Bankim, or a lowly paid clerk in an office, were of petty bourgeois origin. Their occupation ranged between lawyers, doctors, government officials (munsiffs, clerks, collectors, deputy magistrates, etc.) and teachers. Originally, in a position of comparative privilege in the village as owners of petty property, the power of this class was substantially undermined by the new land arrangement policies of colonialism and consequently it lead them to search for alternative routes of livelihood. Throughout the nineteenth century this strata migrated to Calcutta and district towns in search of either jobs or a Western education needed to secure a job. The statistical records of migration in the census of 1911 show clearly that the bulk of the migration to Calcutta was not from the labouring classes of artisans and peasant, though economically the most affected classes under colonialism, but from the higher castes of Brahmins and Kayasthas, in other words, the rural gentry. Brahmins, Kayasthas, and Vaidyas combined made up 50 per cent of the total migration into Calcutta. The late eighteenth and the first half of the nineteenth century saw the gradual but steady decline of the villages from whence this layer had originated. One of the prime arteries of the economy, traditional handicrafts, was hit hard by colonial production, leading finally to its near total extinction.[7]

The upper classes were not necessarily affected by the economic decline, having shifted their allegiance to the new rulers. The economy needed indigenous capital and as a result, till the 1840s, the merchant-*bania* had tremendous influence in the metropolis. The change in trade patterns in

[7] See for example, Nabinchandra Sen, *Amar Jiban*, Vol. 3 (Calcutta: Bharat Mihir Press, 1910), pp. 149, 157, 160.

the subsequent years closed the avenues for such forms of capital accumulation and from the middle of the nineteenth century the sole employment for Indians, above the class of peasants or workers, was office jobs or chakri. The rise of a coherent group of the intelligentsia stands out as the hallmark of this period and we have tried to show the workings of their ideology which emphasized culture, education, and literary symbols.

The problem of the intelligentsia was, however, a complex problem of class position. Stifled as they were by the colonial economy, they lacked both the means and the power to resolve the crisis. A strike by them would not stop the process of production, nor would it halt the course of the 'drain'. As a result, their situation was marked by a profound contradiction. On the one hand, their critique of the political economy of colonialism was not only exhaustive but genuinely revolutionary in its anti-imperialist content. Their rhetoric about culture and education must be placed in this context to be fully appreciated. We have tried to show how this rhetoric was firmly tied to a process of ideological mobilization, by way of which disparities between classes were sought to be removed in the name of a collective bhadralok identity.

On the other hand, however, because this strata did not firmly belong to any one class position, the solutions to the very crisis that they so elegantly outlined were bound to be limited and tinged with revivalism. An excellent example of the choices on offer by the new middle class was an article published in the *Hindoo Patriot* in 1854. Entitled 'English Strikes and Bengallee Dhurmghuts', it was a rare piece of direct political *analysis* of contemporary social concerns. 'Dhurmghuts' among the peasants of Bengal and the strikes by British workers were both, according to the author, 'symptoms of one common social disorder', namely, 'the estrangement of feeling between the upper and lower orders of men'. Having said this, the article makes a strong case for both workers and peasants, in the process outlining the vagaries of a modern economy, the obsession with the 'security of property', and the miserable existence of the majority of people. 'The case is not so clear', it informs us, against the workers and peasants, 'as we are taught to believe'. In conclusion, it rhetorically poses the question of a remedy to modern social ills. The author was evidently acquainted with, what he termed, 'the bolder genius of European Socialists'. Their theories, the article propounded, were 'openly absurd', for it meant nothing but 'the destruction of those inequalities of rank and condition which give so much beauty to the social structure and scope for so many of the finer feelings of our nature'. The 'true remedy' instead lay in the 'upper classes of society attaining to a due sense of the responsibilities of their position and cultivating a close sympathy with the lower orders'.[8] In other words, reform from above.

Marx's analysis of petty bourgeois socialism in nineteenth-century France is a useful analogy to the political sentiments of our author. This brand of socialism, Marx has shown, had a serious critique of capitalism, exemplified in the works of men like Sismondi:

It proved, incontrovertibly, the disastrous effects of machinery and division of labour; the concentration of capital and land in a few hands ... it pointed out the inevitable ruin of the petty bourgeois and peasant, the misery of the proletariat, the anarchy in production, the crying inequalities in the distribution of wealth ... the dissolution of old moral bonds, of the old family relations, of the old nationalities.[9]

The solutions that this political form offered, was again, very close to the social remedies imagined in Bengal:

This form of Socialism aspires either to restoring the old means of production ... and with them the old property relations, and the old society, or to cramping the modern means of production and of exchange, within the framework of the old property relations that have been, and were bound to be exploded by those means ...

Ultimately, when stubborn historical facts had dispersed all intoxicating effects of such self-deception, this form of Socialism ended in a miserable fit of blues.[10]

Saidian theorists in their search for colonial specificities sometimes miss general historical trends of class behaviour. This explanation seems much more valid for both the localized social reforms of the bhadralok and Gandhian dreams of village communes, than attaching to them the glorious project of being critiques of 'Western Enlightenment'.[11]

The substitution of a weak and inadequate bourgeoisie for a dynamic intelligentsia in the national struggle has had some important consequences in the history of colonialism as well as its historiography. The role of the

[8] *Hindoo Patriot*, 13 July 1854, reprinted in Benoy Ghosh, ed., *Selections*, Vol. 3, pp. 152–4.

[9] K. Marx and F. Engels, *Selected Works*, pp. 55–6.

[10] Ibid., p. 56.

[11] Partha Chatterjee argues that Gandhian politics was outside the realm of Western Enlightenment rationality. P. Chatterjee, 'Gandhi and the Critique of Civil Society', pp. 153–95.

colonial state in the context of an economically backward country like India
also needs to be considered in accounting for this difference in class roles. If
we take printing as an example of innovations effected by colonialism, the
unevenness of development between western Europe and the colonized
countries stands out in sharp relief.

In Europe, the time between the introduction of paper (twelfth century)
and the first printed books (mid-fifteenth century) was nearly four hundred
years. These years saw the rise of centres of merchant capitalism (Genoa
and Venice being spectacular instances) whose tentacles spread impressively
over land and sea and whose innovations in banking, insurance, and the
first joint-stock companies laid part of the institutional basis for a later and
wider capitalist development. In other words, by the time printing arrived
in mainland Europe, the ground was already being prepared for new classes
and new social changes.

In Bengal, the contrast is startling. Between the first printed book of
Halhed in 1778 and the flourishing Bengali press of the 1850s there was a
gap of less than a hundred years. In this one century colonialism had
accelerated the otherwise natural development of the political economy to
astounding heights. The development of the intelligentsia in this context
of historical acceleration is significant. In an excellent recent essay Sudipta
Kaviraj has aptly referred to the Bhadralok as "accidental inhabitants of
modernity". The modern, in other words, came to Bengal not as a choice,
but as a tragic corollary to subjection.[12]

The intelligentsia, bred on the exported ideas of a much advanced
political system, had to nonetheless, when the time came for ideological
mobilization, depend on the forces on the ground. In the absence of a
substantial working class this was inevitably the peasantry and the urban
petty bourgeoisie.[13] It is worthwhile to bear in mind that despite the location
of the bhadralok in urban towns, most of them had intimate links with the
countryside, either as intermediate tenure holders, landlords, or as a simple

[12] Sudipta Kaviraj, "Laughter and Subjectivity: The Self-Ironical Tradition in Bengali
Literature", *Modern Asian Studies*, Vol. 34, no. 2, 2000, p. 379.

[13] Even in 1947 the number of workers in large-scale industries was only 2.65
million which comprised 2 per cent of the total labour force. See, Morris. D. Morris,
'The Growth of Large-Scale Industry to 1947', in D. Kumar and M. Desai, eds.,
Cambridge Economic History of India, Vol. II (Cambridge: Cambridge University Press,
1983), p. ***.

connection with the ancestral home in the native village. From 1830, when
the first Tenancy Act was passed, the condition of the peasants was a topic
of active discussion and debate for the intelligentsia. Rammohan Roy, owner
of extensive zaminadari property, called for legislation on the subject.[14] The
learned journals like the *Bengal Spectator*, *Tattobodhini Patrika*, and the
Hindoo Patriot, all called to attention the cause of the ryot.

There were material reasons for this agrarian concern. First, the
peasantry was the only class that a section of the bhadralok had some limited
organic connection with, as opposed to the infant working class whose
relationship to production, till the end of the century, was almost entirely
under British control. Second, the peasants, throughout the nineteenth
century, had repeatedly rebelled against their local oppressors. The sheer
size and militancy of the peasantry in a backward economy made them
appear as a potent force against colonialism. Nationalist imagery, from the
mid-nineteenth century was thus not about industrial development but
about the land and landed relations. Factories and machines did not form
the basis of poetry and songs, the rural landscape did. Last, but not the
least, petty property relations, ideologically bound the peasantry as a class
and the new middle class. The driving force of the bhadralok world of
reforms was a harking back to the past and to tradition. It is important to
understand that both social classes, the urban petty bourgeois and the
peasantry wanted a return to the older order of things. The sole ideological
difference being that while the former had some limited benefits from the
present system the latter had virtually none. This is not to say that when
sections of the peasantry actively demanded a reverting back to the traditional
order, they found bhadralok support. The intelligentsia, throughout the
nineteenth century opposed all forms of peasant uprisings with the sole
exception of the Indigo revolt where the enemy was clearly the white planters.
Theirs was much more a project of what Marx has called 'corporate guilds
for manufacture, patriarchal relations in agriculture', in which the peasant
could be genially included; any kind of revolt from below was actively
denounced.

---

[14] Rammohan Roy, *Expositions of the Practical Operation of the Judicial and Revenue
Systems of India and of The General Character and Conditions of its Native Inhabitants, as
submitted as Evidence to the Authorities in England with Notes and Illustrations etc.* (London:
Smith, Elder, 1832), pp. 70–2.

The working class, in contrast, did not win much favour with the bhadralok. In 1857, the *Hindoo Patriot* complained of the arrogance acquired by the 'serving class', due to an improvement in their living standard:

The state of labour market in Calcutta and its suburbs suggests the inference that either capital has increased or population decreased. Without either of these causes wages would not have risen to their present status .... The result is that the day laborer and the artizan have adopted habits of life which they formerly could but aspire .... Men, women and even children ... obtain ready employment from capitalists engaged in the business [of jute and the railways]. The work performed in the course of a single day puts into the pocket of the working man more than three times the amount he could earn as a servant of field laborer. And while the pecuniary advantage is so extraordinary his social position has become much more independent. The ryot who only a few years ago could not find courage to talk to a well dressed person except with down-cast eyes and folded hands, now knows the value of his position, and the insolence of the labouring class is becoming a thorn in the way of respectable men.[15]

According to Amiya Bagchi, the real wages of unskilled workers, which were already very low in the 1870s, actually fell by the end of the century. Skilled workers just about managed to maintain their real earnings, but did not improve their condition. The daily wage of an unskilled worker (the majority) was equal to a return journey fare on the newly introduced trams of the 1880s. The drivers and conductors of the trams had to work a sixteen-hour day in order to earn Rs 20. As a result, from the 1880s, several strikes by coach-builders, municipal sweepers, and jute-mill workers are known to taken place.[16]

The historiography of colonialism, particularly of peasant movements, often underestimates the merging of ideological interests between the petty bourgeois and the peasant. Ranajit Guha, for example, has claimed that the 'unrealised potential' of the nationalist struggle was to be found in the radical peasant jacqueries of the past century: 'all mass struggles will tend inevitably to model themselves on the unfinished projects of Titu, Kanhu, Birsa and Mangher Singh'.[17] This is clearly not a Marxist position. Marx believed that the act of validating the present or the future in terms of the past was a

---

[15] *Hindoo Patriot*, cited in Benoy Ghosh, ed., *Selections*, Vol. 3, pp. 55–6.

[16] Amiya Bagchi, 'Wealth and Work in Calcutta: 1860–1921', pp. 222–3.

[17] Ranajit Guha, *Elementary Aspects of Peasant Insurgency* (New Delhi: Oxford University Press, 1983), p. 336.

feature peculiar to bourgeois movements, not a universal or inevitable strategy for all social change. His thoughts on this relationship between tradition and revolution is best outlined at the beginning of *The Eighteenth Brumaire of Louis Bonaparte*:

Men make their own history, but they do not make it just as they please, they do not make it under circumstances chosen by themselves, but under circumstances directly encountered, given and transmitted from the past. The tradition of all dead generations weighs like a nightmare on the brain of the living. And just when they seem engaged in revolutionizing themselves and things, in creating something that has never yet existed, precisely in such periods of revolutionary crisis they anxiously conjure up the spirits of the past to their service and borrow from them names, battle-cries and costumes in order to present the new scene of world history in this time-honoured disguise and this borrowed language. Thus Luther donned the mask of the Apostle Paul, the revolution of 1789 to 1814 draped itself alternately as the Roman Republic and the Roman Empire, and the revolution of 1848 knew nothing better to do than to parody, now 1789, now the revolutionary tradition of 1793 to 1795.[18]

Marx here is categorical in his distinction between a capitalist model of emancipation and the true liberation of humanity. Bourgeois revolutions merely aspire to emancipate capitalism. Their mobilizing rhetoric is thus necessarily mystified and seeks justification from a usually mythologized past. Hence the resurrection of the glorious Hindu tradition by even the most progressive and liberal of the bhadralok. Mobilizations by revival is not limited to only the bourgeoisie. The peasantry, for their part, dependent on property relations on land, ideologically manifest, even at the height of radical uprisings, not the rhetoric of a new future, but a future forged in the past. This is not limited to Sidhu, Kanhu, and Birsa alone. A tragic corroboration of this argument lies in the historic experience of peasant movements elsewhere in the non-European world. The peasant guerrilla war in Zimbabwe (1972), for instance, began with the avowed goal of establishing socialism, the war brought death and destruction on a catastrophic scale. The resultant social change, however, was not socialism but the creation and consolidation of a new black elite. In his account of the struggle David Lan has noted:

All nationalisms make use of metaphors of land, of soil and earth, of territory and boundary, of monuments and graves, of the heroes of the past who are ancestors of

---

[18] K. Marx and F. Engels, *Selected Works*, p. 96.

the nation. The symbolism of the *mhondoro* [spirits of past chiefs] gains its extraordinary effectiveness as an expression of the struggle for Zimbabwe from its ability to combine the economic and political aspects of the struggle in a single unforgettable image: the chiefs of the past, independent and prosperous, benign and generous to their followers, in sole possession and control of their bountiful fertile lands.[19]

National liberation struggles cannot thus be passed under a banner of either socialism or the liberation of humanity. The class ridden past of human history, according to the laws of historical materialism, cannot form either inspiration or model for a future that hopes to be free of class. Again Marx and Engels leave no room for doubt on the matter. A socialist struggle, they argue 'cannot draw its poetry from the past, but only from the future'.[20]

This work has not, however, been a study of the working class or their organizations. It is perhaps worth mentioning, in conclusion, why we consider the study of the bhadralok to be of relevance.

There has been a particular form to the national liberation struggles of the global south in the twentieth century. They have tended to be mass movements dominated by the peasantry and led by a vocal and professional intelligentsia. The colonial intelligentsia's birth in the crucible of the colonial state is well recorded. What is perhaps less documented is its substitutive status in attempting to provide to the nationalist movement what the European bourgeoisie as a class provided to the anti-feudal struggles of eighteenth and nineteenth centuries. Within the freedom movements of the south, however, an independent demand for worker's power never emerged amongst the various viable alternative visions of the future. The fundamental struggle that lay at the heart of the postcolonial state, was thus not between the worker and the bourgeoisie but between the two faces of the bourgeoisie itself: the urban and the rural. From this, Nigel Harris has correctly surmised that after independence the central debate was not between the proletariat and the bourgeoisie, but between 'the urban petty bourgeoisie, pressing for an extension of the State and public employment, and the rural petty bourgeoisie, pressing for the devotion of more national resources to agriculture'. This struggle, according to Harris, manifested itself

---

[19] David Lan, *Guns and Rain: Guerillas and Spirit Mediums in Zimbabwe* (London: Currey, 1985), pp. 218–19.

[20] K. Marx and F. Engels, *Collected Works*, Vol. XI (London: Lawrence and Wishart, 1975), p. 106.

in the 'political debate between State ownership, identified by the urban petty bourgeoisie as "socialism" (from Mao to Nasser and Nehru) and rural capitalism'.[21]

The outcome of this historical trend in the theoretical understanding of colonialism and postcolonial societies has meant two things: one, the rise of the claim that Marxism cannot make sense of third world developments, and two, that Marxism needs to be remodelled along Maoist lines, that is, according to the peasantry the role of liberators. It should be of considerable concern to Marxists that the subaltern studies collective, with one sole exception, does not deal at all with any working class movement. The bulk of historical writing on Bengal, has thus concentrated either on peasant and tribal movements or on the bhadralok. This is not strange given the fact that these two forces played the most significant role in nationalist mobilization and struggle. It is one thing, however, to study class forces and quite another to ascribe to them roles beyond their historic scope. It is thus not surprising that Marxists like Asok Sen comment dejectedly that 'Modern India has now lost most of the ideological and practical means of revolutionary community that might have been available'.[22] The reason for such cynicism is not hard to understand. The failure of the proletariat isolated most sections of the Left, leaving socialists with no other weapons except intellectual or actual guerrilla warfare. The first steps of opposition, both in the academia and the political arena tend to unconsciously revive pre-Marxist utopian socialist thought. The working class is scarcely ever considered the agency for the achievement of socialism, and the 'proletariat' is equated with any force that happened to be in opposition to the status quo.[23]

Our attempt here, has been to set a portion of the record straight on the class nature of the bhadralok and their role in the task of nation-building. It is important to understand the specificities of backward capitalism and the class forces that it generates in order to secure analysis of the present. It is also important for the present, as well as the future, to identify clearly the classes that are structurally capable of forming an alternative.

[21] Nigel Harris, *Of Bread and Guns: the World Economy in Crisis* (Harmondsworth: Penguin, 1983), p. 37.

[22] Asok Sen, 'Subaltern Studies: Capital, Class and Community', p. 221.

[23] The term 'subaltern' is a classic instance of this trend whereby it stretches far enough to include any oppressed group, whether along class, caste, or gender lines.

In 1950, Walter Benjamin writing his *Theses on the Philosophy of History* was convinced that 'even the dead will not be safe from the enemy if he wins'. He thus placed upon historians the task of rescuing from the past the 'spark of hope' about human redemption.[24] Despite having witnessed the systematic annihilation of a militant worker's movement in post-First World War Germany by the fascists, Benjamin had increasingly come to identify redemption with socialist revolution. Our analysis of the past is thus primarily urged in order to place our hopes in the forces of the future.

[24] Walter Benjamin, *Illuminations* (London: Fontana Press, 1992), p. 247.

Bibliography

I. Official Records, Publications, and Newspapers

(a) Official Records and Annual Reports

The principal official sources used were the General and Education Proceedings of the Government of Bengal, housed in the West Bengal State Archives, Calcutta.

Annual Report on the Presidency Division for 1872–3, no. 77JG (dated 16 Sept 1873), WBSA.

Government of Bengal, General Proceedings: 1850–80.

Government of Bengal, General Proceedings (Education Department): 1850–80.

Government of Bengal, Judicial Proceedings: 1860–80.

The Bengal and Agra Directory and Annual Register for 1848 (Calcutta, 1848).

The Bengal Directory and Fourth Quarterly Register for the Year 1838 (Calcutta, 1838).

Bengal, Miscellaneous Public Documents 1843–87 in the British Library Collection.

Banerjee, B.N., 'Raja Radhakanta Deb's Services to the Country' in *Indian Historical Records Commission*, Vol. 9 (Calcutta, 1926).

Calendar of Persian Correspondence 1767–69, Vol. 2 (Calcutta, 1914).

O'Donnell, C.J., ed., *Census 1891, Volume III (Bengal)* (Calcutta, 1893).

Imperial Gazetteer of India, Provincial Series: Bengal, Vol. 1 (Calcutta, 1909).

Sanskrit College Files for Letters Collection, Vol. 6 (…?).

Selections from the Records of the Government of India, No. LIV (Calcutta, June 1867).

Selections from Records of the Bengal Government Papers on the Establishment of the Presidency College of Bengal, Vol. 14 (Calcutta, 1854).

Selections from the Records of the Bengal Government, No. XXXIII (Calcutta, 1859).

Selections from the Records of the Government of India, Home Revenue and Agricultural Department, No. LIX (Calcutta, 1879).

Selections from the Record of the Bengal Government, No. XXXII (Calcutta, 1859).

BMS Mss, Carey to Sutcliff, dated 9 August 1794.

Imperial Gazetteer of India: Provincial Series, Bengal, Vol. 1 (Calcutta, 1909).

Minutes and Proceedings of the General Committee of Public Instructions, Vol. V (Calcutta, October 1831).

Annual Report of the Calcutta Literary Society (Calcutta, 1875).

Report of the Transactions of the Vernacular Literature Society From July 1st. 1858 to December 31st. 1859 (Calcutta, 1860).

Report on the Administration of Bengal 1874–75 (Calcutta, 1876).

Report on the Native Papers 1889 (Calcutta, 1889).

Report of the Commission Appointed by the Government of India to Inquire into the Condition and Prospects of the University of Calcutta, Vol. 2, Part 1 (Calcutta, 1919).

The First Report of the Institution for the Encouragement of Native Schools in India (Serampore, 1817).

Report of Public Instruction (Calcutta, 1863–4).

Reports of the Proceedings of the Calcutta School Book Society (Calcutta, 1818–56).

Selected Chapters of the Report of the Calcutta University Commission (Calcutta, 1919).

Second Report of the General Council of Education in India Formed With a View to the Promotion of the General Education of the People on a National Basis as Laid Down in the Education Despatch of 1854 (London, 1883).

(b) Journals and Newspapers

Bangadoot (Calcutta) 13 June 1829.

Bengal Past and Present, Vol. XXIX, 1925.

Bengal Spectator (Calcutta) 16 March 1843.

Friend of India (Serampore) 1820–59.

Gyananeshawn (Calcutta) February 1838–June 1838.

Hindu Pioneer, 1, 5 (Calcutta) January 1836.

India Gazette (Calcutta) 21 October 1831.

Indian Mirror (Calcutta) 23 September 1889.

Samachar Darpan (Calcutta) 30 January 1830.

Sambad Prabhakar (Calcutta) 23 November 1853.

Somprakash (Calcutta) 29 July 1878.

Tattobodhini Patrika (Calcutta) 1834–1870.

II. Non-Official Books, Articles, Dissertations (English)

A Rapid Sketch of the Life of Raja Radhakanta Deva Bahadur, with some Notices of his Ancestors and Testimonials of his Character and Learning By the Editors of the Raja's Sabdakalpadruma (Calcutta: J.M. Gaumisse, Englishman Press, 1859).

Abdul Kaium, Mohammad, *A Critical Study of the Early Bengali Grammars. Halhed to Haughton* (Dhaka: Asiatic Society of Bangladesh, 1982).

Acharya, Poromesh, 'Indigenous Education and Brahminical Hegemony in Bengal', in Nigel Crook, ed., *The Transmission of Knowledge in South Asia* (Delhi: Oxford University Press, 1996), pp. 98–118.

Althusser, L. and E. Balibar, *Reading Capital*, trans. Ben Brewster (London: New Left Books, 1970).

Althusser, L., *For Marx*, trans. Ben Brewster (Harmondsworth: Penguin, 1977).

_____ *Lenin and Philosophy and Other Essays*, trans. Ben Brewster (London: New Left Books, 1970).

Anderson, Benedict, *Imagined Communities: Reflections on the Origins and Spread of Nationalism* (London: Verso, 1983).

Anderson, Perry, 'The Antinomies of Antonio Gramsci', *New Left Review*, 100 (November–December, 1976), pp. 5–75.

_____ *The Origins of Postmodernity* (London: Verso, 1998).

Anon, Shishubodhak, (Calcutta: Vidyaratna Press, 1857).

'The Application of the Roman Alphabet to All the Oriental Languages', Contained in a Series of Papers by Messrs. Trevelyan, J. Prinsep, and Tytler, Rev. a. Duff, and Mr. A.T. Prinsep. And Published in Various Calcutta Periodicals in the Year 1834 (Serampore, 1834).

Arnold, David, 'Touching the Body: Perspectives on the Indian Plague', in Ranajit Guha ed., *Subaltern Studies II* (New Delhi: Oxford University Press, 1983), pp. 55–90.

Bagchi, Amiya Kumar, 'De-industrialization in India in the Nineteenth Century: Some Theoretical Implications', *The Journal of Development Studies*, 12, 2. (January, 1976), pp. 135–64.

_____ 'Markets, Market Failures, and the Transformation of Authority, Property and Bondage in Colonial India', in B. Stein and S. Subrahmanyam, eds., *Institutions and Economic Change in South Asia* (New Delhi: Oxford University Press, 1996), pp. 48–70.

_____ 'Wealth and Work in Calcutta, 1860–1921', in Sukanta Chaudhuri, ed., *Calcutta: The Living City*, Vol. 1 (Calcutta: Oxford University Press, 1990), pp. 212–23.

_____ *Merchants and Colonialism*, Occasional Paper, 38 (Calcutta: Centre for Studies in Social Sciences, 1981).

_____ *Private Investment in India 1900–1939* (Cambridge: Cambridge University Press, 1972).

_____ *The Evolution of the State Bank of India: Roots: 1806–1876, Parts I and II* (Bombay: Oxford University Press, 1987).

Balibar, Renee, *Le Francais National: Politique et Pratiques de la Langue Nationale sous la Revolution Francaise* (Paris: Hachette, 1974).

Bandopadhyay, Asit Kumar, *Unabingsha Satabdir O Bangla Sahitya* (Calcutta, 1959).

Bandyopadhyay, Sekhar, *Caste, Politics and the Raj: Bengal 1872–1937* (University of Calcutta, Dept. of History, Monograph No. 5: South Asia Books, 1990).

_____ *Caste, Protest and Identity in Colonial India: The Namasudras of Bengal, 1872– 1947* (Richmond: Curzon Press, 1997).

Bandyopadhyay, Upendrakrishna. *Handbook of Proverbs: English and Bengali* (Calcutta: Bengal Medical and School Book Library, 1891).

Banerjea, Runga Lal, *On the Importance of Physical Education* (Calcutta: n.p., 1860).

Banerjee, Sumanta, 'Marginalisation of Women's Popular Culture in Nineteenth-century Bengal', in K. Sangari and S. Vaid, eds., *Recasting Women: Essays in Colonial History* (Delhi: Kali for Women, 1989), pp. 127–79.

_____ *The Parlour and the Streets: Elite and Popular Culture in Nineteenth Century Calcutta* (Calcutta: Seagull Books, 1989).

Barnard, H.C., *A Short History of Education in England 1760–1944* (London: University of London Press, 1961).

Basak, N.L., *History of Vernacular Education in India* (Calcutta: Educational Publishers, 1974).

Basu, Ranu, 'Some Aspects of the Composition of the Urban Elite in Bengal, 1850– 1872', in *Studies in Bengal*, Papers presented at the Seventh Annual Bengal Studies' Conference (East Lansing: Asian Studies Centre, Michigan State University, 1975), pp. 107–23.

Bayly, C.A., 'Colonial Rule and the "Informational Order" in South Asia', in Nigel Crook, ed., *The Transmission of Knowledge in South Asia* (Delhi: Oxford University Press, 1996), pp. 280–315.

Benjamin, Walter, *Illuminations* (London: Fontana Press, 1992).

Bhadra, Gautam, 'Four Rebels of Eighteen Fifty Seven', in Ranajit Guha, ed., Subaltern Studies IV (New Delhi: Oxford University Press, 1985), pp. 229–75.

238   Bibliography

Bhaduri, Amit, 'The Evolution of Land Relations in Eastern India Under British Rule', *IESHR*, 13, 1 (January–March, 1976), pp. 45–8.

Bhattacharya, D. and B.B. Bhattacharya, eds., *Census of India 1961: Report of the Population Estimates of India (1820–1830)* (New Delhi: Manager of Publications, 1965).

Bose, N.K., 'Calcutta—a Premature Metropolis', *Scientific American* (September, 1965), pp. 90–102.

Bose, N.S., *The Indian Awakening and Bengal* (Calcutta: Firma KLM, 1960).

Breckenridge, Carol A. and Peter van der Veer, eds., *Orientalism and the Postcolonial Predicament* (Philadelphia: University of Pennsylvania Press, 1993).

Broomfield, J.H., *Elite Conflict in a Plural Society: Twentieth-Century Bengal* (Berkeley: University of California Press, 1968).

Callinicos, Alex, 'The "New Middle Class"', in A. Callinicos and C. Harman eds., *The Changing Working Class* (London: Bookmarks, 1989), pp. 13–51.

——— *Making History: Agency, Structure and Change in Social Theory* (Ithaca: Cornell University Press, 1988).

Cameron, C.H., *An Address to Parliament on the Duties of Great Britain to India in Respect of the Education of the Natives and their Official Employment* (London: Longman, Brown, Greem and Longmans, 1853).

Cannon, Garland, ed., *The Letters of Sir William Jones*, Vol. II (Oxford: Clarendon Press, 1970).

Carey, Eustace, ed., *Memoir of William Carey* (Hartford: Canfield and Robins, 1837).

Carey, S.P., *William Carey* (London: The Carey Press, 1934).

Carey, William, 'On the Importance of Sungskrita to the Future Improvement of India', *Friend of India*, Vol. 2, No. XVI (1819), pp. 373–82.

——— *A Grammar of the Sungskrit Language Composed from the Works of the Most Esteemed Grammarians* (Serampore: Mission Press, 1806).

——— *Hints Relative to Native Schools, Together with the Outline of An Institution for their Extension and Management* (Serampore: Mission Press, 1816).

Carrère d'Encausse, Hélène and Stuart R. Schram, eds., *Marxism and Asia: An Introduction with Readings* (London: Allen Lane The Penguin Press, 1969).

Chakrabarty, Dipesh, 'The Colonial Context of the Bengal Renaissance: A Note on Early Railway-Thinking in Bengal', Paper presented at the 33rd Session of the Indian History Congress at Muzaffarpur, Decmber 1972.

——— *Provincializing Europe: Postcolonial Thought and Historical Difference* (Princeton: Princeton University Press, 2000).

Chakravarti, Satish Chandra, ed., *The Father of Modern India* (Calcutta: Rammohan Roy Centenary Committee, 1935).

Chandravarkar, Rajnarayan, 'Industrialization in India before 1947: Conventional Approaches and Alternative Perspectives', *Modern Asian Studies*, 19, 3 (1985), pp. 623–68.

Chartier, Roger, ed., *The Culture of Print: Power and Uses of Print in Early Modern Europe* (Cambridge: Polity, 1984).

Chatterjee, Partha, 'Agrarian Relations and Communalism in Bengal, 1926–35', in Ranajit Guha, ed., *Subaltern Studies I* (New Delhi: Oxford University Press, 1982), pp. 9–38.

_____ 'Gandhi and the Critique of Civil Society', in Ranajit Guha, ed., *Subaltern Studies III* (New Delhi: Oxford University Press, 1983), pp. 153–95.

_____ 'More on the Modes of Power and the Peasantry', in Ranajit Guha ed., *Subaltern Studies II* (New Delhi: Oxford University Press, 1982), pp. 311–49.

_____ *Nationalist Thought and the Colonial World: A Derivative Discourse?* (London: Zed for the United Nations University, 1986).

_____ *Texts of Power: Emerging Disciplines in Colonial Bengal* (Calcutta: Samya, 1996).

_____ *The Nation and its Fragments: Colonial and Postcolonial Histories* (New Delhi: Oxford University Press, 1993).

Chattopadhyay, Suniti Kumar, and Priyoranjan Sen, eds., *Manoel da Assumpcam's Bengali Grammar. Facsimile reprint of the Original Portuguese, with Bengali translation and selections form his Bengali–Portuguese vocabulary* (Calcutta: Calcutta University Press, 1931).

Chaudhuri, Benoy, 'Land Market in Eastern India 1793–1940 Part 1: The Movement of Land Prices', *IESHR*, 12, 1 (January–March, 1975), pp. 1–42.

Chaudhuri, K.N., ed., *The Economic Development of India Under the East India Company* (London: Cambridge University Press,1971).

Chuckerbutty, Takoordass, *Thoughts on Popular Education* (Calcutta: City Press, 1870).

Cliff, Tony, 'Deflected Permanent Revolution', in *Trotskyism After Trotsky* (London: Bookmarks, 1999), pp. 60–9.

Cohen, G.A., *Karl Marx's Theory of History: A Defence* (Oxford: Clarendon Press, 1979).

Cohn, Bernard S. 'Representing Authority in British India' in E. Hobsbawm and T. Ranger, eds., *The Invention of Tradition* (Cambridge: Cambridge University Press, 1992).

Combe, George, *The Constitution of Man* (Hartford: S. Andrus & Son, 1854).

Cronin, Richard, 'The Government of Eastern Bengal and Assam and "Class Rule" in Eastern Bengal, 1905–1912', in J.R. Mclane, ed., *Bengal in the Nineteenth and Twentieth Century* (East Lansing: Asian Study Center, Michigan State University, 1975), pp. 99–117.

Darnton, Robert, *The Business of Enlightenment: A Publishing History of the Encyclopédie, 1775–1800* (Cambridge, Mass. London: Belknap Press, 1979).

———— *The Forbidden Best-Sellers of Pre-Revolutionary France* (London: Harper Collins, 1997).

Das, Sisir Kumar, *Sahibs and Munshis: An Account of the College of Fort William* (New Delhi: Orion Publications, 1978).

Dasgupta, Prabal, 'On Sanskrit and Indian English: Some Linguistic Considerations', *New Quest*, 67 (January–February, 1988), pp. 15–25.

Datta, Akshay Kumar, *Charupath* (Calcutta: Tattvabodhini Press, 1854).

Datta, Kalikinkar, *Studies in the History of the Bengal Subah 1740–70* (Calcutta: University of Calcutta, 1935).

De, Barun, 'A Critique of the Historiography of the Trend Entitled "Renaissance" in Nineteenth Century India', Paper presented at the Indo-Soviet symposium on India and Russia in Moscow, May 1973.

De, Sushil Kumar, *Bengali Literature in the Nineteenth Century* (Calcutta: Firma KLM, 2nd ed., 1962).

Deb, Raja Binaya Krishna, *The Early History and Growth of Calcutta* (Calcutta: Riddhi, 1977, first edn, 1905).

Derrett, J.D.M., *Religion, Law and the State in India* (London: Faber and Faber, 1968).

Derrida, J., *Of Grammatology*, trans. Gayatri Chakravorty Spivak (Baltimore, London: Johns Hopkins Press, 1976).

Dey, Lal Behari, 'Calcutta and Those that Live in it', *Bengali Magazine* (November, 1873), pp. 173–85.

———— *Recollections of Alexander Duff* (London: T. Nelson and Sons, 1879).

Dirks, Nicholas B., ed., *Colonialism and Culture* (Ann Arbor: University of Michigan Press, 1992).

Dutt, Hurchandra, *Bengali Life and Society* (Calcutta: Sanders, Cones and Co., 1853).

Dutt, Shoshee Chunder, *Bengaliana: A Dish of Rice and Curry, and other Indigestible Ingredients* (Calcutta: Thacker, Spink and Co. 1858).

Eagelton, Terry, 'Awakening from Modernity', *Times Literary Supplement*, 20 February 1987.

Eisenstein, E., *The Printing Press as an Agent of Change: Communication and Cultural Transformation in Early Modern Europe* (Cambridge: Cambridge University Press, 1979).

Elster, Jon, *Making Sense of Marx* (Cambridge: Cambridge University Press, 1985).

Fabian, Johannes, *Language and Colonial Power: The Appropriation of Swahili in the Former Belgian Congo 1880–1938* (Berkeley: University of California Press, 1991).

Febvre, L. and H. Martin, *The Coming of the Book: The Impact of Printing, 1450–1800* (London: Verso, 1986).

Fisher, Michael, *Indirect Rule in India: Residents and the Residency System 1757–1857* (Delhi: Oxford University Press, 1991).

Foucault, M., *Discipline and Punish: The Birth of the Prison*, trans. Alan Sheridan (Harmondsworth: Penguin, 1979).

_____ *The Archaeology of Knowledge, and the Discourse on Language*, trans. Alan Sheridan and Rupert Swyer (New York: Pantheon Books, 1972).

_____ *The Order of Things: An Archaeology of the Human Sciences* (London, New York: Routledge, 1994).

Ganguli, Syamacharan. 'Bengali, Spoken and Written', *Calcutta Review*, 65, 130 (July–December, 1877), pp. 395–417.

Ghose, C., 'Essay on Mill's British India', *Calcutta Gazette*, 14 February 1828.

Ghose, N.N., *Memoirs of Maharaja Nubkissen Bahadur* (Calcutta: K.B. Basu, 1901).

Ghosh, B., 'Some Old Family Founders in Eighteenth Century Calcutta', *Bengal Past and Present*, 79 (January–June,1960), pp. 42–55.

Ghosh, Benoy, 'A Critique to Bengal Renaissance', *Frontier*, 4, 24–6 (September, 1971), pp. 4–12.

_____ 'Social Change' in *Renascent Bengal*, foreword by R.C. Majumdar (Calcutta: Asiatic Society, 1972), pp. 12–20.

_____ ed., *Selections from English Periodicals of Nineteenth-Century Bengal*, Vol. 3 (Calcutta: Papyrus, 1980).

_____ ed., *Selections from English Periodicals of Ninettenth-Century Bengal*, Vol. 5 (Calcutta: Papyrus, 1980).

Ghosh, Girish Chunder. *A Lecture on the Life of Ramdoolal Dey, The Bengali Millionaire* (Calcutta: Riddhi-India, 1978, Ist edn 1868).

Ghosh, Jogesh Chunder, ed., *The English Works of Raja Rammohan Roy*, Vol. II (Calcutta: Oriental Press, 1901).

Giddens, Anthony, *The Class Structure of the Advanced Societies* (London: Unwin Hyman, 1981).

Gilloch, Graeme, *Myth and Metropolis: Walter Benjamin and the City* (Cambridge: Polity Press, 1997).

Goldthorpe, J, 'On the Service Class, its Formation and Future', in A. Giddens and G. Mackenzie, eds., *Social Class and the Division of Labour* (Cambridge: Cambridge University Press, 1982), pp. 162–85.

Goswami, Manu, *Producing India: From Colonial Economy to National Space* (Chicago: The University of Chicago Press, 2004).

Gramsci, Antonio, *Selections from the Prison Notebooks* (New York: International Publishers, 1971).

Guha, Arabinda, ed., *Unpublished Letters of Vidyasagar* (Calcutta: Ananda Publishers, 1971).

Guha, Ranajit, *History at the Limit of World History* (New York: Columbia University Press, 2002).

—— 'Dominance without Hegemony and its Historiography', in Ranajit Guha, ed., *Subaltern Studies VI* (New Delhi: Oxford University Press, 1992).

—— *Elementary Aspects of Peasant Insurgency* (New Delhi: Oxford University Press, 1983).

—— *History at the Limit of World History* (New York: Columbia University Press, 2002).

—— 'On Some Aspects of the Historiography of Colonial India', in Ranajit Guha ed., *Subaltern Studies I* (New Delhi: Oxford University Press), pp. 1–8.

Gupta, A., ed., *Studies in the Bengal Renaissance* (Calcutta: National Council of Education, 1958).

Halhed, Nathaniel Brassey, *A Grammar of the Bengali Language* (Calcutta: Ananda Publishers, 1980, first edn, 1778).

Hallas, Duncan, *The Comintern* (London: Bookmarks, 1985).

Hamilton, W., *The East India Gazetteer* (London: Printed for J. Murray by Dove, 1815).

Harris, Nigel, *Of Bread and Guns: the World Economy in Crisis* (Harmondsworth: Penguin, 1983).

Hatcher, Brian A., *Idioms of Improvement: Vidyasagar and the Cultural Encounter in Bengal* (Calcutta: Oxford University Press, 1996).

Hindustani, A., 'The Babu', *Bengali Magazine* (April 1874), pp. 413–29.

Hoch, Paul, *White Hero, Black Beast: Racism, Sexism and the Mask of Masculinity* (London: Pluto Press, 1979).

Hunter, W.W., *A Statistical Account of Bengal*, Vol. 1 (London: Trübner and Co., 1875).

Inden, Ronald, *Imagining India* (Oxford: Blackwell, 1990).

Jack, J.C., *The Economic Life of a Bengal District: A Study* (Oxford: Clarendon Press, 1916).

Jaffar, S.M., *Education in Muslim India: Being an Inquiry into the State of Education During the Muslim Period of Indian History, 1000–1800 AC* (Delhi: Idarah-iAdabiyat-iDelli, 1973).

Jameson, Frederic, *The Cultural Turn: Selected Writings on the Postmodern, 1983–1998* (London: Verso, 1998).

Jones, Gareth Stedman, *Language of Class: Studies in English Working Class History 1832–1982* (Cambridge: Cambridge University Press, 1983).

Jones, William, 'On the Gods of Greece, Italy and India', *Asiatic Researches*, Vol. 1 (Varanasi: Bharat-Bharati, 1972, first edn 1784), pp. 188–235.

Joshi, P.C., 'A Dedicated Teacher—Some Memories' in Barun De, ed., *Essays in Honour of Prof. S.C. Sarkar* (New Delhi: People's Publishing House, 1976), pp. 3–12.

Joshi, Svati, ed., *Rethinking English: Essays in Literature, Language, History* (New Delhi: Oxford University Press, 1991).

Joshi, V.C., *Rammohan Roy and the Process of Modernization in India* (Delhi: Vikas, 1975).

Junius, *Two Letters on the Education of the People of India* (Serampore: Serampore Press, 1835).

Kaviraj, Sudipta, Literary Culture in History: Bengali, unpublished paper.

⸻ 'Laughter and Subjectivity: The Self-Ironical Tradition in Bengali Literature', *Modern Asian Studies*, Vol. 34, No. 2 (2000), pp. 379–406.

⸻ *The Unhappy Consciousness: Bankimchandra Chattopadhyay and the Formation of Nationalist Discourse in India* (New Delhi: Oxford University Press, 1995).

Kejariwal, O.P., *The Asiatic Society of Bengal and the Discovery of India's Past: 1784–1838* (New Delhi: Oxford University Press, 1988).

Kesavan, B.S. *History of Printing and Publishing in India, A Story of Cultural Reawakening, South Indian Origins of Printing and its Efflorescence in Bengal* (New Delhi: National Book Trust, 1985).

Kling, Blair B., *Partner in Empire: Dwarkanath Tagore and the Age of Enterprise in East India* (Berkeley: University of California Press, 1976).

Kopf, David, *British Orientalism and the Bengal Renaissance 1773–1835* (California: University of Calfornia Press, 1965).

Kumar, Ravinder, ed., *Essays on Gandhian Politics: The Rowlatt Satyagraha of 1919* (Oxford: Clarendon Press, 1971).

Lan, David, *Guns and Rain: Guerillas and Spirit Mediums in Zimbabwe* (London: Currey, 1985).

Lethbridge, Roper, ed., *A History of the Renaissance in Bengal, Ramtanu Lahiri: Brahman and Reformer* (Calcutta: Editions Indian, 1972, first edn 1904).

Lipner, Julius J., *Brahmabandhab Upadhyaya: The Life and Thought of a Revolutionary* (Delhi: Oxford University Press, 1999).

Lockwood, David, *The Blackcoated Worker: A Study in Class Consciousness* (London: Allen and Unwin, 1958).

Long, James, 'Calcutta in the Olden Times—Its People', *Calcutta Review*, 35, 69 (September, 1860), pp. 164–227.

_____ 'Early Bengali Literature and Newspapers', *Calcutta Review*, 13, 25 (January–June, 1850), pp. 124–61.

_____ *A Descriptive Catalogue of Bengali Works* (Calcutta: Sanders, Cones, 1855).

_____ ed., *Adam's Report on Vernacular Education in Bengal and Behar, With a Brief View of its Past and Present Conditions* (Calcutta: Home Secretariat Press, 1868).

_____ *Five Hundred Questions on the Social Condition of the Natives of India* (London: Trübner and Co., 1865).

_____ *How I Taught the Bible to Bengal Peasant Boys* (Christian Vernacular Society for India, n.d.).

Loomba, Ania, *Colonialism/Postcolonialism* (New York: Routledge, 1998).

Majumdar, B.B., *History of Political Thought from Rammohun to Dayananda(1821–84)* (Calcutta: University of Calcutta, 1934).

Majumdar, J.K., *Raja Rammohan Roy and Progressive Movement in India: A Selection from Records* (Calcutta: Art Press, 1941).

Majumdar, R.C., ed., *Renascent Bengal* (Calcutta: Asiatic, Society, 1972).

Mani, Lata, 'Contentious Traditions: The Debate on *Sati* in Colonial India', in K. Sangari and S. Vaid, eds., *Recasting Women: Essays in Colonial History* (Delhi: Kali for Women, 1989), pp. 88–126.

Mann, M., *The Sources of Social Power: A History of Power from the Beginning to A. D. 1760*, Vol. 1 (Cambridge: Cambridge University Press, 1986).

Marx, Karl, *Capital*, Vol. 1 (London: Lawrence and Wishart, 1976).

Marx, Karl, and F. Engels, 'Manifesto of the Communist Party', in *Selected Works* (London: Lawrence and Wishart, 1973), pp. 31–63.

_____ *Collected Works*, Vol. V (London: Lawrence and Wishart, 1975).

_____ *Collected Works*, Vol. XI (London: Lawrence and Wishart, 1975).

_____ *Selected Works* (London: Lawrence and Wishart, 1968).

McCully, B.T., *English Education and the Origin of Indian Nationalism* (New York: Columbia, 1940).

McGuire, John, *The Making of a Colonial Mind: A Quantitative Study of the Bhadralok in Calcutta, 1857–1885* (Canberra: Australian National University, 1983).

Metcalf, Thomas R., *Ideologies of the Raj* (Cambridge: Cambridge University Press, reprint 1998).

'The Midnapore System of Primary Education', *Calcutta Review*, 63, 125 (January–June), pp. 125–72.

Mill, James, *History of British India*, Vol. 2 (London: James Madden; Piper, Stephenson and Spence, 1858, first edn 1815).

Mitra, Barada Charan, 'English Influence on Bengali Literature', *Calcutta Review*, 80, 162 (January–June, 1885), pp. 330–45.

Mitra, Pearychand, *A Biographical Sketch of David Hare*, ed., G. G. Sengupta (Calcutta: Jijnasa, 1979, Ist edn 1877).

Mitra, Subolchandra, *Life of Pundit Iswar Chandra Vidyasagar* (New Delhi: Ashish Publishers, 1975, first edn 1907).

Monteath A.M. and A.P. Howell, eds., *Selections from the Education Records of the Government of India*, Parts 1 and 2 (Delhi: National Archives of India, 1960).

Morris. D. Morris, 'The Growth of Large-Scale Industry to 1947', in D. Kumar and M. Desai, eds., *Cambridge Economic History of India*, Vol. II (Cambridge: Cambridge University Press, 1983), pp. 553–676.

Mukherjee, D.N., *A Monograph on Paper and Paper Mache in Bengal* (Calcutta: The Bengal Secretariat Book Depot, 1908).

Mukherjee, Rudrangshu, 'The Azimgarh Proclamation and some Questions on the Revolt of 1857 in the Northwestern Provinces' in Barun De, ed., *Essays in Honour of Prof. S.C. Sarkar* (New Delhi: People's Publishing House, 1976), pp. 477–98.

Mukherjee, S.N., 'Class, Caste and Politics in Calcutta, 1815–38' in E. Leach and S.N. Mukherjee, eds., *Elites in South Asia* (Cambridge: Cambridge University Press, 1970), pp. 33–78.

_____ *Calcutta: Myths and History* (Calcutta: Subarnarekha, 1977).

_____ *Sir William Jones: A Study in Eighteenth Century British Attitudes to India* (London: Cambridge University Press, 1968).

Murdoch, John, *India's Greatest Educational Need: The Adequate Recognition of Ethics in her Present Transition State* (London and Madras: Christian Literature Society for India, 1904).

_____ *Letter to Babu Iswarchandra Bidyasagar on Bengali Typography* (Calcutta: Christian Vernacular Education Society, 1865).

Nair, P.T., *A History of the Calcutta Press: The Beginnings* (Calcutta: Firma KLM, 1987).

_____ ed., *Calcutta Gazette: Introductory Volume* (Calcutta: Bibhash Gupta, 1989)

Nandy, Somendra Chandra. *Life and Times of Cantoo Baboo* (Calcutta: Allied Publishers, 1978).

Naoroji, Dadabhai, *Admission of Educated Natives into the Indian Civil Service* (London: Macmillan and Co., 1868).

Naregal, Veena, *Language Polities, Elites and the Public Sphere* (New Delhi: Permanent Black, 2001).

'The Native Press of Bengal', *Calcutta Review*, 43, 86 (July–December, 1866), pp. 358–79.

O'Brien, Mark, *Perish the Privileged Orders* (London: Redwords, 1995).

Omissi, David, '"Martial race": Ethnicity and Security in Colonial India, 1858–1939', *War and Society*, 9, 1 (1991), pp. 1–27.

Ong, Walter J., *Orality and Literacy: The Technologizing of the Word* (London: Routledge, 1990).

Pahl, R.E. and J.T. Winkler, 'The Economic Elite: Theory and Practice', in A. Giddens and P. Stanworth, eds., *Elites and Power in British Society* (London: Cambridge University Press, 1974), pp. 102–22.

Paine, Thomas, *Rights of Man*, edited with an introduction by Henry Collins (Harmondsworth: Penguin, 1976).

Pal, K., *The Young Bengal Vindicated* (Calcutta: Stanhope Press, 1856).

Palit, Chittabrata, 'The Young Bengal: A Self Estimate', in Ramesh C. Majumdar ed., *Renascant Bengal (1817–1857)* (Calcutta: Asiatic Society 1972), pp. 65–74.

Pandey, Gyanendra, 'Rallying around the Cow: Sectarian Strife in the Bhojpur Region, c. 1887–1917', in Ranajit Guha, ed., *Subaltern Studies II* (New Delhi, Oxford University Press, 1983), pp. 60–129.

Pecheux, Michel, *Language, Semantics and Ideology: Stating the Obvious*, trans. Harbans Nagpal (London: Macmillan, 1982).

Prakash, Gyan, 'Postcolonial Criticism and Indian Historiography', *Social Text*, 31/32 (1992), pp. 8–19.

Quine, Willard Van Orman, 'Five Milestones of Empiricism', in *Theories and Things* (Cambridge, Mass., London: Harvard University Press, 1981), pp. 67–72.

Rahim, M.A., *Social and Cultural History of Bengal* (Karachi: Pakistan Historical Society, 1963).

Ray, Rajat K., *Social Conflict and Political Unrest in Bengal* (New Delhi: Oxford University Press, 1984).

Ray, Ratna, 'Land Transfer and Social Change Under the Permanent Settlement', *IESHR*, 11, 1 (1974), pp. 1–45.

Raya, Lalitmohan, *Meyeli, A Collection of Sayings and Proverbs in Use by Bengali Women* (Mymensingh: Ananda Press, 1877).

Rhodes, Dennis E., *The Spread of Printing, Eastern Hemisphere India, Pakistan, Ceylon, Burma and Thailand* (Amsterdam: A.L. van Gendt, 1969).

Richey, J.A. *Selections from Education Records*, Part II (Calcutta: Superintendent, Government Printing, 1920).

Robinson, Francis, 'Islam and the Impact of Print in South Asia', in Nigel Crook ed., *The Transmission of Knowledge in South Asia* (New Delhi: Oxford University Press, 1996), pp. 62–97.

Roy, Debesh, *Pre-British Bengali Prose: Search for Sources*, Occasional Paper No. 48 (Calcutta: Centre for Studies in Social Sciences, 1982).

Roy, Rammohan, *Expositions of the Practical Operation of the Judicial and Revenue Systems of India and of the General Character and Conditions of its Native Inhabitants, as Submitted as Evidence to the Authorities in England, with Notes and Illustrations etc.* (London: Smith, Elder, 1832).

Roy, Tapti, 'Disciplining the Printed Text: Colonial and Nationalist Surveillance of Bengali Literature', in Partha Chatterjee, ed., *Texts of Power, Emerging Disciplines in Colonial Bengal* (Calcutta: Samya, 1996), pp. 30–62.

S. Taniguchi, H. Yanagisawa, T. Shinoda and F. Oshikawa, eds., *Economic Changes and Social Transformation in Modern and Contemporary South Asia* (Tokyo: Hitotsubashi University Press,1994)

Saniyal, S.C., 'History of the Press', *Calcutta Review*, 132, 236 (January, 1911), pp. 1–47; 132, 264 (April, 1911), pp. 141–200.

Sanyal, Hitesranjan, *Social Mobility in Bengal* (Calcutta: Papyrus,1981).

Sanyal, Rajat, *Voluntary Associations and the Urban Public Life in Bengal 1815–1876: An Aspect of Social History* (Calcutta: Riddhi, 1980).

Sarkar, Sumit, 'Post-modernism and the Writing of History', *Studies in History*, 15, 2 (1999), p 293–322.

_____ 'Rammohan Roy and the Break with the Past', in V.C. Joshi, ed., *Rammohan Roy and the Process of Modernization in India* (Delhi: Vikas, 1975), pp. 46–68.

_____ *A Critique of Colonial India* (Calcutta: Papyrus, 1985).

_____ *The Swadeshi Movement in Bengal: 1903–1908* (New Delhi: People's Publishing House, 1973).

_____ *Writing Social History* (New Delhi: Oxford University Press, 1997).

Sarkar, Susobhan, *Notes on the Bengal Renaissance* (Calcutta: Papyrus, reprint 1985).

Sarkar, Tanika, 'Jitu Santal's Movement in Malda 1924–1932: A Study in Tribal Protest', in Ranajit Guha, ed., *Subaltern Studies IV* (New Delhi: Oxford University Press, 1985), pp. 136–64.

_____ 'Rhetoric Against Age of Consent', *Economic and Political Weekly*, 28, 36 (1993), pp. 1869–78.

_____ *Hindu Wife, Hindu Nation: Community, Religion and Cultural Nationalism* (Bloomington: Indiana University Press, 2001)

Seal, Anil, *Emergence of Indian Nationalism* (Cambridge: Cambridge University Press, 1971).

Sen, Asok, 'Subaltern Studies: Capital, Class and Community', in Ranajit Guha, ed., *Subaltern Studies V* (New Delhi: Oxford University Press, 1987), pp. 203–35.

_____ 'The Bengal Economy and Rammohan Roy' in V.C. Joshi, ed., *Rammohan Roy and the Process of Modernization in India* (Delhi: Vikas, 1975), pp. 103–35.

_____ *Iswarchandra Vidyasagar and his Elusive Milestones* (Calcutta: Riddhi-India, 1977).

Sen, Dinesh Chandra, *History of Bengali Language and Literature* (Calcutta: Calcutta University, 1911).

Sen, Pannalal, *The Master of Printing or the Manual of a Printing Office* (Calcutta: The Hindusthan Publishing Company, 1921).

Sen, Sudipta, *Empire of Free Trade: The East India Company and the Making of the Colonial Marketplace* (Philadelphia: University of Pennsylvania Press, 1998).

Sen, Sukumar, 'Early Printers and Publishers in Calcutta', *Bengal Past and Present*, 87 (January–June, 1968), pp. 59–66.

_____ *History of Bengali Literature* (Delhi: Sahitya Akademi, 1960).

Sengupta, Prabodhprakasa, *Dictionary of Proverbs* (Calcutta: A. Mukherjee, 1899).

Seton-Kerr, W.S., 'Charters and Patriots', *Calcutta Review*, 18, 36 (July–December, 1852), pp. 403–26.

Shahidullah, Kazi, 'The Purpose and Impact of Government Policy on *Pathshala Gurumohashoys* in Nineteenth-Century Bengal' in Nigel Crook, ed., *The Transmission of Knowledge in South Asia* (New Delhi: Oxford University Press, 1996), pp. 119–34.

Sharp, H. and J.A. Richey, *Selections from Educational Records*, Part I (Calcutta: Superintendent, Government Printing, 1920).

Shaw, Graham, *Printing in Calcutta to 1800—A Description and Checklist of Printing in Late 18th Century Calcutta* (London: Bibliographical Society, 1981).

Siddiqi, Majid H., *Agrarian Unrest in North India: The United Provinces 1918–22* (New Delhi: Vikas, 1978).

Singh, Jyotsna G., *Colonial Narratives/Cultural Dialogues: 'Discoveries' of India in the Language of Colonialism* (London and New York: Routledge, 1996).

Singh, S.B., *European Agency Houses in Bengal (1783–1833)* (Calcutta: Firma KLM, 1966).

Sinha, Mrinalini, *Colonial Masculinity* (Manchester and New York: Manchester University Press, 1995).

Sinha, N.K., *The Economic History of Bengal from Plassey to the Permanent Settlement*, 1 and 3 (Calcutta: Firma KLM, 1956–62).

Sinha, Pradip, *Calcutta in Urban History* (Calcutta: Firma KLM, 1978).

Slater, T.E., ed., *Keshub Chandra Sen and the Brahmo Samaj* (Madras: Society for Promoting Christian Knowledge, 1884).

Smith, Adam, *An Inquiry into the Nature and Causes of the Wealth of Nations*, Edited and with an Introduction by Kathryn Sutherland (Oxford: Oxford University Press, 1993).

Spivak, Gayatri Chakravorty, 'Can the Subaltern Speak?' in C. Nelson and L. Grossberg, eds., *Marxism and the Interpretation of Culture* (London: Routledge, 1988), pp. 271–313.

Ste Croix, G.E.M. de, *The Class Struggle in the Ancient Greek World* (London: Duckworth, 1981).

Tagore, Rabindranath, *My Reminiscences* (London: Macmillan, 1917).

Therborn, Göran, *The Ideology of Power and the Power of Ideology* (London: Verso, 1980).

Thompson, E.P., *The Making of the English Working Class* (Harmondsworth: Penguin, 1991).

_____ *The Poverty of Theory and Other Essays* (London: Merlin Press, 1978).

Tomlinson, B.R., *The Economy of Modern India: 1860–1970* (Cambridge: Cambridge University Press, 1996).

Tripathi, Amales, *Trade and Finance in the Bengal Presidency 1793–1833* (Bombay: Orient Longman, 1956).

Trotsky, L., 'The Peculiarities of Russian Historical Development', in *The Permanent Revolution and Results and Prospects* (New York: Pathfinder, 1978), pp. 37–45.

_____ *The History of the Russian Revolution* (London: Pluto Press, 1977).

Viswanathan, Gouri, *Masks of Conquest: Literary Study and British Rule in India* (London: Faber and Faber, 1990).

Volosinov, V.N., *Marxism and the Philosophy of Language*, trans. L. Matejka and I. R. Titunik (Cambridge, Massachusetts, London: Harvard University Press, 1996).

Ward, William, *View of the History, Literature, Religion of the Hindus including a Minute Description of their Manners and Customs and Translations from their Principal works*, 2 Vols (Serampore: Mission Press, 1818).

Wenger, J., 'Popular Literature of Bengal', *Calcutta Review*, 13, 26 (January–June, 1850), pp. 257–84.

Wilson, Horace Hayman, *The Religious Sects of the Hindus. Based on the 'Stetch' by H.H. Wilson ... with additions from later sources of information*, Compiled by J. Murdoch, (London and Madras: Christian Literature Society for India, 1904).

Wolf, Eric., *Europe and the People Without History* (Berkeley and Los Angeles: University of California Press, 1982).

Wolpert, Stanley, *A New History of India* (Oxford: Oxford University Press, 1997).

Wright, Eric Olin, *Class, Crisis and the State* (London: New Left Books, 1978).

———— *Classes* (London: Verso, 1985).

Young, William Gordon, *Tracts on the Rural Population of Bengal and Behar* (Calcutta: Sanders, Cones and Co., 1858).

———— *Training Schools for Teachers of the Ryots* (Calcutta: Sanders, Cones and Co., 1858).

III. Non-Official Books, Articles, and Dissertations (Bengali)

Abdul Jalil, Muhammad, *Madhyajuger Bangla Sahitye Bangla O Bangali Samaj* (Dhaka: Bangla Academy, 1986).

Adhikary, Aghornath, *Vidyalaya Vidhayak Vivida Vidhan* (Calcutta: Sanyal and Co., 1909).

Anisuzzaman, *Puratan Bangla Gadya* (Dhaka: Bangla Academy, 1984).

Anonymous, 'Durgeshnandini [Book Review]', *Rahasya Sandarbha*, 2nd series, Vol. 21 (1854), p. 142.

———— *Hak Katha* (Calcutta: Local Press, 1873).

———— *Hemantakumari* (Calcutta: Hitaishi Press, 1868).

———— *Suraloke Banger Parichay* (Calcutta, 1882).

Bagal, Jogeshchandra, *Banglar Janashiksha* (Calcutta: Viswabharati Press, 1949).

———— *Banglar Uchchashiksha* (Calcutta: Vishwabharati Press, n.d.).

Bamasundari, *Ki Ki Kusanskar* (Calcutta: n.p, 1876).

Bandyopadhyay, Asit Kumar, *Bangla Sahityer Itibritta*, Vol. 3 (Calcutta: Modern Book Agency, 1993).

Bandyopadhyay, Bhabanicharan, *Kalikata Kamalalaya and Kalikata Kalpalata*, Bishnu Basu, ed., (Calcutta: Pratibhash, 1986).

_____ *Nabababubilash* (Calcutta: Madanmohan De, 1825).

_____ *Rasarachanasangraha* (Calcutta: Nabapatra Prakashan, 1987).

Bandyopadhyay, Bibhutibhushan, *Bibhutirachanabali*, Vol. 3, edited by Gajendrakumar Mitra, Chandidas Chattopadhyay, and Taradas Bandyopadhyay (Calcutta: Mitra Ghosh, 1972).

Bandyopadhyay, Brajendrakumar, and Sajanikanta Das, eds., *Rammohan Granthabali* (Calcutta: Bangiya Sahitya Parishad, n.d.)

Bandyopadhyay, Brajendranath, 'Rammohan Roy', *Pashchimbanga*, 12–16 (September–October 1996), pp. 27–40.

Bandyopadhyay, Brajendranath, and Sajanikanta Das, eds., *Rammohan Granthabali* (Calcutta: Bangiya Sahitya Parishad, n.d.).

_____ *Sahitya Sadhak Charitmala: Ishanchandra Bandyopadhyay* (Calcutta: Bangiya Sahitya Parishad, 1945).

_____ *Sahitya Sadhak Charitmala: Kangal Harinath* (Calcutta: Bangiya Sahitya Parishad, 1954).

_____ *Sahitya Sadhak Charitmala: Pearychand Mitra* (Calcutta: Bangiya Sahitya Parishad, 1948).

_____ *Sahitya Sadhak Charitmala: Rajkrishna Roy* (Calcutta: Bangiya Sahitya Parishad, 1948).

_____ *Sahitya-Sadhak Charitmala: Haraprasad Shastri* (Calcutta: Bangiya Sahitya Parishad, 1949).

Bandyopadhyay, Brajendranath, ed., *Sambad Patre Sekaler Katha*, Vol. 1 (Calcutta: Bangiya Sahitya Parishad, 1970).

_____ *Sambad Patre Sekaler Katha*, Vol. 2 (Calcutta: Bangiya Sahitya Parishad, 5th ed, 1994).

Bandyopadhyay, Chandicharan, *Vidyasagar* (Calcutta: Standard Publishers, 1990.)

_____ *Vidyasagar Chatrajiban* (Calcutta: 1896).

Bandyopadhyay, Gopalchandra, *Hita Shiksha*, Part 1 (Calcutta: Hitaishi Press, 1869).

_____ *Hitashiksha*, Part 4 (Calcutta: Hitaishi Press, 1869).

_____ *Shikshapranali: An Elementary Treatise on Education* (Calcutta: Hitaishi Press, 1868).

Bandyopadhyay, Maheshchandra, *Anubadsar* (Calcutta: n.p., 1864).

Bandyopadhyay, Rangalal, *Padmini Upakhyam*, 2nd edition (Calcutta: Baptist Mission Press, 1865).

Banerjee, Woomeshchandra, *The New Infant Teacher*, Part 3 (Calcutta: n.p., 1877)

Bangal, Byomchand, (Harishchandra Mitra), *Ghar Thakte Babui Bheje* (Dhaka: Girish Press, 1872).

Barua, Hem, *Lakshmikanta Bejbarua*, trans. Asit Gupta (New Delhi: Sahitya Akademi, 1970).

Basak, Radhanath, *Sharirtatvasar* (Calcutta: Vidyaratna Press, 1863).

Basu Chaudhury, Tarinicharan, *Jamidari Mahajani Hishab* (Dacca: Sulabh Press, 1875).

Basu, Asutosh, *Samaj Kalanka* (Calcutta: n.p., 1885).

Basu, Chandranath, *Hindutva* (Calcutta: Medical Library, 1892).

Basu, Manomohan, *Baktritamala* (Calcutta: Madhyastha Press, 1873).

_____ *Hindu Achar Byabahar* (Calcutta: Madhyastha Press, 1876).

_____ *Samajchitra, Purba O Bartaman Athaba Kereler Jiban* (Calcutta: Nepalchandra Ghosh, reprint 1981).

Basu, Rajnarayan, *Atmacharit* (Calcutta: Kuntalin Press, 1909).

_____ *Bangla Bhasha O Sahitya Bishayak Baktrita* (Calcutta: Nutan Bangla Press, 1878).

_____ *Sekal Ar Ekal* (Calcutta: Valmiki Press, 1874).

Bhadra, Gautam, *Iman O Nishan: Banglar Krishak Chaitanyer Ek Adhyaya* (Calcutta: Subarnarekha, 1994).

Bhattacharya, Asutosh, ed., *Baish Kabir Manasamangal Ba Baisha* (Calcutta: Calcutta University, second edn 1962).

Bhattacharya, Debipada, 'Bangla Samayikpatra', in Chittaranjan Bandyopadhyay, ed., *Dui Shataker Bangla Mudran O Prakashan* (Calcutta: Ananda Publishers, 1981), pp. 283–300.

Bhattacharya, Jatindramohan, 'Punthir Pare Bai', in Chittaranjan Bandyopadhyay, ed., *Dui Shataker Bangla Mudran O Prakashan* (Calcutta: Ananda, 1981), pp. 21–8.

_____ ed., *Bangla Mudrita Granther Talika*, Vol. 1: 1743–1852 (Calcutta: A. Mukherjee, 1990).

_____ *Mudrita Bangla Granther Panji 1853–1867* (Calcutta: Pashchim Bangla Academy, 1993).

Bhattacharya, Kalikrishna, *Naba Niti Sara*, Part 1 (Calcutta: Sudharnab Press, 1858).

Bhattacharya, Kantichandra, *Udiya Svatantra Bhasha Nahe* (Calcutta: Girish Vidyaratna Press, 1870).

Bhattacharya, Nandakumar Kabiratna, *Gyan Saudamini* (Calcutta: Vidyaratna Press, 1863).

Bhattacharya, Surendranath, ed., *Jagajjiban Birachita Manasamangal* (Calcutta: Calcutta University, 1960).

Biswas, Dilip, *Rammohan Samiksha* (Calcutta: Saraswat Library, 2nd edn 1994).

Biswas, Sukumar, ed., *Bangla Academy Punthi Parichay*, Vol. 1 (Dhaka: Bangla Academy, 1995).

Chakrabarti, Bani, *Samaj Sanskarak Raghunandan* (Calcutta: Bani Chakrabarti, 1970).

Chakrabarti, Batabihari, *Kalir Kulta Prahasan* (Calcutta: Kar Press, 1877).

Chakrabarti, Shyamal, *Chapa Harafer Hat* (Calcutta: Sahitya Sadan, 1970).

Chakrabarty, Chintaharan, 'Nadiar Bhasha', *Sahitya Parishad Patrika*, 51, 1–2 (1964), pp. 40–2.

Chakravarty, Bholanath, *Sei Ekdin ar Ei Ekdin, Arthath Banger Purba o Bartaman Abastha* (Calcutta: Cornwallis Press, 1875).

Chanda, Srinath, *Bramho Samaje Challish Bachar* (Dacca: Bharat Mahila Press, 1913).

Chattopadhyay, Bankimchandra, 'Babu' in *Bankim Rachanabali*, Vol. 2 (Calcutta: Sahitya Samsad, 1969) pp. 10–12.

——— 'Sanjibchandra Chattopadhyay', in Asitkumar Bandyopadhyay, ed., *Sanjib Rachanabali* (Calcutta: Mandal Book House, 1973), pp. 23–6.

Chattopadhyay, Becharam, *Griha Karma* (Calcutta: Presidency Press, 1864).

Chattopadhyay, Chandramohan, *Shishuranjan* (Calcutta: Stanhope Press, 1868)

Chattopadhyay, Gangadhar, *Ekei Ki Bole Bangali Saheb* (Calcutta: 1874), p. ****.

Chattopadhyay, Kedarnath, 'Upendrakishor: Satabarshik Sraddhanjali', *Viswabharati Patrika* (Kartik–Poush, 1963), pp. 108–19.

Chattopadhyay, Nabinchandra, *Baruni Bilash* (Calcutta: School Book Press, 1867).

Chattopadhyay, Umacharan, *Balak Ranjan* (Halishahar: n.p., 1855).

Chattopadhyaya, Basantakumar, ed., *Jyotirindranather Jiban Smriti* (Calcutta: Subarnarekha, 2002, first edn 1920).

Chaudhuri, Pramatha, 'Atibhashan', in *Prabandha Sangraha* (Calcutta: Viswabharati Press, 1974), pp. 77–82.

Chaudhuri, Saratchandra, 'Shikshaker Upajogita', *Shiksha Parichar* (Baishakh and Jaishtha, 1890), pp. 8–12; 33–9.

Chaudhuri, Satyajit, et al., eds., *Haraprasad Shastri Rachana-Sangraha*, Vol. 2 (Calcutta: Paschim Banga Rajya Pustak Parishad, 1981).

Choudhury, Kamal, *Kalkatar Tinsho Bacharer Itihas: Sanskriti Kendra* (Calcutta: Pratibhash, 1990).

Das, Nirmal, *Bangla Bhashar Byakaran O Tar Kramabikash* (Calcutta: n.p., 1987).

Datta, Akshay Kumar, *Bahyabastur Sange Manab Prakritir Bichar*, (Calcutta: Tattvabodhini Press, 1851–53).

Datta, Mahendranath, *Jibankahini* (Calcutta: Shishir Kumar Mitra, 1924).

Dhar, Jaharlal, *Kalikata Rahasya, Adhunik Kalikatar Jibanta Pratibha* (Calcutta: n.p., 1896).

Dutt, Michael Madhusudan, 'Ekei Ki Bole Sabhyata' in Brajendranath Bandyopadhya and Sajanikanta Das, eds., *Madhusudan Rachanabali* (Calcutta: Bangiya Sahitya Parishad, 1954).

Dutta, Bijitkumar, and Sunanda Dutta, eds., *Manikram Ganguli: Dharmamangal* (Calcutta: Calcutta University, 1960).

Ghatak, Kalimoy, *Charitashtak*, (Hooghly, 1967)

Ghosh, Abinashchandra, ed., *Naradeb Sibchandra Deb O Tatsahadharminir Adarsha Jibanalekshya* (Calcutta: Birendranath Mitra, 1918).

Ghosh, Benoy, *Badshahi Amal* (Calcutta: Aruna Prakashani, 1967).

—— *Banglar Bidyotsamaj* (Calcutta: Prakash Bhaban, 1979).

—— *Banglar Nabajagriti* (Calcutta: Orient Longman, reprint 1979).

—— *Bidrohi Derozio* (Calcutta: Bak Sahitya, 1961).

—— ed., *Samayikpatre Banglar Samajchitra*, Vol. 4 (Calcutta: Papyrus, 1963).

Ghosh, Dasarathi, 'Asamia ki Svatantra Bhasha?', *Nabya Bharat*, 12, 4 (Shravan, 1894), pp. 197–202.

Ghosh, Hemendraprasad, 'Mastermahashay', *Sahitya* (Jaishtha, 1898), pp. 101–11.

Ghosh, Jogendranath, *Bangla Mudrankaner Itibritta O Samalochana* (Calcutta: Nutan Bangla Press, 1870).

Ghosh, Manmathanath, *Manishi Bholanath Chandra* (Calcutta: Gurudas Chattopadhyay and Sons, 1924).

—— *Sekaler Lok* (Calcutta: Gurudas Chattopadhyay and Sons, 1923).

Ghosh, Manomohan, *Bangla Gadyer Char Jug* (Calcutta: Dasgupta and Co., 1942).

Ghosh, Nibaranchandra, *Smritividya Ba Swaranshakti Bardhaner Upay* (Calcutta: Samya Press, 1898).

Ghosh, Sankhya, 'Iswarchandra Vidyasagar', in Sudhirkumar Gangopadhyay et al., eds., *Banglar Manisha*, Vol. 2 (Calcutta: Sarat Publishing House, 1987), pp. 411–16.

Goswami, Jayanta, *Samjchitre Unabingsa Satabdir Bangla Prahasan* (Calcutta: Sahityasree, 1974).

Goswami, Prasad Das, *Amader Samaj* (Serampore: Tamohar Press, 1895).

Guhathakurata, Manoranjan, *Chatrera Khabe Ki* (Calcutta: n.p., 1917).

Gupta, Ambikacharan, *Kalir Maye Choto Bou Orofe Ghor Murkho* (Calcutta: Cornwallis Press, 1881).

Gupta, Kshetra, ed., *Madhusudan Rachanbali*, 11th edition (Calcutta: Sahitya Samsad, 1990)

Gupta, Nabakumar, *Niti Kaumudi* (Dhaka: Nandakumar Guha and Co., 1867).

Gupta, Rajanikanta, *Amader Vishwavidyalaya* (Calcutta, n.d.).

Haldar, Tarakrishna, *Chamtkar Swapnadarshan* (Calcutta: N.L. Sheel's Press, 1867).

Kaviraj, Narahari, 'Banglar Jagoron O Bhadralok', in Narahari Kaviraj, ed., *Unish Shataker Banglar Jagoran: Tarka O Bitarka* (Calcutta: K.P. Bagchi and Co., 1984), pp. 249–70.

Laha, Narendranath, *Ashtadash Satabdi Porjonto Europeogan Kartrik Bharate Shiksha Bistar* (Calcutta: Oriental Press, 1923).

Lahiri, Durgadas, *Bangalir Gaan* (Calcutta: Bangabasi-Electro-Machine Press, 1905).

Maitra, Bishnuchandra, 'Bangabhasha O Sahitya', *Nabya Bharat* (Shravan, 1897), pp. 182–90.

_____ *Apachay O Unnati* (Calcutta: Nabakrishna Press, 1890).

Maitreya, Akshaykumar, 'Shiksha Samasya', *Utsaha* (Magh, 1900), pp. 348–55.

Majumdar, Kedarnath, *Bangla Samayik Sahitya* (Mymensingh: Narendranath Majumdar, 1917).

Mandal, Panchanan, ed., *Chithipatre Samajchitra*, Vol. 1 (Calcutta: Vishwabharati Press, 1968).

_____ *Punthi Parichay*, Vol. 1 (Calcutta: Vishwabharati Press, 1951).

Mitra, Anandachandra, *Prachin Bharat O Adhunik Europe Sabhyatar Bhinna Murti* (Mymensingh: Bharatmihir Press, 1876).

Mitra, Benoychandra, *Rajarampur Srikrishnapur Mitrabangsha* (Burdwan: n.p., 1942).

Mitra, Dinabandhu, 'Sadhadar Ekadashi' in Gopal Haldar, ed., *Dinabandhu Rachanasangraha* (Calcutta: Saksharata Prakashan, 1973), pp. 161–214

Mitra, Dwarkanath, *Mushalang Kul Nashanang* (Calcutta: Bhaskar Press, 1864).

Mitra, Harishchandra, *Ghar Thakte Babui Bheje* (Dhaka: Sulabh Press, 1863).

Mitra, Krishnakumar, *Atmacharit* (Calcutta: Prabasi Press, 1937).

Mitra, Shibratan, ed., *Bangla Prachin Punthir Bibaran*, Vol. 2 (Calcutta: Bangiya Sahitya Parishad, 1919).

Moitra, Harimohan, *Shasthyarakshar Prosnottar* (Calcutta: H.C. Gangooly and Co., 1872).

Mookerjee, Hiralall, *Watt's Improvement of Mind or Nitirutnahara*, Part 1, (Calcutta: Nuton Bangla Press, 1870).

Mukherjee, Madhusudan, *Sushilar Upakhyam* (Calcutta: Vernacular Literature Committee, 1864).

Mukhopadhyay, Bholanath, *Apnar Mukh Apni Dekho* (Calcutta: Hindu Press and Sahashi Yantra, 1863).

_____ *Koner Ma Kande Ar Takar Puntli Bandhe* (Calcutta: Hindu Press, 1863).

Mukhopadhyay, Bhudev, *Shikshabishayak Prastab* (Hooghly: Budhodoy Press, 1864).

Mukhopadhyay, Dinanath, *Jamidari Bigyan* (Hooghly: Budhodoy Press, 1866).

Mukhopadhyay, Harimohan, ed., *Bangabhashar Lekhak*, Part I (Calcutta: n.p., 1904).

Mukhopadhyay, Harimohan, *Krishi Darpan* (Calcutta: Chanpatala Bangla Press, 1859).

Mukhopadhyay, Harisadhan, *Kalikata Sekaler O Ekaler* (Calcutta: K.P. Bagchi, 1915).

Mukhopadhyay, Jadunath, *Sharirpalan* (Hooghly: Budhodoy Press, 1868).

Mukhopadhyay, Nilkantha, *Balya Kahini* (Hetampur: Harinath Bhattacharya, 1904).

Mukhopadhyay, Somnath, *Shikshapadhdhati* (Calcutta: New Sanskrit Press, 1866).

Mukhopadhyay, Upendranath, *Hindujati O Shiksha*, Vol. 1 (Calcutta: Srikali Ghosh, 1915).

Nag, Arun, ed., *Satik Hutom Penchar Naksha* (Calcutta: Subarnarekha, 1991).

Nayaratna, Ramgati, *Banglabhasha O Banglasahitya Bishayak Prastab: A Treatise on the Bengali Language and Literature* (Hooghly: Budhoday Press, 1872–3).

Neogi, Dwijendranath, *Uchcha Shikshak Sahachar* (Calcutta: n.p., 1902).

Patra, Prafulla Kumar, ed., *Vidyasagar Rachanabali* (Calcutta: Patra's Publications, 2nd edn 1991).

Prasannamayi Devi, *Purba Katha* (Calcutta: Adi Brahmo Samaj Press, 1917).

Ray, Bangachandra, *Amar Jibanalekshya* (Dacca: Umeshchandra Sen, 1913).

Ray, Gopalchandra, 'Bangla Bayer Byabsa', in Chittaranjan Bandyopadhyay ed., *Dui Shataker Bangla Mudran O Prakashan* (Calcutta: Ananda Publishers, 1981), pp. 351–64.

Ray, Kartikeyachandra, *Jibancharit* (Calcutta: Indian Association Publishing Company, reprint 1956).

Ray, Suprakash, *Mukti-yuddhe Bharatiya Krishak*, first published 1966 (Calcutta: Bharati Book Stall, 1980).

Raya, Jadunath, *Shikshabichar* (Calcutta: The New Sanskrit Press, 1870).

Roy, Rammohan, *Subrahmanya Shastrir Sahit Bichar* (Calcutta: Baptist Mission Press, 1820).

Roy, Ramsundar, *Stridharma Bishayak* (Calcutta: Chaitanya Chandradoy Press, 1859).

Rudra, Kaligopal, 'Ashami Bhasha', *Nabya Bharat*, 13, 7 (Kartik, 1895), pp. 346–51.

Sarbadhikari, Debaprasad, *Smritirekha* (Calcutta: Nikhilchandra Sarbadhikari, 1933).

Sen, Abhaycharan, *Abidyar Das Ain*, (Dacca: Bengalee Press, 1853).

Sen, Chandrashekhar, *Ki Holo* (Calcutta: People's Friend Press, 1875).

Sen, Dineshchandra, *Gharer Katha O Jugsahitya* (Calcutta: Shishir Publishing House, 1922).

_____ *Grihasree* (Calcutta: Gurudas Chattopadhyay and Sons, 1915).

Sen, Gaurinath, *Sharirik Shasthya Vidhan* (Calcutta: Sambad Sajjan Ranjan Press, 1862).

Sen, Girishchandra, *Atma Jibanbrittanta* (Calcutta: Gupta, Mukherjee and Co., 1906).

Sen, Nabinchandra, *Amar Jiban*, Vol. 1 (Calcutta: Bharat Mihir Press, 1907).

_____ *Amar Jiban*, Vol. 3 (Calcutta: Bharat Mihir Press, 1910).

Sen, Prasanna Chandra, *Krishi Karjer Mat* (Dhaka: Sulabh Press, 1867).

Sen, Shashibhushan, *Karmakshetra* (Calcutta: City Book Society, 1903).

Sen, Sukumar, 'Battalar Besati', *Visva Bharati Patrika* (Shravan, 1948), pp. 16–25.

_____ *Battalar Chapa O Chabi* (Calcutta: Ananda, 1984).

Sengupta, Kaliprasanna, *Jamidari Darshan* (Hooghly: Budhodoy Press, 1863).

Sharma, Taran, *Keranipuran* (Calcutta: Tarinicharan Das, 1886).

Shastri, Haraprasad, 'Kaleji Shiksha', in *Haraprasad Granthabali* (Calcutta: Basumati Sahitya Mandir, n.d.), pp. 321–4.

Shastri, Priyonath, ed., *Pujyapad Srimanmaharshi Debendranath Thakurer Swarachita Jivan-charit O Parishishta* (Calcutta: Bannerjee Press, 1898).

Shastri, Shibendranarayan, *Banglar Paribarik Itihas*, Vol. 2 (Calcutta: Sachindralal Biswas, 1935).

_____ *Kalikatar Paribarik Itihas*, Vol. 1 (Calcutta: Ramkrishna Sahitya Kutir, 1933).

Shastri, Shibnath, *Atmacharit* (Calcutta: Pashchimbanga Niraksharata Durikaran Samiti, 1979).

_____ *Ramtanu Lahiri O Tatkalin Bangasamaj* (Calcutta: S.K. Lahiri and Co., second edn 1909).

Sheel, Nemaichand, *Erai Abar Borolok* (Calcutta: Stanhope Press, 1867).

Sripantha (Nikhil Sarkar), *Jokhon Chapakhana Elo* (Calcutta: Bangasanskriti Sammelan, 1977).

Sur, Atul, 'Kagaj O Kali', in Chittaranjan Bandyopadhyay, ed., *Dui Shataker Bangla Mudran O Prakashan* (Calcutta: Ananda Publishers, 1981), pp. 400–7.

Swarnakumari Devi, 'Sekele Katha', in *Swarnakumari Devi Granthabali* (Calcutta, n.d.), pp. 107–12.

Tagore, Prasanna Kumar, (Parashar), *Krishi Sangraha* (Calcutta: Vidyaratna Press, 1862).

Tagore, Satyendranath, *Amar Balyakal O Amar Bombai Prabash* (Calcutta: Kantik Press, 1915).

Thakur, Abanindranath, 'Gharoa', in *Abanindra Rachanabali*, Vol. 1 (Calcutta: Prakash Bhaban, 1975), pp. 59–172.

Thakur, Rabindranath, *Jiban Smriti* (Calcutta: Vishwabharati Press, 1970).

————— *Rabindra Rachanabali*, Vol. 9 (Calcutta: Government of West Bengal, 1988).

Trivedi, Ramendrasundar, 'Charit Katha', in Brajendranath Bandyopadhyay and Sajanikanta Das, eds., *Ramendra Rachanabali* (Calcutta: Bangiya Sahitya Parishad, 1949), pp. 178–262.

Vidyalankar, Mrityunjay, *Vedantachandrika* (Calcutta: Government Gazette Press, 1817).

Vidyaratna, Sambhuchandra, *Vidyasagar Jibancharit* (Calcutta: Chirayat Prakashan, reprint 1992, first edn 1891).

Index

petty-bourgeoisie 61–4, 221–4
printing strategies 99–100
role in nation-building 232
salaried class 54–63
social composition of 52
social location of 7
social reforms of 226
sociological account of 36–40, 51–2
and status 25–6
working class and 229, 232
Bhaduri, Amit 50n
Bharatchandra 200
 Bharatchandra Granthavali 115
Bhattacharjea, Woomesh Chandra 70
Bhattacharya, Gangakishor 39, 114, 126n, 139
Bhattacharya, Haridas 105n
Bhattacharya, Jatindramohan 91n, 115n, 136n, 140n, 141
Bhattacharya, Kalikrishna 70, 82n
Bhattacharya, Nandakumar Kabiratna 74n
Bhattacharya, Sridhar 118
Bhattacharya, Surendranath 123n
Bhugol Sutra 142
Birch, W. 44
Bishop's College Press 142
Bodhodoy 99, 71, 130
Bolts, William 133n
Bornoporichoy 148
Bose, Basanta Kumar 123
Bose, Gopalchandra 142
Bose, H. 130n
Bose, Iswarchandra 143
Bose, Jagadishchandra 130n
Bose, N.S. 12n
Bourgeoisie 60–4, 222, 224, 226, 232
 movement 230
 national movement 222

peasantry and 227
socialism 224
Brahma Samaj 16, 79, 102, 142
Breckenridge, Carol A. 14n
British India Society 103
Broomfield, J.H. 2, 27n–8n, 35n, 38n
Buckland, C.T. 146n
Butrisha Singhasun, The 111
Byakaran 142
Byron, Lord 216

Calcutta,
 banias of 41–9, 51–3
 Bhabanicharan Bandyopadhyay's account of 36–40
 migration to 224
 population of 44–5
 salaried class in 54–6
Calcutta Gazette 128, 204
Calcutta Literary Society 34
Calcutta Madrassa 179
Calcutta Review 103, 173, 184, 214
Calcutta School Book Society 174
Calcutta School Society 75, 174
Calcutta Trades Association 151
Callinicos, Alex 52, 68
Cameron, C.H. 107n
Campbell, George 107
Cannon, Garland 198n
Capitalism, and printing 109
Carey, Eustace 128, 137, 199n
Carey, S.P. 201n
Carey, William 110–11, 133, 135n, 137n, 199, 202n, 204
Carr, Tagore and Company 83
Chaitanya 200
Chakrabarti, Batabihari 92n
Chakrabarty, Dipesh 6, 18n
Chakrabarty, Tarachand 105
Chakraborty, J. 171
Chakraborty, W.C. 171